Developing Intermediate Vocabulary

Previously published by Georgian Press

Simon Haines

CAMBRIDGE UNIVERSITY PRESS
Cambridge, New York, Melbourne, Madrid, Cape Town, Singapore,
São Paulo, Delhi, Dubai, Tokyo, Mexico City

Cambridge University Press
The Edinburgh Building, Cambridge CB2 8RU, UK

www.cambridge.org
Information on this title: www.cambridge.org/9780521140454 (without key)
www.cambridge.org/9780521140478 (with key)

First published by Georgian Press (Jersey) Limited 2003
Reprinted and published by Cambridge University Press 2010 (twice)

Printed in India by Replika Press Pvt. Ltd

A catalogue record for this publication is available from the British Library

ISBN 978-0-521-14045-4 Paperback without key
ISBN 978-0-521-14047-8 Paperback with key

Produced by AMR Design Ltd (www.amrdesign.com)

Contents

The Key begins on page 97 of the With Key edition.

Acknowledgements

The authors and publishers acknowledge the following sources of copyright material and are grateful for the permissions granted. While every effort has been made, it has not always been possible to identify the sources of all the material used, or to trace all copyright holders. If any omissions are brought to our notice we will be happy to include the appropriate acknowledgement on reprinting.

The BBC for the extract from 'Stressed out in Sweden' by Rosie Goldsmith (page 28).

Far & Near Travel Magazine (www.far-and-near.com) for the adapted extract from 'Historic Antigua' by A.K. Lee (page 44).

Lorraine Gregoire for the adapted version of *The Big Blue Shirt* (page 80).

The Guardian for the extract from 'By gum, here's something for the memory to start chewing on', © Helen Carter (page 24), and for 'The future is purple', © The Guardian 2002 (page 72).

The Institute for Social Inventions for the extract from the www.internet-free-day.org home page (page 8).

The New York Times for the extract from 'Camera rage strikes Hawaii drivers', © The New York Times company (page 20).

OK PetGazette for the extract from 'The shepherd's dog' by Hugh Jones, © Ashworth Publishing LLC 2000–01 (pages 56–7).

Time Warner Books UK for the extract from *Weird Weather* by Paul Simons (pages 60–61).

Weekend Magazine for 'A short history of frozen food' by Julian Champkin (page 33).

Illustrations by: Josephine Blake (pages 80, 81, 82), Martyn Ford (pages 8, 48) and David Woodroffe (pages 34, 35, 60, 69)

Photographs by permission of: imagestate.com (pages 16, 32, 44), Marinepics Limited (page 40) and popperfoto.com (pages 56, 68)

Cover image: © Shutterstock

Introduction

The purpose of *Developing Intermediate Vocabulary* is to enable intermediate-level students to discover, learn and practise words and phrases in authentic contexts. Learners using the book will develop an awareness of a wide range of vocabulary, including collocation, word-building, topic vocabulary, and related words.

The book is suitable for use in the classroom or for homework. The With Key edition is essential if the book is to be used for self-study.

How the book is organised

There are 20 four-page topic-based units, followed by five Review units. The topic-based units are not grouped or sequenced in any particular way, so they may be studied in any order. If the book is being used in conjunction with a general English coursebook, it might be possible for teachers to choose units to complement coursebook topics.

Review units
Each Review unit recycles and consolidates some of the most useful words and phrases from the group of four units it relates to.

Collocation lists
On pages 93 and 94 there are lists of collocations, which are cross-referenced to the main units.

Index
Pages 95 and 96 contain a detailed Index of exercises dealing with particular vocabulary items and topics.

Key
The With Key edition contains answers to all the exercises.

How each unit is organised

Each unit is based on a text of 250–350 words in length from an authentic source. Texts are of different types, including magazine articles, newspaper stories, emails and short stories. A small number of the texts are written in American English. Units follow this basic pattern:

Introduction
This introduces key vocabulary from the text which follows. Students match selected words and phrases with their meanings, checking in a dictionary any they do not already know.

Reading
Students read the text and fill the gaps with correct words and phrases from the Introduction. In some units a short comprehension exercise follows this gap-filling task.

Following the reading are a variety of exercise types, all based on vocabulary occurring in the text. In addition there are **Extension** exercises which further develop other related vocabulary. The final exercise in each unit is either a **Practice** or a **Puzzle**. Both these recycle words and phrases from the unit.

The following are exercise types which occur frequently throughout the book.

Related words
A table, usually with the headings *noun, verb, adjective* and *adverb*, contains a number of words from the reading text. Students complete the remaining gaps in the table with related words. See Exercise C on page 9 for an example.

Collocation

The purpose of the numerous collocation exercises is to draw students' attention to pairs of words which are commonly used together. These are of various types:

- Verb + noun   *to lose your temper*
- Adjective + noun   *an expensive mistake*
- Verb + adverb   *to sleep lightly*

Students match appropriate pairs of words, then use the collocations they have formed to complete gapped sentences.

Topic vocabulary

Some students find it helpful to learn words in thematic groups. So, if a reading text contains a number of words or phrases related to a particular subject, one of the exercises may focus on this thematic vocabulary. For example, Unit 10, *A journey to remember*, groups travel nouns together.

Phrasal verbs

A number of units include phrasal verb exercises. These generally focus on one particular verb, for example, *carry, set* or *turn*.

Idioms

The idiom exercises are of different types. They may focus on particular words used idiomatically, e.g. **cut** *someone dead*, **cut** *corners*. They may deal with word types such as adjectives, e.g. **thick**-*skinned, out of* **thin** *air*. Or the focus may be thematic, as in the exercise on animal idioms: *an early* **bird**, *a dark* **horse**, etc.

Word building

The word-building exercises draw attention to particular features of words. For example:

- Prefixes and suffixes (e.g. **re**wind, **low**-fat, duty-**free**)
- Noun endings, as in words for jobs (e.g. act**or**, econom**ist** , music**ian**)
- Adjective endings (e.g. bor**ed** / bor**ing**)
- Verbs ending in -en (e.g. sharp**en**, wid**en**)
- Adjectives starting with a- (e.g. **a**wake, **a**sleep)

Other vocabulary exercises

There are various other exercises which occur occasionally, including:

- British and American English (e.g. *rubbish / trash*)
- Confusing words (e.g. *house / home*)
- Formal and informal words (e.g. *injured / hurt*)
- Compound nouns (e.g. *street corner*)
- Compound adjectives (e.g. *long-legged*)
- Homophones (e.g. *our / hour*)

These, and many other exercises which focus on vocabulary items specific to particular units, are listed in the Index on pages 95–6.

Extension exercises

These develop an aspect of vocabulary which has featured in a previous exercise. For example, in the verb-noun collocation exercise on page 10, students learn that the verb *lose* is used with the following nouns and phrases:
a chance / contact with someone / an election / interest in something / your job / sight of / your temper / your way.

Extension 2, which follows, focuses on three verbs which are used as the opposites of *lose*: *find / keep / win*.

Notes to teachers

If you are using this book in class with your students, remember that units can be done in any order, as texts and exercises are not graded in any way. Choose texts or topics that you think your students will find interesting or useful.

Each unit ends with a final practice exercise, in the form of a short gapped text or puzzle, which recycles vocabulary from the unit. These would make ideal homework exercises. The Review units could be set as occasional tests.

Although the exercises are designed to be done by students working individually, you could ask students to work in pairs on certain exercises. Section A, Introduction, would be suitable for this, as students are encountering a new topic and a new text for the first time. One way of approaching pairwork is to get students to work individually in the first instance, and then to compare their answers with a partner, before a final check in the Key or with the teacher.

Notes to students working alone

The units in this book can be used in any order. Choose texts or topics that you think you will find interesting and useful.

You probably already have your own favourite way of recording and learning vocabulary, but if you don't, here are a number of ways you could try:

- Divide a notebook into several sections. For example, you could use the headings

    TOPICS   VERB + NOUN COLLOCATIONS   WORD-BUILDING   PHRASAL VERBS

    Each time you come across words you want to learn, list them in the appropriate section of your notebook. Try to learn ten new words or combinations of words each day.

- Design a 'spidergram' to include a set of words you would like to remember. These work particularly well for groups of words related by topic. Example:

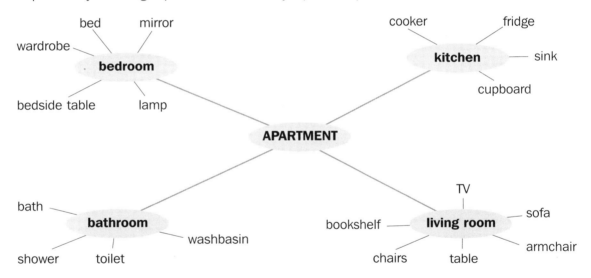

- Write sentences incorporating the words or phrases you want to remember, then make a tape recording of these sentences. Listen to the tape from time to time and repeat the sentences until you feel you know them. (This method works best if you write your own sentences, but if you are short of time use the sentences from the book.)

- From each unit, choose 10 words or phrases you think you will find useful. Write them down and stick them somewhere you will see them every day, for example on a noticeboard at home, on the fridge, or even on a mirror you look in regularly. Every time you see them, say them aloud and check you know the meanings. Think of different situations in which you could use them.

And finally ...
The main purpose of this book is to help you develop your vocabulary. We hope you will find the texts and the exercises interesting and useful. Try to use words and phrases you have learned from the book as often as possible – in fact whenever you are speaking or writing English. Remember, it is only by using new words and phrases that you will really learn them.

A day without the Internet

A Introduction

1 These words and phrases are from the article below. Try to match them with their meanings.

a	*big business*	1	something that happens
b	*controversial*	2	unhealthy, low quality, bad for you
c	*event*	3	a person who studies something to discover new information
d	*isolate*	4	a device for controlling a computer
e	*junk (food)*	5	not actively
f	*mouse*	6	causing disagreement and discussion
g	*passively*	7	not real, only on a computer or the Internet
h	*researcher*	8	dangerous
i	*risky*	9	powerful companies and financial organisations
j	*virtual*	10	to keep separate from things or people

2 Check in a dictionary the meaning of any of these words you do not understand.

B Reading

Read the article and fill each gap with a word or phrase from **A1**.

Put down your mouse

An Internet organisation is trying to persuade people to take part in *International Internet-Free Day*, which would be held every year on the last weekend in January. The idea is that people will leave the **(a)** _____ world and go out into the real world. One supporter of the idea said, 'The Internet can be like addictive **(b)** _____: food you can never get enough of but which you don't really want.'

A spokesman for the Internet-Free Day team explained, 'The Internet **(c)** _____s people socially and damages their eyesight. That is what **(d)** _____ has done with it. It was never meant to be like this. The Internet began as a quick and simple way for **(e)** _____s to communicate and exchange information.'

'But it's so easy to get addicted to a half-life in a virtual world, and to lose touch with your family, friends and neighbours. Human beings need contact with the real world. Email and the Internet are just not enough.'

So, put down your **(f)** _____ and turn off your computer. The real world is open all day every day and welcomes visitors. It offers you the chance to feel human again. An Internet-free day will give you back your real life.

Imagine your perfect day, suggest the idea to some friends and find an exciting **(g)** _____ to take part in. Then go out into the world outside your window, and make your perfect day a reality!

Here are some ideas:

• Organise a *Dice Day*. Write down half a dozen unusual things your group could do on the day, number these things from 1 to 6, then throw a dice. You have to agree to do whichever activity the dice chooses.

• Or choose a less **(h)** _____ activity: go for a country walk, visit an art gallery or museum, have a discussion about a(n) **(i)** _____ subject. Anything as long as it involves more than just **(j)** _____ consuming, watching or listening.

C Related words

1 Fill the gaps in this chart with words related to the words given. Sometimes there are two words in one group. (X = no useful word at this level.)

Noun	Verb	Adjective	Adverb
a _____	X	real	_____
b _____ _____ *	X	addictive	X
c _____	damage	_____	X
d _____	communicate	_____	_____
e contact	_____	X	X
f _____ visitor*	_____	X	X
g _____	_____	perfect	_____
h _____	_____	exciting _____	X
i _____	_____	risky	_____

* These words refer to people.

2 Fill the gaps in these sentences with words you have added to the chart.

a A telly _____ is someone who can't stop watching television.

b If you drink and drive, there's a _____ that you will lose your driving licence.

c Next time you're on a _____ to London, you must come and see us again.

d I know I'm not very _____ this evening, but I've had a hard day and I don't feel like talking.

e When I fell over I hurt my leg, but I don't think I've done any serious _____.

f If I were you I'd _____ the police and report the accident straightaway.

g She's really _____ about starting her new job. She's been looking forward to it for weeks.

D The suffix *-free*

An *Internet-free day* is a day without the Internet. Match these adjectives with the suffix *-free* with nouns they could describe.

alcohol-free   duty-free   fat-free   lead-free   rent-free   trouble-free

accommodation / cigarettes / drink / goods / holiday / journey / lager / paint / petrol / wine / yoghurt

EXTENSION 1

1 Addictions

An alcoholic is someone who is addicted to alcohol. What are these people addicted to?
a chocoholic   a shopaholic   a workaholic

2 *Go for*

The article suggests that people *go for a walk*. Which of these can we *go for*?

a bicycle ride / a drink / a drive / a football match / a picnic / a run / a shop / a swim

E Verb-noun collocations

1 The verbs below are from the article. Which nouns or phrases in the box can follow them? Make four lists. (Some nouns or phrases can follow more than one verb.)

exchange   hold   lose   offer

advice / contact with someone / a conversation / someone a drink / an election / an explanation / glances / greetings / ideas / information / interest in / your job / someone a lift / a meeting / an opinion / phone numbers / sight of / your temper / your way

2 Find the best endings for these sentence beginnings, and fill each gap with the correct form of one of the verbs from above.

Beginnings	Endings
a I've been out of work for over a year, then last week the phone rang and ...	**1** there's no need to _____ your temper.
b We had to postpone the meeting because so many people were ill, so ...	**2** we must _____ addresses and phone numbers.
c I wasn't trying to annoy you –	**3** I _____ my way.
d Sorry I'm late. I don't know the town very well and ...	**4** someone _____ me a job.
e Can I _____ you a drink?	**5** He never _____ an opinion.
f Let's keep in touch. Before you go, ...	**6** Who do you think will win?
g They are _____ the election soon.	**7** We've got beer, wine or orange juice.
h It's difficult to know what he thinks.	**8** we're _____ it next week instead.

EXTENSION 2

1 Opposites of *lose*

What are the opposites of the *lose* collocations from **E1**? Make expressions with these verbs.

find   keep   win

a _____ your temper   **d** _____ in contact with

b _____ your way   **e** _____ an election

c _____ your job

2 Collocations with *change*

Answer the questions with words or phrases from the box.

> channels / your clothes / currency / jobs / your mind / the subject / trains

a What do you sometimes have to change when you travel by rail?
b What could you change if you were too warm or too cold?
c What do you sometimes need to change when you go from one country to another – so that you can buy things?
d What do you change when you alter your opinion?
e What do you change when you want to talk about something different?
f What do you change when you're fed up with the work you are doing?
g What do you change when you want to watch a different TV programme?

F Phrasal verbs with *turn*

The article tells you to **turn off** your computer.

1 Match these *turn* verbs with one or more of meanings a–g.

turn down   turn off   turn on   turn up

a arrive at a place or event
b increase sound or heat from something like a radio or a cooker
c leave one road to go along another
d move a switch so that something starts working
e move a switch so that something stops working
f reduce sound or heat from something like a radio or a cooker
g refuse an offer or the person who makes it

2 Complete each sentence with the correct form of a *turn* verb from **F1**.

a I can't work because the TV's too loud. Please _____ it _____ .

b Go along the motorway for about 10 kilometres and then _____ _____ when you see signs for London.

c It was a great game, but unfortunately only a few people _____ _____ .

d I'm really cold. Can you _____ the heating _____ , please?

e He applied for a job as a policeman, but they _____ him _____ .

G Practice

Read this letter from someone reacting to the idea of an Internet-free day. Fill the gaps with words and phrases from sections **A–F** above.

I think the idea of an Internet-free day is really brilliant. Lots of my friends – myself included – are completely **(a)** _____ to their computers and spend hours and hours every day in their own **(b)** _____ world. Another friend just can't stop working – he admits himself that he's a **(c)** _____ . So I am definitely going to **(d)** _____ my mouse, **(e)** _____ my computer and **(f)** _____ my friends to persuade them to get involved in an **(g)** _____ or activity where we can actually do something **(h)** _____ for a change. We're thinking about **(i)** _____ a bike ride or perhaps helping to tidy up the local park. I'm not very brave, so I don't want to do anything too **(j)** _____ .

The future of music

A Introduction

1 These words are from the article below. Try to match them with their meanings.

a	accessible	1	involving large numbers of people / the majority
b	consumer	2	able to change easily
c	download	3	the amount something is worth
d	duplicate	4	melodies
e	flexible	5	to choose
f	luxury	6	a person who buys and uses products
g	mass	7	to copy from the Internet to a computer
h	select	8	easy to get
i	tunes	9	great comfort or wealth
j	value	10	to copy, to reproduce

2 Check in a dictionary the meaning of any of these words you do not understand.

B Reading

1 Read the article and fill each gap with the correct form of a word from **A1**.

Digital and free

The fact that technology is changing music is nothing new. The arrival of the phonograph in the late 19th century made it possible to (**a**) _____ performances, with the result that there is no music made today that has not been shaped by the fact of recording.

As recording technology spread throughout the world, it had some surprising effects. Folk (**b**) _____, for example, which had always been (**c**) _____, changing with each performance, were transformed by recording into fixed songs that could be exactly repeated.

Consumerism grew in the last century as technology improved. What (**d**) _____ consumed – whether books, CDs or videos – were exact copies. The ability to make huge quantities of copies was the key ingredient of (**e**) _____ culture.

The massive upset that music is now experiencing is the change from analogue copies to digital copies. The analogue copies of the industrial age were perfect and cheap. The information age is driven by digital copies, which are perfect and **free.**

Of course, it's not just music that is being copied for free: it is text, pictures, movies, entire websites. But the moment something becomes free, its (**f**) _____ changes. When electric lighting was new and expensive, the poor burned candles. When electricity became easily (**g**) _____ and cheap, candles at dinner became a sign of (**h**) _____. Now, the only truly valuable things are those which cannot be copied.

What kinds of things can't be copied? A friend may pass on a recording by your favourite group, but if you pay, the group will e-mail it to you seconds after the performance. Similarly, you may (**i**) _____ the music of a rock band from the Internet, but the only way to get the full details of each track is to contact the band and pay.

Free music brings other problems. No matter what your tastes, there are not enough hours in a lifetime to listen to more than a tiny fraction of the music which is recorded each year. So people will pay to have someone (**j**) _____, edit and present the music to them in an easy and fun manner. Music will continue to be sold, because it will be easier to buy music you really like than to find it for free.

2 Read the article again and decide if these statements are true (**T**) false (**F**).

    a The phonograph was invented during the last century.   **T / F**

    b Recording technology helped folk music to become more flexible.   **T / F**

    c Analogue copies were cheaper than digital copies.   **T / F**

    d Things that can be copied are worth less than things that cannot be copied.   **T / F**

    e The writer predicts that in the future nobody will pay for music.   **T / F**

C Related words

1 Fill the gaps in this chart with words related to words given. Sometimes there are two words in one group. (X = no useful word at this level.)

Noun	Verb	Adjective
a _____	_____	accessible
b electricity _____ *	X	electrical _____
c _____	_____	industrial _____ (country)
d luxury	X	_____
e performance _____ *	_____	X
f _____	repeat	_____
g _____	select	_____
h technology _____ *	X	_____
i _____	transform	X
j value	_____	valuable

* These words refer to people.

2 Fill the gaps in these sentences with the correct form of words you have added to the chart.

    a The car _____ used to employ millions of workers. Now a lot of the work is done by robots.

    b Have you ever _____ in front of a live audience?

    c My best friend's family is very wealthy – they live in a really _____ house.

    d In the twentieth century steam trains were replaced by _____ trains.

    e If you want a new car, look in the local paper – there is a huge _____ to choose from.

    f This job is terribly _____. I have to do the same thing hundreds of times a day.

EXTENSION: Adjective pairs

Look at these pairs of adjectives and their meanings, then choose the correct word in sentences **a–f**.

Adjective	Meaning	Example
economic	relating to business or industry	economic theories
economical	cheap, not expensive to run	an economical heating system
electric	using electricity	an electric cooker
electrical	concerned with electricity	an electrical engineer
historic	important, significant	a historic speech
historical	happening in the past	a historical event

a This is a very *economic / economical* car. It does 20 kilometres to the litre.
b Tomorrow's meeting between the two leaders will be a *historic / historical* occasion.
c In the future, *electric / electrical* cars will be more common.
d The government is bringing in a new *economic / economical* policy.
e My brother is the manager of an *electric / electrical* store.
f I've just read a fantastic *historic / historical* novel. It's set during the French Revolution.

D Adjective-noun collocations

1 Which nouns in the box can follow these adjectives from the article? Make four lists.

cheap   expensive   free   valuable

experience / fares / gift / holiday / imitation / information / mistake / newspaper / seat / ticket

2 Complete these sentences using adjective-noun collocations from **D1**.

a When you order your first three books from the club, we will send you a(n)
_____ _____ worth at least £10.

b That's not a real diamond ring. It's just a(n) _____ _____.

c Some companies are prepared to pay a lot of money for _____ _____
about their competitors.

d Buying that second-hand car was a(n) _____ _____. It's broken down three
times already.

e Most _____ _____s are full of advertisements and contain hardly any news.

f For many people, going to university is a very _____ _____. They learn
a lot about the world and themselves.

g During its Shakespeare season, the theatre is offering _____ _____
to students.

h For their honeymoon they went on a really _____ _____ to the Seychelles.

E Music words

1 The words in the box are all related to music and recording. Group them under the four
headings which follow. One example of each is given.

band / cassette / CD / composer / group / folk / instrument / jazz / mini-disc / opera / orchestra / performance / pop / rhythm / rock / singer / song / studio / track / tune

Kinds of music	People	Words connected with recording	Other words
folk	*group*	*CD*	*instrument*

2 Check in a dictionary the meaning of any of these words you do not understand.

3 Add any more words you know to the lists.

F Word groups

Here are some groups of words. In each group, one word is a general word and the others are examples of this general word.
Example:

> *gold / metal / silver / steel*
>
> **Metal** is the general word; *gold*, *silver* and *steel* are different kinds of metal.

Which are the general words in these groups?

a *electricity / energy / gas / nuclear power / solar power*
b *cinema / entertainment / theatre / television*
c *breakfast / dinner / lunch / meal / supper*
d *century / month / time / week / year*
e *cassette / CD / DVD / mini-disc / recording*

G Puzzle

Find the following words in this puzzle. They can be horizontal, vertical or diagonal.

a Two 'price' adjectives with opposite meanings
b Someone who buys things
c Another word for *choose*
d Traditional musicians make this kind of music.
e Able to change easily
f Two modern jobs
g A melody
h An adjective related to *economy*
i The noun related to *repeat*
j The adjective related to *luxury*
k A late meal
l A recording of film or television

```
E  L  U  N  C  T  U  N  E  P  I  T
R  X  F  L  E  X  I  B  L  E  L  E
E  C  P  R  O  D  F  V  S  C  U  C
C  H  H  E  N  E  O  A  E  O  X  H
O  A  S  E  N  N  L  L  L  N  U  N
N  C  R  U  A  S  K  U  E  S  R  O
O  C  H  I  P  P  I  M  C  U  I  L
M  E  A  S  I  P  V  V  T  M  O  O
I  S  T  I  L  T  E  I  E  E  U  G
C  T  V  I  D  E  O  R  N  R  S  I
P  R  E  P  E  T  I  T  I  O  N  S
E  L  E  C  T  R  I  C  I  A  N  T
```

3 Mobile phones

A Introduction

1 a Which of these does not have a *screen*?

A a television   B a watch   C a cinema   D a mobile phone

b Which of these does not have *keys*?

A a video recorder   B a piano   C a computer   D a mobile phone

2 Complete sentences **a–j** with words from the box. You may have to change the words slightly. (Use your dictionary to check the meanings of any words you are not sure of.)

> character / communicate / company / compose / emergency / peaktime /
> pre-paid / ring / text

a _____ calls are the most expensive because that's the most popular time for people to use their phones.

b When mobile phones were first introduced, many people only used them in _____.

c For many young people, mobile phones are the most popular way of _____ with friends.

d It can be embarrassing if your phone _____ when you are in a public place.

e If you are musical, you can _____ your own ring tones.

f The name for a written phone message is a _____ message.

g I couldn't understand the notice because it was written in Chinese _____.

h Vodaphone and Orange are two well-known mobile phone _____.

i _____ calls are those you pay for before you make them.

B Reading

Read the article and fill each gap with the correct form of a word from **A1** or **A2**.

Look who's talking

When parents buy their children a mobile phone, they probably imagine them on a street corner somewhere, needing to phone home. They intend it for **(a)** _____ and for short, important calls. They do not expect them to send silly messages to their friends in the school classroom. This is **(b)** _____ messaging, or 'texting', which allows kids to **(c)** _____ with each other easily and quickly. According to phone **(d)** _____, it's a rapidly growing habit.

To a 16-year-old, the attraction of text messaging over old-fashioned phone calls is obvious: it is silent and secret. It is also cheap. Most British under-18s now have mobiles, and many of these

16

phones are on **(e)** _____ packages, which means that parents have some control over how much their children spend. A **(f)** _____ call might cost 30 pence, but for about 10 pence they can type in a message of up to 160 **(g)** _____ and send it anywhere in the country.

15-year-old Sunita goes to a school in London where teachers take away mobiles if they **(h)** _____ during lessons. 'Texting is good fun,' she says. 'Nobody can see which **(i)** _____ you're pressing, so they've no idea what you're writing.'

A survey of 10- to 21-year-olds asked them why they liked text messaging. 'Fun' came at the top of the list; then 'cheap', 'silent, 'private' and 'immediate'.

'Mobile phones are like toys,' says Nigel O'Brien of *Mobile Choice* magazine. 'You can **(j)** _____ your own ring tone, send picture messages, play games on their little **(k)** _____ , or even programme them to ring out your favourite pop song.' And soon, of course, more of us will be using them to take and send instant photos too!

C Verb-noun collocations

1 The verbs below are from the article. Which nouns in the box can follow them? Make four lists. (Some nouns can follow more than one verb.)

play   press   send   spend

> *a button / a CD / chess / energy / football / a key / a letter / a message / money / the piano / a present / a signal / a switch / time / a trick on someone*

2 Find the best endings for these sentence beginnings, and fill each gap with the correct form of one of the verbs from **C1**.

Beginnings	Endings
a It's really easy to start the computer –	**1** It's someone _____ the violin.
b I can't afford to come out tonight –	**2** I _____ it by airmail.
c What's that dreadful noise?	**3** Why don't you have a break for lunch?
d Let's _____ a trick on your brother.	**4** you just _____ this button.
e They should have got my letter by now –	**5** Yes, but I haven't _____ for months.
f If you want to get rid of what you've written, ...	**6** _____ the delete key.
g Are you still interested in golf?	**7** Good idea! Let's hide his car keys.
h You've _____ all morning writing that report.	**8** I _____ all my money.

EXTENSION 1

You can **kill** time, **save** time, **spend** time or **waste** time. What other nouns can go with these verbs? Tick the spaces in this table.

	time	energy	food	your life	a person	money
kill	✔					
save	✔					
spend	✔					
waste	✔					

D Compound nouns

1 A compound noun is a noun with two or more parts. Here are some examples from the article.

> *mobile phone / street corner / text messaging / school classroom / phone companies / phone calls / under-18s / picture message / pop songs*

How are these compound nouns made? Match each noun in the box with one of these descriptions:

- noun + noun
- noun + noun + noun
- noun + -*ing*
- adjective + noun
- preposition + noun

2 We often use compound nouns instead of longer phrases. For example:

a street corner = the corner of a street
under-18s = people who are under 18 years old

Make compound nouns to use instead of these phrases:

a a conversation on the phone
b people who are over 30 years old
c the tone which a phone makes when it rings
d a phone box in a public place
e a message on a machine which answers the phone

E Related words

1 Fill gaps in this chart with words related to the words given. Sometimes there are two words in one group. (X = no useful word at this level.)

Noun	Verb	Adjective	Adjective with opposite meaning
a _____ _____	X	mobile	_____
b _____	imagine	_____ _____	_____
c _____	intend	_____	_____
d _____	_____	growing	X
e attraction	_____	_____	_____
f _____		silent	X
g _____ _____	X	secret	X
h _____	X	private	X
i _____	X	immediate	X

2 Fill the gaps in these sentences with words you have added to the chart.

   a I'm sorry I offended you. It wasn't _____.

   b Recently there has been a dramatic _____ in the use of mobile phones.

   c I can't _____ her attention even though I've been calling to her for several minutes.

   d I can't concentrate on reading unless there is complete _____ in the room.

   e When I was a child, I had a(n) _____ friend who lived under my bed. At the time, I really thought he was real.

   f When they become famous, many pop stars and film stars lose their _____.

EXTENSION 2: Adjectives and their opposites

Here are some pairs of adjectives with opposite meanings. Notice how the second word is different from the first.

mobile / immobile
legal / illegal
responsible / irresponsible
polite / impolite

Now replace the adjectives in these phrases with words which have the opposite meanings.

   a *regular* mealtimes
   b a *patient* teacher
   c *legible* handwriting (*legible* = possible to read)
   d a *mature* teenager (*mature* = grown up)
   e a *relevant* question

F Practice

Read this summary of a report from an anti-smoking organisation. Fill the gaps with words or phrases from sections **A–E** above.

Smoking and mobiles

Doctors think that the recent steady **(a)** _____ in the use of mobile phones among the **(b)** _____ -18s may be one explanation for the dramatic decrease in teenage smoking since 1996. Experts are suggesting that mobile phones may meet some of the same needs as cigarettes for this age group. It's more than just something to do with the hands. Mobiles are cool – they're **(c)** _____ because they are adult. Like cigarettes, they help young people to create a self-image and to feel part of a group. If they see their friends **(d)** _____ with each other, either by **(e)** _____ them or by **(f)** _____ them text **(g)** _____, they will almost certainly regard mobile phones as essential.

   With pay-as-you-go mobile phones, young people are even **(h)** _____ their money in the same way and at the same places as they would if they were buying cigarettes. Some can't afford to do both, others might get all they want from having a mobile, and for them smoking may become unimportant. For some of today's teenagers, smoking might even seem like 'old technology'.

4 Camera rage in Hawaii

A Introduction

1 These words and phrases are from the article below. Try to match them with their meanings.

a	drop	1	to object to, to complain about
b	furious	2	to drive faster than the limit
c	gesture	3	to go down, to fall
d	major	4	where people live
e	pack	5	with nothing to show its identity
f	protest against	6	a movement of hands
g	rage	7	a group that moves around together
h	residential	8	great anger
i	speed	9	extremely angry
j	unmarked	10	main, important

2 Check in a dictionary the meaning of any of these words you do not understand.

B Reading

1 Read the article from an American newspaper and fill the gaps with the correct form of words from **A1**.

Slow down! This ain't the Mainland!

Bumper stickers in Hawaii say "Slow down! This ain't the Mainland!" But now drivers **(a)** _____ (3 words) a programme forcing them to drive more slowly. Recently the state began using digital cameras – operated from **(b)** _____ vans – to catch drivers who **(c)** _____ and run red lights on certain state roads and highways.

The response has been rapid. Several thousand **(d)** _____ drivers have bought illegal covers to hide their license plates. They have written letters to the local papers trying to persuade people not to pay their tickets. Cellphone brigades call morning radio shows to tell them where the vans are, and there are hundreds of reports of drivers making angry **(e)** _____ and even throwing trash at the vans.

One group says the problem is not speeding, but the speed limits. At 55 miles per hour, Hawaii's speed limit is the lowest in the USA. On many **(f)** _____ highways, which often go past schools and **(g)** _____ areas, the limit **(h)** _____ to 45 or 35 m.p.h.

Some officials are even saying that the program may be working too well. "People are now driving too slowly," said a spokeswoman for the City of Honolulu. "They're driving in **(i)** _____ so their plates can't be seen by the cameras. There are people who speed around these packs. And, of course, the vans themselves are being attacked by drivers."

The scheme has caused such **(j)** _____ that some lawmakers are thinking about abandoning it. They say it makes people drive badly.

In one respect, though, the program is a clear success. In its first eight days, it produced nearly 1,300 traffic citations. Normally, there are about 800 citations in an eight-day period.

2 How much do you remember about the article? Answer these questions, then read the article again to check your answers.

    a Where are the digital cameras?
    b Who do the angry motorists telephone to say where the cameras are?
    c What is the speed limit in Hawaii?
    d How do motorists try to avoid the cameras?
    e How many speeding motorists did the cameras catch in the first eight days?

C Strong adjectives

1 The motorists of Hawaii were *furious* about the speed cameras. *Furious* is stronger than *angry*.
Put these sets of adjectives in order, starting with the weakest and ending with the strongest. Use a dictionary to check your ideas.

    a *angry / furious / irritated*
    b *cold / cool / freezing*
    c *good / excellent / satisfactory*
    d *exhausted / sleepy / tired*
    e *amazing / surprising / unexpected*

2 Now complete these sentences with one of the 'strongest' adjectives from **C1**

    a I've been working since 6 o'clock this morning. I'm completely _____!
    b The heating broke down last night. I woke up absolutely _____!
    c The firework display was totally _____. I've never seen anything like it.
    d It was the fourth time that week that the train had been late. The passengers were absolutely _____!
    e He got 98% for his assignment. His work was simply _____!

EXTENSION 1: Related words

What are the nouns related to these adjectives from **C1**?

a *amazing*	_____	**e** *good*	_____
b *cool*	_____	**f** *irritated*	_____
c *excellent*	_____	**g** *satisfactory*	_____
d *furious*	_____	**h** *surprising*	_____

D American English

1 The article you have just read is from the *New York Times* and is written in American English. Match these words from the article with their British English equivalents.

    a *cellphone*   **1** number plate
    b *citation*   **2** rubbish
    c *highway*   **3** summons (an order to appear in a law court)
    d *license plate*   **4** to cross, to drive through
    e *run (red lights)*   **5** mobile
    f *trash*   **6** main road

2 There are some spelling differences between British and American English.
For example, *program* in American English is spelt *programme* in British English.
Can you fill the gaps in this chart with the missing words?

	American	British
a	program	programme
b	center	_____
c	_____	humour
d	license (*noun*)	_____
e	_____	catalogue
f	traveled	_____

E Verb-noun collocations: *Make* and *do*

1 Some of the drivers in Hawaii *make angry gestures* at the unmarked vans. Which words and phrases in the box follow *make* and which follow *do*? Write two lists of ten words and phrases in your exercise book.

> your best / business with someone / the cooking / a crossword / damage / a decision /
> an effort / exercises / housework / a job / a mistake / a noise / someone an offer /
> a painting / a phone call / progress / room for something / the shopping /
> a suggestion / trouble

make	do

2 Now complete these conversations using expressions with *make* or *do* from **E1**.

a We've run out of food. Shall I go to the supermarket and _____?

b I'm sorry, it's all my fault. I _____ a terrible _____.

c If you want to pass your exams, you'll have to _____ a much bigger _____.

d Last night's storm _____ a lot of _____ to our roof. It'll need replacing.

e You'll have to move the piano if you want to _____ the new TV.

f Can I _____? Why don't you learn to drive? You'd have an easier life.

g The people next door _____ so much _____ last night that I couldn't get to sleep.

EXTENSION 2: Meanings of *make* and *do*

The verbs *make* and *do* have many meanings. What do they mean in sentences **a–f**?
Choose synonyms from the box.

> come to / cut or style / earn / equal / spend / travel at

a My brother *makes* about £1000 a week.
b The driver admitted to the police that he had been *doing* over 200 kilometres an hour.
c He *did* five years in prison for burglary.
d Fifty-three and forty-seven *makes* exactly a hundred.
e I'm sorry we couldn't *make* your party on Friday. We didn't get back until midnight.
f I'm having my hair *done* this afternoon.

F Verb-adverb collocations

1 Which adverbs in the box can follow these verbs? Make five lists.

drive   sleep   speak   walk   work

> carefully / carelessly / clearly / dangerously / fast / hard / heavily / lightly / loudly /
> noisily / quickly / slowly

2 Complete these sentences with verb-adverb collocations from **F1**.

a I can't hear what you're saying. Can you _____ more _____, please?

b We'll have to _____ a little more _____ if we want to get there on time.

c He was arrested for _____ _____. He admitted doing over 100 mph.

d You won't wake him. He always _____ _____.

e She's one of our best employees. She always _____ _____.

3 Someone who *eats noisily* is a *noisy eater*. What do we call these people?

a someone who *drives carefully* _____

b someone who *speaks clearly* _____

c someone who *sleeps lightly* _____

d someone who *works hard* _____

e someone who *walks slowly* _____

G Puzzle

Read the clues and complete the puzzle. All the answers are words from this unit.

a An adjective describing an area where people live
b Great anger
c American English for *rubbish*
d Extremely angry
e A hand movement
f The opposite of *carelessly*
g Extremely good
h Extremely surprising
i The American English spelling of *catalogue*
j American English for *mobile phone*
k The noun related to *irritated*

k

a — — — | — — — — — — — —
b | — — —
c — | — — —
d — — — | — — —
e — — — | — — —
f — — — | — — — — — —
g — — — — — — — | —
h — — — | — —
i — — — — | —
j — — — — — — | —

5 Is chewing gum good for you?

A Introduction

1 These words are from the article below. Try to match them with their meanings.

a *assessment*	1 to connect or relate
b *concentration*	2 to investigate, to look into
c *evidence*	3 a test or measurement
d *explore*	4 related to the human mind and its abilities
e *imitation*	5 an idea which might explain facts
f *associate*	6 the ability to focus your attention on something
g *mental*	7 not real, a copy
h *theory*	8 proof, information which makes us believe something

2 Check in a dictionary the meaning of any of these words you do not understand.

B Reading

1 Read the article and decide whether these statements are true (**T**) or false (**F**). Do not try to fill the gaps yet.

a Two groups took part in the chewing gum experiments. **T / F**
b Gum chewers had a better long-term memory than the others. **T / F**
c The scientists understand clearly why chewing gum improves memory. **T / F**
d People's heart rate increases when they chew gum. **T / F**
e Chewing gum helps people to concentrate on their studies. **T / F**

To chew or not to chew

Experiments suggest that chewing gum can assist the memory.

The habit of chewing gum is usually (a)_____ with young people, pop stars, and football managers. But researchers now believe that it's a habit which can improve your memory. Experiments carried out by Lucy Wilkinson and Dr Andrew Scholey, at the University of Northumbria, studied the positive effects of chewing gum on people's (b)_____ abilities.

A group of 75 adults was split into three groups: one group chewed sugar-free gum, a second group copied the process of chewing but without gum – (c)_____ chewing, and a third group did nothing. During the experiments, a computerised (d)_____ took place of the subjects' attention abilities, their long-term memory, and their working memory.

The results showed that chewing gum in a natural way improved people's abilities in a number of memory tests, compared with imitation chewing and not chewing at all. The gum chewers showed an improvement in immediate and long-term memory: their ability to remember words was 35% better than the two other groups.

Dr Scholey said the researchers did not know exactly why chewing gum improved these abilities, but they were (e)_____ a number of (f)_____.

He said: "We found that people who chewed gum had better memory for word lists and holding information. We think the improvement may be to do with having something in your mouth. We checked heart rate and found it increased during chewing."

There was no concrete (g)_____ from the experiments to support the idea that chewing gum improved (h)_____ while studying.

2 Now read the article again and fill each gap with the correct form of one of the words from **A1**.

C Related words

1 Fill the gaps in this chart with words related to the words given. Sometimes there are two words in one group. (X = no useful word at this level.)

Noun	Verb	Adjective	Adverb
a assessment _____ *	_____	X	X
b concentration	_____	_____	X
c evidence	X	_____	_____
d _____ _____ *	explore	_____	X
e imitation _____ *	_____	_____	X
f _____	associate	X	X
g _____	X	mental	_____
h theory	X	_____	_____

* These words refer to people.

2 Fill the gaps in these sentences with words you have added to the chart.
   a Amundsen was a famous Norwegian _____ who reached the South Pole.
   b Children often _____ the behaviour of their older brothers or sisters.
   c Someone had _____ been smoking in the room.
   d I find it difficult to _____ on my work when other people are talking.
   e _____, we could win the lottery this week, but it's very unlikely.
   f After two 3-hour exams in one day, I was _____ exhausted.

D Adjective-noun collocations

1 The adjectives **a–e** are from the article. Match them with their opposites **1–5**.
   a *long-term*   **1** artificial
   b *mental*   **2** theoretical
   c *natural*   **3** negative
   d *positive*   **4** physical
   e *concrete*   **5** short-term

2 Which adjectives in **D1** can be used with these nouns?

   ability / effects / evidence / light / memory

3 Complete these sentences using adjective-noun collocations from **D1** and **D2**.

    a He seems to have a _____ _____ to get on with people.

    b There is no _____ _____ that using mobile phones is harmful.

    c Most people don't like rain, but it does have some _____ _____ : like helping plants to grow.

    d My grandmother can clearly remember her schooldays but her _____ _____ is very poor. She can't remember what she did yesterday.

    e Our office has no windows, so we have to work in _____ _____ .

EXTENSION: 'Memory' verbs

Apart from *remember*, there are a number of other verbs related to memory and remembering.

1 Match the verbs with their meanings.

a *memorise*	**1** make you remember something you have to do
b *recall*	**2** make you remember something similar
c *recognise*	**3** bring something back to your memory
d *remind you **of** something*	**4** learn by heart so that you can remember it exactly
e *remind you **to do** something*	**5** identify something or someone you have seen before

2 Choose the best verb in the these sentences.

    a Haven't we met before? I'm sure I *remind / recognise* you from somewhere.

    b I'm terrible at *memorising / recognising* telephone numbers.

    c She *reminds / recalls* me of my sister. She's got the same laugh.

    d I'm sorry, but I can't *recall / memorise* having a phone conversation with you.

    e Could you *remind / remember* me to buy my dad a birthday present tomorrow?

E Phrasal verbs with *carry*

The article says that Lucy Wilkinson and Andrew Scholey **carried out** experiments. *Carry out* means *do* or *perform*. Here are some more phrasal verbs with *carry* and their meanings.

• *get carried away*	behave in a strange way because you are enthusiastic about something
• *carry something off*	succeed in doing something difficult
• *carry on*	continue
• *carry something through*	finish doing something planned

Now choose the best *carry* verb in these sentences.

a Scientists have been *carrying out / carrying on* tests to discover how the virus is spread.

b Politicians are determined to *carry away / carry through* their plan to improve schools.

c Sorry, I didn't mean to interrupt you. Please *carry off / carry on*.

d That was a fantastic performance. I know you were nervous, but you *carried it off / carried it on* brilliantly.

e I'd never seen such a fantastic selection of CDs! I got a bit *carried away / carried off* and spent all my money.

F Nouns + prepositions

*The gum chewers showed an improvement **in** long-term memory.*
Fill the gaps in these sentences with one of the prepositions from the box.

> between / for / in / into / on / to

a Last year politicians got a 10% increase _____ their salaries.

b Chewing gum has a definite effect _____ people's ability to remember words.

c I have no objection _____ your chewing gum if it helps you to study.

d We had a choice _____ going by taxi or catching a train.

e She seems to have lost all interest _____ her studies.

f Everyone knows about his financial dependence _____ his parents.

g Has anybody got an explanation _____ his absence?

h Researchers have been doing research _____ the connection _____ chewing gum and memory.

i They have been getting support _____ their research from the makers of chewing gum.

G Practice

Read this short article about someone's bad memory. Fill the gaps with words and phrases from sections **A–E** above.

> I've got a terrible **(a)** _____ for detailed facts. For example, I often
> **(b)** _____ people by their faces, but I find it completely impossible to
> **(c)** _____ their names. My **(d)** _____ memory is particularly bad. I can
> **(e)** _____ the names of all my school friends but be completely unable to
> **(f)** _____ the name of someone I met yesterday! The problem is worse if
> I'm tired, and getting plenty of sleep seems to bring about an **(g)** _____ in
> the situation.
> All this may be associated with my inability to **(h)** _____ on what I'm
> doing. For example, if I'm trying to read a book or watch TV, every little noise
> or movement disturbs me. My friends point out that it's a **(i)** _____ problem
> rather than a physical one, and not very serious, but that doesn't really help.

Job stress in Sweden

A Introduction

1 These words and phrases are from the article below. Try to match them with their meanings.

a	*burned out*	**1**	a person with special knowledge or skill
b	*campaign*	**2**	something that happens to you
c	*casualty*	**3**	ill, unwell
d	*clinic*	**4**	to concentrate (on), to give your attention (to)
e	*experience*	**5**	achieving or producing a lot
f	*expert*	**6**	a person who suffers as a result of something bad
g	*focus on*	**7**	exhausted due to overwork over a long period
h	*high-pressure*	**8**	a series of planned activities intended to achieve an aim
i	*productive*	**9**	stressful, demanding
j	*sick*	**10**	a place where people go for specialist medical help

2 Check in a dictionary the meaning of any of these words you do not understand.

B Reading

Read the article and fill each gap with the correct form of a word or phrase from **A1**.

My personality had gone

Rosie Goldsmith describes making a radio programme about the problems of stress in Sweden.

I thought I was well prepared to make a programme about stress among Sweden's young high-tech workers. But I was in for a shock. Many young Swedes are not only stressed, they're completely **(a)** _____. Change has happened so quickly in Sweden and young people are **(b)** _____ of that change.

First I met Torbjorn Levin – a tall Swede in his thirties who used to run his own advertising business and worked on average 50–70 hours a week. He burned out. He describes the **(c)** _____ : 'I felt empty. My personality had gone.' Torbjorn stopped work, went to his parents' home and slept for three months. Today he is working again, but differently: 'I take it one day at a time. I question *why* I do things.'

Next I went to talk to one of the country's leading **(d)** _____ on stress, Professor Alexander Perski,

who runs a burnout **(e)** _____. He says that Swedes are not used to **(f)** _____ work. There's a feeling that they're losing control over their own lives.

But stress doesn't just affect individuals – it also involves enormous costs to the country. This worries the Swedish Social Affairs Minister, Ingela Thalen. 'The government is investing more money in research and support, and there are education **(g)** _____. But in the end,' she says, 'people are responsible for their own health.'

My final visit was to meet an inspiring boss, Jurgen Lerjestad, who has come up with a brilliant new idea: you work only six hours a day. You then have time for a real life – at home with the kids and doing sports and other leisure activities. When you're at work, you **(h)** _____ work – no long phone calls to the boyfriend or the bank. His staff are never **(i)** _____, they are more **(j)** _____ and more enthusiastic, and very few of them leave the company. They earn a full salary, and their clients are happier too.

C Adjective-noun collocations

1 Which nouns in the box can follow these adjectives from the article? Make four lists.

brilliant   enthusiastic   inspiring   leading

expert / idea / meeting / politician / teacher / worker

2 Complete these sentences using adjective-noun collocations from **C1**.
(You will have to change the form of some of the nouns.)

a He is one of the country's _____ _____ on climate change.

He's always being interviewed on television.

b I've just had a(n) _____ _____. Why don't we start our own business?

c I was never interested in maths, probably because I didn't have a very _____

_____.

d Bill Clinton was one of the world's _____ _____ in the 1990s.

e The firm has a lot of _____ _____. They are always keen to get to work.

D Related words

Fill the gaps in this chart with words related to the adjectives given. Sometimes there are two words in one group. (X = no useful word at this level.)

	Noun	Verb	Adjective	Adverb
a	_____	X	brilliant	_____
b	_____ _____ *	_____	enthusiastic	_____
c	_____	_____	inspiring	X
d	_____ *	_____	leading	X
e	_____ _____ _____ *	_____	productive	_____

* These words refer to people.

EXTENSION 1: *High- / Low-*

The compound adjectives *high-tech* and *high-pressure* are used in the article. Make adjectives using *high-* or *low-* with these words to complete the sentences **a–g**.

class / cost / fat / level / lying / risk / speed

a A car that can go very fast is a _____ car.

b When you want to lose weight, you eat _____ food.

c Dangerous sports like bungee jumping or mountaineering are _____ sports.

d If you haven't got much money, you live in _____ housing.

e Rich or famous people might stay in a _____ hotel.

f A meeting between important people, for example between presidents of the most powerful countries in the world, is a _____ meeting.

g Land which is near the sea is _____ land.

E Phrasal verbs with *out*

The article tells us that Torbjorn Levin **burned out**. Phrasal verbs with *out* often have the meaning of an activity ending completely. Use the correct form of these verbs to fill the gaps in the sentences.

blow out   die out   knock out   run out   sell out   tire out

a The car won't start. I think it may have _____ _____ of petrol.

b I need a lot of sleep. Staying up late at night _____ me _____.

c Mike Tyson _____ _____ his opponent in the first round of their fight.

d Many rare birds and animals are _____ _____ because of pollution.

e The wind was so strong that it _____ _____ the fire.

f The latest Madonna CD is incredibly popular. The shops _____ _____ of it on the first day.

EXTENSION 2

What other meanings can **out** have? Match the verbs with **out** in these sentences with meanings **1–4**.

a I don't feel like cooking tonight. Shall we *eat out*?

b We need to *set out* early if we want to arrive by midday.

c There isn't room for all those clothes. You'll have to *throw* some of them *out*.

d The teacher asked one of the students to *give out* the books.

1 remove, get rid of
2 go to a restaurant
3 distribute
4 start a journey

F Three-part phrasal verbs

The article says that Jurgen Lerjestad **came up with** a brilliant new idea. This means he *thought of* or *produced* an idea.

Match the three-part phrasal verbs in sentences **a–f** with meanings **1–6**.

> **Note**
> The three parts of these verbs almost always stay together. Example:
> A   *Did he come up with that idea?* [NOT *Did he come up that idea with?*]
> B   *No, I came up with it.* [NOT *I came up it with.*]

a I must *get down to* my geography essay today.

b She never buys a train ticket. I don't know how she *gets away with* it.

c I wish you'd stop *going on about* your rich relatives!

d Many young children *look up to* their teacher when they first start school.

e Our hotel was disappointing, but the wonderful weather *made up for* it.

f I can't *put up with* that noise any longer. Please turn your music down.

1 admire and respect
2 talk for a long time about something, in an annoying way
3 escape without criticism or punishment for something wrong you have done
4 provide something good to compensate for something bad
5 start making an effort to do something
6 tolerate, bear, endure

G Confusing words

Choose the correct word to complete each sentence.

a Stress can have a terrible *affect / effect* on some people.
b When he was at school, he hated doing scientific *experiences / experiments*.
c When I was 18, I left *home / house* and went to university.
d I can only sunbathe for half an hour – I've got very *sensible / sensitive* skin.
e Her ring looks expensive, but actually it's completely *priceless / worthless*.
f I don't mind being *alone / lonely* – I've always enjoyed my own company.

H Practice

Read this short news report about what a German company is doing to make its workers' lives easier. Fill the gaps with the correct form of words and phrases from the box. There are **two words** you do not need to use.

> *affect / come up with / effect / employees / enthusiasm / experiences / experiments / expert / idea / productive*

German Town Promotes Sleeping on the Job

A German town has found that sleeping on the job, even for limited periods, can have the **(a)** _____ of making workers more **(b)** _____.

For two years, civil servants in the small town of Vechta near Hamburg have been allowed twenty minutes after lunch to nap* in their office chairs or to relax in other ways. In the beginning workers didn't think much of the **(c)** _____, but then they were happier and they started working with more **(d)** _____.

The town **(e)** _____ the scheme because it had too much work for too few **(f)** _____, and no money to take on new civil servants. A local health insurance company gave them courses in napping. **(g)** _____ carried out by the Institute of Sleep Research and Medicine in Regensburg found that 22 percent of the entire German population naps regularly. But according to an **(h)** _____ at the Institute, Juergen Zulley, only Vechta had put the idea of sleeping on the job into practice.

'Work and sleep are normally seen as opposites, and many firms don't want to admit that their employees sleep at work,' Zulley said.

* *to nap = to sleep for a short time*

7 A short history of frozen food

A Introduction

1 You are going to read an article about using ice to keep food fresh. Here are some words and phrases from the article.

> crammed / crystal / to defrost / to freeze / freezer / freezing / frozen / to keep /
> mushy / naturalist / to preserve / to stuff / to thaw out

a Underline the **seven** words and phrases which are connected in some way with **ice**.

b What do you notice about **five** of these words?

c Match the words connected with ice with these meanings:
  1 a place to keep food very cold
  2 a small shape with many sides, made of ice
  3 to make something ice-cold and solid
  4 to allow something which was ice-cold to return to its normal condition
  5 in an ice-cold, solid condition
  6 very cold

d Find other words in the box that mean:
  1 filled with a lot of things pushed together
  2 to fill something tightly
  3 to prevent from going bad
  4 a person who studies living things
  5 soft and wet
  6 to stay fresh

2 Check in a dictionary the meaning of any of these words you do not understand.

B Reading

1 Read the article and answer these questions. Do not try to fill the gaps yet.

  a Who first used ice to keep fish fresh?
  b Where did Clarence Birdseye discover the idea of keeping fish fresh by using ice?
  c How and why is slow-frozen fish horrible?
  d What was the 'Springfield Experiment'?

THANK YOU MR BIRDSEYE

The Chinese invent everything first. In the 15th century they used to fill their fishing boats with lumps of ice, so that the fish would still be fresh when it was brought to land. And in 1626, Francis Bacon, an Englishman who some people think may have written Shakespeare's plays, died of pneumonia which he caught while he was **(a)** _____ a dead chicken with snow to see if it would keep. But we have Clarence Birdseye to thank for modern **(b)** _____ food.

Clarence was a **(c)** _____ and wild man of the woods. He dropped out of university to become a trapper and to study wildlife for the American Government in the Canadian Arctic north. He spent the three long winters of 1910 to 1913 in a small wooden hut with Mrs Birdseye, lots of dead fish and a bathtub. To **(d)** ____ the fish, he filled the bath with them and packed ice round them.

At some point food obviously ran short, so he **(e)** _____ some of the fish and cooked it. He learned, from the local Eskimos, that the faster he **(f)** _____ the fish, the better it tasted later. Slow-frozen fish is **(g)** _____ and horrible because big ice **(h)** _____ form inside it and break up the flesh, but a fish caught in **(i)** _____ winds and laid flat on the ice as soon as it is caught tastes lovely. There are lots more ice crystals inside it, but they are microscopic in size.

Back in New York, Clarence invented a machine to flash-freeze packets of fish by squeezing them between two very cold steel plates, and started Birdseye Frozen Sea-foods Inc. On March 6 1930, in the 'Springfield Experiment', 26 different frozen foods were sold from a **(j)** _____ in a shop in Massachusetts.

Today, your home freezer, which is probably **(k)** _____ with piles and piles of delicious frozen meals just waiting to **(l)** _____, is the result.

---

2 Now read the article again and fill each gap with the correct form of a word or phrase from **A1**.

C Verbs + prepositions

*In 1626, Francis Bacon stuffed a dead chicken **with** snow. He died **of** pneumonia.*
Fill the gaps in the sentences with one of these prepositions.

> *for / from / in / of / on / with*

a After a day's fishing, his hands and all his clothes *smelt* _____ fish.

b Clarence Birdseye *succeeded* _____ finding a way of freezing fish.

c He *filled* the bath _____ fish and ice.

d These days many people *rely* _____ frozen food for their everyday meals.

e The taste of frozen food *depends* _____ how quickly it was frozen.

f We have Clarence Birdseye to *thank* _____ inventing a machine which froze fish quickly.

g Now we *pay* less _____ frozen fish than _____ fresh fish. *(Same word twice.)*

h After three nights in sub-zero temperatures, he was *suffering* _____ severe frostbite.

D Near synonyms

1 Find **five** groups of **three** words from this list which are similar in meaning.

> appalling / appetising / awful / delicious / to fill / heaps / horrible / loads / microscopic /
> minute / to pack / piles / to stuff / tasty / tiny

2 Fill the gaps in these sentences with words from **D1** in the correct form. Usually three words are possible, but in one case only two are possible.

a That was probably the worst film I've ever seen. It was absolutely _____.

b When the stone hit the car, the windscreen smashed into thousands of _____ pieces.

c We _____ so many clothes into our cases that we could hardly close them.

d Everyone was very kind this year. I got _____ of presents for my birthday.

e Everything on the menu sounds really _____.

EXTENSION: Word stress

The word *minute* has two meanings, depending on whether the stress is on the first syllable or the second syllable:
I'll be there in a 'minute.   When my daughter was born she had mi'nute fingers.

Here are some more words which can have different meanings, depending on where the stress is. Choose the correct alternative in each sentence.

a I don't really want to change jobs. I'm quite '*content / con'tent* where I am.
b It took them several days to cross the '*desert / de'sert* from north to south.
c Would anyone '*object / ob'ject* if I smoked a cigarette in here?
d You'll need a special '*permit / per'mit* to work here.
e I wonder who's going to '*present / pre'sent* the prizes at the school this year?
f Let's put the rubbish out. The '*refuse / re'fuse* collectors will be here soon.

E Materials

Mr and Mrs Birdseye lived in a small **wooden** hut for three years.
Clarence Birdseye's machine froze fish by squeezing it between two very cold **steel** plates.

> **Notes**
> Most words for materials have only one form: **Steel** plates / The plates are made of **steel**.
>
> But *wood* and *wool* have two forms: *A **wooden** hut / The hut was made of **wood**.*
> *A **woollen** jacket / This jacket is made of **wool**.*

What are these objects made of? Match each picture with a word or words from the box on **page 35**.

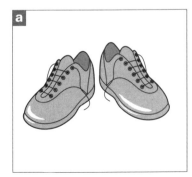

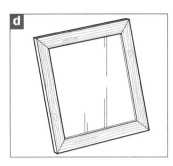 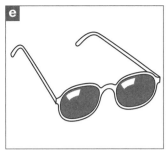  

cloth (material) / glass / leather / metal / paper / plastic / pottery / rubber / wood

F Occupations

Clarence Birdseye was a *trapper* (someone who traps animals) and a *naturalist* (someone who studies living things).

Using one of the suffixes **-er / -ian / -ist / -or**, write the words used for someone who …

a … studies or plays *music* _____

b … plays the *guitar* _____

c … *cleans windows* _____

d … *acts* in films _____

e … studies *biology* _____

f … has a job in *politics* _____

g … studies *economics* _____

h … *directs* a film or play _____

i … *manages a company* _____

j … *operates a computer* _____

G Puzzle

Find the following words in this puzzle. They can be horizontal, vertical or diagonal.

a Two 'ice' words
b Two words which mean *very small*
c Two words which mean *very bad*
d Two words with two different stress patterns for each
e Two different materials
f A theatrical occupation
g A musician

```
A  D  E  F  R  O  S  T  K  O
A  P  D  A  C  T  O  R  F  G
W  G  P  E  A  C  T  T  R  U
F  L  E  A  S  L  A  I  E  I
U  A  T  A  L  E  P  N  E  T
L  S  E  B  C  L  R  Y  Z  A
T  S  R  I  C  H  I  T  E  R
I  M  I  N  U  T  E  N  R  I
M  P  L  A  S  T  I  C  G  S
Y  O  C  O  N  T  E  N  T  T
```

A Introduction

1 These words and phrases are from the two emails below. Try to match them with their meanings.

a	*area*	**1**	very busy
b	*backpacker*	**2**	a port, a place where ships stop to load and unload
c	*body clock*	**3**	wonderful
d	*cut costs*	**4**	a place where there is a natural spring of water which is good
e	*harbour*		for drinking or bathing in
f	*hectic*	**5**	a geographical region, a part of a country
g	*impressive*	**6**	to reduce what you spend
h	*recover*	**7**	a traveller who carries his/her possessions in a rucksack
i	*spa*	**8**	the human body's natural time to do certain things, e.g. sleep
		9	to return to a normal condition after tiredness or illness

2 These sets of words and phrases are also from the emails. Make up your own sentences using the words and phrases in each set in any order.
Example: *body clock / long flight*   *A long flight can affect / upset your body clock.*

   a *hire / bike / explore / area*
   b *beach / sand*
   c *camp / sleeping bag / tent*

3 Check in a dictionary the meaning of any of the words in **A1** and **A2** you do not understand.

B Reading

Read the two emails and fill each gap with the correct form of a word or phrase from **A1** or **A2**.

Hi Dad,
We're safe and sound in Auckland, although totally exhausted. It's been a pretty
(a) _____ few days exploring, finding our way around and **(b)** _____ from the longest flight you could imagine.

Auckland is quite **(c)** _____ – lots of good places to eat and stay and it's really quite hot! Our **(d)** _____ are still wrong. This morning we woke after 16 hours sleep at 5.30 a.m., wide awake and ready for a nice walk around the town and the **(e)** _____ . We've decided to **(f)** _____ some bikes and then set about some proper exploration.

Anyway, as you can imagine, there's not a lot to tell you yet. We're just getting very hot and tired – all in the name of adventure.

I'll be checking my emails at least once a week so I should be able to keep up to date.

Hope all's well.

Lots of love,

Matthew xx

Hi!

How's it all going? We're back in Auckland after a week at Piahia, in a region called the Bay of Islands. It was fantastic – lots of harbours, bays and lovely beaches. We slowed right down and spent time just relaxing. It was a good place to have a break after the busy city.

Tomorrow we're going north-east to an area called the Coramandel. It's most amazing feature is a hot water beach – a kind of natural **(g)** _____ right on the sand! Sounds strange, doesn't it? We have now decided to camp with our new tent and sleeping bags and really **(h)** _____. It'll be cheaper and healthier than the special hostels for **(i)** _____.

I sent a few postcards out a week or so ago. Have they arrived yet? Anyway, I hope you are all well and happy.

Love to everyone,

Matt xx

C Verb-noun collocations

1 Which nouns and phrases in the box can follow these verbs?

cut   find   have

> the answer to a question / a bath / bread / a break / breakfast / costs /
> a cure for a disease / dinner / a holiday / prices / a rest / a scene from a film /
> a shower / the solution to a problem / taxes / your way (somewhere)

2 Fill the gaps in these conversations with verb-noun collocations from **C1** in the correct form.

a A I've been working non-stop all morning.

    B Why don't you _____?

b A The video seems shorter than the film we saw at the cinema.

    B Yes, I think they've _____ several _____.

c A Do you think they'll ever _____ for cancer?

    B Of course. They're making progress all the time.

d A Why are you so late? Was there a lot of traffic?

    B No, I couldn't _____. In the end I had to ask someone.

e A Have you _____ this year?

    B Yes, we went to Italy for three weeks. The weather was fantastic.

f A Do you know when people first started drinking coffee?

    B No, I don't, but you could _____ in an encyclopedia or on the Internet.

g A Why have you started shopping at the old supermarket again?

    B Because they've _____ their _____.

EXTENSION 1: Idioms with *cut*

Match the **cut** idioms in these sentences with meanings **1–5**.

a I saw my best friend in town yesterday and she just *cut me dead*.
b The fire alarm went off just after lunch, so we had to *cut* our meeting *short*.
c The children were making a terrible noise until the teacher told them to *cut it out*.
d The builders had to *cut corners* to finish the house on time, but the owner made them do some of the work again.
e The headteacher phoned the boy's parents to tell them he had been *cutting lessons*.

1 do quickly and cheaply, but not properly
2 finish early
3 ignore someone completely
4 miss, be absent from
5 stop doing something

D Phrasal verbs with *set*

In his email Matt says: *We've decided to hire some bikes and then* **set about** *some proper exploration.* Here *set about* means *start doing something enthusiastically or seriously*.

These are some more phrasal verbs with *set* and their meanings.

- *set back*   delay, hold up
- *set down*   write / put into writing
- *set off / out*   leave or start on a journey
- *set up*   establish or start something

Now choose the best *set* verb in these sentences.

a Last year my brother *set down / set up* a new Internet company selling CDs.
b As soon as the hurricane was over, they *set about / set up* repairing the damage.
c We've got a long journey tomorrow. We'll have to *set about / set off* early.
d The bad weather *set back / set down* the road repair programme by two months.
e Write a letter to the director, *setting down / setting off* your ideas clearly.

E Adverbs meaning 'completely'

In the first email, the writer says he was **wide** awake at 5.30.
Here *wide* means *completely* or *totally*. We can also use the following words with certain adjectives to mean *completely* or *totally*.

> dead / fast / flat / wide

Fill the gap in each sentence with a word from the box.

a The children had such a tiring day that they were _____ asleep by 6 o'clock.
b He seemed to be asleep although his eyes were _____ open.
c I passed the exam first time. I found it _____ easy.
d Sorry I can't come out tonight. I'm _____ broke.
e We all wanted to hear the president's speech – so everyone was _____ quiet.

F Comparative adjectives

In the second email, Matt says *It'll be **cheaper** and **healthier** than the special hostels.*

Cheaper is the comparative form of *cheap*.
Healthier is the comparative form of *healthy*.

What are the comparative forms of these adjectives from the emails?

a *busy* _____   g *lovely* _____

b *exhausted* _____   h *new* _____

c *good* _____   i *safe* _____

d *happy* _____   j *special* _____

e *hot* _____   k *strange* _____

f *impressive* _____   l *tired* _____

G Practice

Read Matt's father's reply to the two emails. Fill each gap with a word or phrase from the box. There are **two** words or phrases you do not need to use.

> amazing / area / beach / body clock / camp / exhausted / harbour / hectic / hire /
> sleeping bag / tent / wonderful

Hi Matt,

Thanks for your emails – I'm glad to hear everything's working out OK. Funny to think you're over the other side of the world, yet keeping in touch is so easy.

I'm glad you're enjoying New Zealand. It sounds like a(n) **(a)** _____ place, although it's not surprising that you were **(b)** _____ to start with. It will probably be several weeks before your **(c)** _____ gets back to normal again.

It's a good idea to **(d)** _____ bikes to explore the **(e)** _____. A few weeks hard cycling should get you back in shape! The sunshine will make a big difference, too.

Have you started to **(f)** _____ yet? If so, I hope you bought a warm **(g)** _____ – it can get bitterly cold at night in a **(h)** _____.

I expect you'll have been to Coramandel by now. The hot water **(i)** _____ sounds **(j)** _____. I can't quite imagine it. Send me a photo of it if you can. By the way, your postcard arrived yesterday. Thanks.

We're all okay. Take care.

Love, Dad

9 Rowing across the Atlantic

A Introduction

1 These words and phrases are from the article below. Try to match them with their meanings.

a	*complete*	**1**	to start to have or feel
b	*develop*	**2**	a feeling
c	*loneliness*	**3**	great unhappiness
d	*misery*	**4**	the way in which someone is welcomed
e	*phobia*	**5**	to move a boat through water using two oars (pieces of wood)
f	*pull out*	**6**	unhappiness because of being alone
g	*reception*	**7**	to decide not to continue
h	*row*	**8**	an extreme and unreasonable fear
i	*sensation*	**9**	good times and bad times
j	*ups and downs*	**10**	to finish

2 Check in a dictionary the meaning of any of these words you do not understand.

B Reading

Read the article and fill each gap with the correct form of a word or phrase from **A1**.

Debra carries on alone

27-year-old rower Debra Veal has **(a)** _____ a journey across the Atlantic alone. As she landed in Barbados to a warm **(b)** _____ from excited islanders she announced: "It's an amazing **(c)** _____."

Debra, a former physical education instructor from London, who now runs her own Internet company, was supposed to make the 3,000-mile trip with her 35-year-old husband Andrew, but after only two weeks, he **(d)** _____ a terrible **(e)** _____ about the ocean and had to abandon the trip. The couple had decided to make the trip, which started from the Canary Islands on 7 October, so they could spend 'quality time' together.

When Andrew **(f)** _____, Debra decided to carry on **(g)** _____ the 750kg Troika Transatlantic across the ocean alone, avoiding passing ships and sharks, and living on beef stew. She got up every day at 5.30 to row, resting when she needed to, as she made the crossing from Tenerife to Barbados.

When she was asked about the experience she replied: "It has been a really mixed journey with lots of **(h)** _____. Strong winds and heavy seas were real problems, and I had a very bad moment when I was nearly run down by a supertanker which passed me by a few hundred metres. I used to think the sharks would be a danger, but they were more interested in the fish under my boat than what was in it. The **(i)** _____ was the really hard part. But in many ways the ocean has been a fantasy world for me. I've heard no world news, so have no knowledge of the wars, death, **(j)** _____ and destruction that have no doubt been going on. In my world, there has only been peace and beauty."

C Related words

1 Fill the gaps in this chart with words related to the nouns from the article.
(X = no useful word at this level.)

Noun	Verb	Adjective	Adverb
a beauty	X	_____	_____
b destruction	_____	_____	_____
c instructor	_____	_____	X
d knowledge	_____	_____	_____
e loneliness	X	_____	X
f misery	X	_____	_____
g peace	X	_____	_____
h sensation	_____	_____	_____

2 Fill the gaps in these sentences with adjectives you have added to the chart.
Do not use any adjective more than once.

a We found our lessons very _____ – she was an excellent teacher.

b People who read a lot are often _____ about many subjects.

c Newspapers often have _____ stories on their front page to attract more readers.

d We escaped from the city and spent a _____ weekend in the country.

e Why are you looking so _____? Have you had some bad news?

f High winds are quite often very _____. They can blow trees and houses down.

g She could be a model – she has an absolutely _____ face.

h If you go out to work, you have contact with people. People who work from home are often _____.

D Adjective-noun collocations

1 Which nouns in the box can follow these adjectives from the article?

hard   heavy   strong

coffee / decision / disk / leader / luck / opinion / rain / smoker / taste
traffic / wind / work

2 Fill the gaps in these conversations with the correct form of one of the collocations from **D1**.

a A He gets through thirty or forty cigarettes a day.

  B Really? I didn't know he was such a _____ _____.

b A Don't you like dark chocolate?

  B No the _____ is too _____ for me.

c A That must have been a really _____ _____ to take?

  B Yes, it was – I was awake all night trying to make up my mind what to do.

d A I've failed my driving test again.

  B Oh no – that's really _____ _____!

e A Why were you late for work this morning?

  B The _____ was _____ than usual – probably because of the weather.

f A Why do you think the new president is so popular?

  B Because most people like a _____ _____.

EXTENSION: Adjectives ending in *-ed* and *-ing*

1 Choose the correct adjectives in these sentences.

  a Debra Veal was met in Barbados by *excited / exciting* islanders.

  b She told reporters it was an *amazed / amazing* sensation.

2 What can you say about the difference between the following adjectives?

The students were all *bored*.
It was a *boring* lesson.

3 Choose the best adjectives in these sentences.

  a Did you see that TV programme about earthquakes last night? It wasn't very *interested / interesting*.

  b You look very *relaxed / relaxing*. Did you have a good holiday?

  c It's been a *tired / tiring* week. I've had to work late every night.

  d My brother sings in the shower. It's his most *annoyed / annoying* habit.

  e The dull winter weather makes some people feel *depressed / depressing*.

E Phrasal verbs

Find these phrasal verbs in the article and notice how they are used. Then complete sentences **a–e** using the appropriate form of each verb.

carry on   **get up**   **go on**   **pull out**   **run down**

a Andrew _____ _____ of the trip when he found he was afraid of the sea.

b Debra was very brave to _____ _____ alone.

c She had to _____ _____ early every day and start rowing.

d The most dangerous moment was when a big ship almost _____ her _____.

e She didn't know what had been _____ _____ because she hadn't heard the news during her trip.

F Phrasal verbs with *pull*

1 Match these *pull* verbs with one or more of meanings **a–g**.

pull down   **pull in**   **pull out**   **pull off**   **pull through**

  a destroy (a building)

  b succeed in doing something difficult

  c withdraw from / stop doing something

  d stop by the side of the road (a car)

  e recover from a very serious illness

  f remove quickly (e.g. clothes)

  g leave the side of the road (a car)

2 Now complete these sentences with the appropriate form of *pull* verbs from **F1**.

   a In last night's match, Manchester United _____ _____ one of their best wins ever.

   b James was very ill after his operation, but he _____ _____.

   c The apartment block they _____ _____ yesterday was only 20 years old.

   d The champion had to _____ _____ of the race after he fell and injured his leg.

   e We nearly had an accident when the bus _____ _____ in front of us.

G People

Match these words for people with the correct definitions.

a *instructor*		**1**	someone who comes to live permanently in another country
b *islander*		**2**	someone who works for a company or organisation
c *pedestrian*		**3**	someone who sees an event take place and can describe it to others (e.g. a crime or accident)
d *resident*		**4**	someone who is noisy and violent in public
e *motorist*		**5**	someone who teaches other people how to do something
f *hooligan*		**6**	someone who is walking, not driving a car or using public transport
g *passer-by*		**7**	someone who lives on an island
h *employee*		**8**	someone who lives in a place, not a visitor
i *witness*		**9**	someone who is going past a place (especially when an unusual event takes place)
j *immigrant*		**10**	someone who is driving a car

H Puzzle

Read the clues and complete the puzzle. All the answers are words from this unit.

a An extreme fear of something – e.g. insects, flying

b To damage something so badly that it no longer exists

c A computer has a _____ *disk* for storing information.

d The opposite of *war*

e Someone who is not a visitor but lives in a place

f The way in which someone is welcomed

g The opposite of *weak*

h Great unhappiness

i An adjective which describes a smoker who smokes a lot

j Fed up, irritated, a bit angry

k Someone who is walking, not using transport

A journey to remember

A Introduction

1 These words are from the article below. Try to match them with their meanings.

a	*confidently*	**1**	empty of people
b	*contrast*	**2**	in a way which shows pleasure and satisfaction
c	*deserted*	**3**	very sadly
d	*destroy*	**4**	to use a car horn to make a noise
e	*found*	**5**	to buy
f	*honk*	**6**	to ruin completely, to cause extreme damage to
g	*proudly*	**7**	not nervously, in a way which shows you believe you can do something
h	*purchase*		
i	*timidly*	**8**	shyly and nervously
j	*tragically*	**9**	to establish, to begin
		10	a clear difference

2 Check in a dictionary the meaning of any of these words you do not understand.

B Reading

Read the article and fill each gap with the appropriate form of a word from **A1**.

Arrival in Antigua

We flew into Guatemala City on a cool morning. Ours was the first flight of the day, so the airport was practically **(a)** _____. We knew we had to catch a bus to Antigua.

Uncertain what to do next, we walked **(b)** _____ out of the airport building. A strong-looking young man appeared.

"Taxi?"

We didn't know whether we needed a taxi, so we asked, "Bus station? Antigua? "

"Yes, taxi," he replied

(c) _____ and took us to an old blue Chevrolet.

Although there was little traffic on the roads, he **(d)** _____ frequently and drove as fast as he could. We reached the bus station in no time. As we were paying the driver, our bus started to pull away. We yelled desperately, and it slowed just enough for us to jump on.

About an hour-and-a-half later, we arrived in Antigua. It was still early morning and the air was cool. At the tourist office, we met a very friendly Antiguan who **(e)** _____ told us about his city. Antigua was **(f)** _____ in 1543 as the capital of Central America and the home of the Spanish colonial government. For more than 200 years, it was an important cultural and political centre. **(g)** _____, however, many of its beautiful old buildings had been **(h)** _____ in earthquakes in 1773 and 1976.

Of all the people we met that day, the children made a lasting impression on me because of the sharp **(i)** _____ with children at home. A common sight was young girls dressed in the famous orange, violet, red and indigo colours of Guatemala, carrying baskets filled with bright, hand-woven belts, coin purses and bracelets.

"You want to buy bracelet?" asked one particularly remarkable girl selling handmade goods. "Business not good today. You buy something?"

"Where did you learn to speak English so fluently?" I asked. "In school?"

"No, I don't go to school."

"Did you learn by talking to customers?" I asked.

She nodded. We **(j)** _____ a couple of coin purses, which made her very happy.

C Related words

1 Complete this chart with words related to the adverbs from the article. (X = no useful word at this level.)

Adverb	Adjective	Noun
a confidently	_____	_____
b desperately	_____	_____
c fluently	_____	_____
d frequently	_____	_____
e particularly	_____	X
f proudly	_____	_____
g timidly	_____	_____
h tragically	_____	_____

2 Fill the gaps in these sentences with adjectives or nouns you have added to the chart.

a Some athletes are so _____ to win that they take dangerous drugs.

b It's a _____ that she died so young. She had her whole life to look forward to.

c It was simply his _____ that prevented him from answering the teacher's question. He's very intelligent, but he lacks self- _____.

d Is there a _____ reason why you want to meet him? Or is it just out of interest?

e If you are bilingual, it means you are _____ in two languages.

f She's a _____ visitor to this country. She comes five or six times a year.

g Her parents are very _____ of her achievements. They are always telling everyone how clever she is.

D Adjective-noun collocations

1 Which nouns in the box can follow these adjectives from the article? One noun goes with two different adjectives.

common   lasting   sharp

bend (in the road) / contrast / effect / flower / impression / increase / knife / name / relationship / sight / teeth

2 Which collocations from **D1** could be used to refer to the following?

a a rose or a daisy
b a friendship which continues for many years
c John or Anne
d somewhere you ought to drive very carefully

EXTENSION 1: Verbs ending in -en

If you want to make a pencil *sharp*, you *sharpen* it. Make verbs ending in *-en* from the adjectives in the box, then use them to complete the sentences.

loose / short / straight / sweet / tight / wide

a Your trousers are too long. You should _____ them.

b That picture looks crooked. Shall I _____ it for you?

c This road is dangerously narrow. They should _____ it.

d My bicycle wheel was coming loose so I had to _____ it.

e People put sugar in their coffee to _____ it.

f He can't breathe! _____ his tie!

Note If you want to make something *longer*, you *lengthen* it.
If you want to make something *stronger*, you *strengthen* it.

E Verb-noun collocations

1 Which nouns in the box can follow these travel verbs and phrases? (Some nouns can follow more than one verb.)

catch   drive   miss   ride   travel by

bicycle / boat / bus / car / coach / horse / motorbike / plane / taxi / train

2 Find the best endings for these sentence beginnings, and fill each gap with the correct form of one of the verbs or phrases from **E1**.

Beginnings	Endings
a Sorry I can't stop – I'm in a hurry ...	**1** I learnt to _____ a bike when I was three.
b She's frightened of flying ...	
c I've always been a keen cyclist –	**2** as soon as they are 17 years old.
d When I go to work ...	**3** so she's going to _____ boat.
e Many British people learn to _____ a car ...	**4** because I'm frightened of animals.
	5 because I don't want to _____ my bus.
f I've never learnt to _____ a horse ...	**6** I usually _____ the 6.45 train.

EXTENSION 2: Expressions with *catch*

Replace *catch* or *caught* in each sentence with the correct form of a verb from the box.

attract / capture / find / get / hear

a While he was on holiday he *caught* flu and was in bed for several days.
b I've been trying to *catch* the waiter's attention for ten minutes already.
c The police *caught* the criminals as they made their getaway.
d Can you say that again? I didn't quite *catch* what you said.
e It was so embarrassing – my friend *caught* me reading her private diary.

F Travel nouns

Complete the table with nouns from the box. You will need to use one noun twice.

> bus / bus station / driver / pilot / plane / port / sailor / railway station

Place	Vehicle	Person
a airport	_____	_____
b _____	boat	_____
c _____	_____	driver
d _____	train	_____

G Compound adjectives

1 The girls were selling **hand-woven** belts, purses and bracelets.
Match these compound adjectives with the correct descriptions of how they are formed.

> curly-haired / fast-moving / handmade / hand-woven / long-legged / strong-looking

a noun + past participle
b adjective + -ing word
c adjective + noun + -ed

2 Which compound adjectives could be used to describe the following?

a a business which is financed by the government   _____

b something which is shaped like an egg   _____

c someone who has a warm heart   _____

d a film in which the action moves very slowly   _____

e a flower which smells sweet   _____

f someone who writes with their left hand   _____

H Practice

Read this short article about a journey and fill each gap with a word from the box.

> attention / catch / deserted / driver / fluently / long / missed / railway / timidly / train

I was alone in a strange country. I knew a bit of the language, but I couldn't speak it **(a)** _____ . I had arrived at the **(b)** _____ station two minutes late and had **(c)** _____ the last **(d)** _____ . I stood there on the **(e)** _____ platform, wondering what to do. Perhaps I could **(f)** _____ a bus back into town and stay in a hotel. As I left the station a **(g)** _____ -haired man waved to attract my **(h)** _____ . "Taxi?" he said. Before I could answer, he took my case and put it into his car. "How much?" I asked **(i)** _____ . I was worried because I didn't have much money. "Tonight my taxi is free," announced the taxi **(j)** _____ . "I've just won the lottery!"

Claiming compensation

A Introduction

1 These words and phrases are from the article below. Try to match them with their meanings.

a *blame*		**1**	money paid to make up for injury or inconvenience
b *fault*		**2**	connected with the law
c *claim*		**3**	money paid for professional services, e.g. to a lawyer
d *compensation*		**4**	physical harm or damage
e *be entitled to*		**5**	to say someone or something is responsible for something bad
f *fees*		**6**	a hard path for walking on at the side of a road
g *injury*		**7**	an increase
h *legal*		**8**	responsibility for something bad
i *pavement*		**9**	to have a right to something
j *rise*		**10**	a demand for money you think you have a right to

2 Check in a dictionary the meaning of any of these words you do not understand.

B Reading

1 Read the article and fill each gap with the correct form of a word or phrase from **A1**.

Oy! Watch out where you're going!

Whose fault is it?

An advertisement in Britain tells the public: "If you have been injured while playing a sport, you may **(a)** _____ a large sum of money in compensation." The advert also promises **(b)** _____ assistance in obtaining compensation for accidents at work, for car crashes and for other **(c)** _____. One company which provides this legal service says that it receives 30,000 requests for help every month. Some companies guarantee that if they lose a compensation **(d)** _____, the customer will not have to pay them any **(e)** _____.

Local councils are having to pay out larger and larger amounts of compensation in a wide range of cases – for example, to people who have fallen in towns and are (**f**) _____ the bad condition of (**g**) _____ , or to parents who blame a school because their children have failed their exams. The head of an insurance company which deals with some of these cases says "More and more people believe that when things go wrong, it must be someone's (**h**) _____ . If you can find someone to blame, you claim (**i**) _____ . People don't want to take responsibility for anything these days. If you walk into a wall, it's the wall's fault for being there. Many people think of this as an easy way of making money."

Doctors, dentists and social workers are also being blamed for things that go wrong in people's lives, and this is costing the country billions of pounds every year. Does this really mean that Britain is becoming more like America, where people go to court first and ask questions later? And if there is a sudden (**j**) _____ in compensation claims, who will end up paying? As usual, it will be ordinary members of the public or the customers of insurance companies who will lose.

2 Answer these questions about the article, using appropriate phrases from the box.

blame the school / claim compensation / insurance companies / legal assistance / lose their claim / make money

a What may people injured in car crashes be able to do?
b What are the companies who advertise offering?
c In what situation do customers not have to pay legal fees?
d What do some parents do if their children fail exams?
e Why do so many people make compensation claims?
f Who usually pays the money in compensation claims?

C Verb-noun collocations

1 Which nouns in the box can follow these verbs from the article?

make   pay   take

advice / care / an exam / fees / fun of someone / a joke / medicine / money / notes / a photo / a profit / rent / responsibility (for) / tax(es)

2 Complete these sentences using collocations from **C1**.

a There's no point in suggesting anything to him – he never _____ _____ .
b The doctor gave me two different kinds of _____ to _____ .
c In their first year of business the company _____ a small _____ .
d Don't _____ _____ of him – even if you don't mean it. He just can't _____ a _____ .
e If you own your house, you don't have to _____ _____ .
f _____ _____ when you cross the road – the traffic is very busy at this time of day.

D Expressions with *go* + adjective

In the article, the head of the insurance company says *People believe that when things* **go wrong**, *it must be someone's fault.* When something *goes wrong*, it doesn't happen in the way it should. For questions **a–h**, choose the appropriate answers **1–8**.

a What should you do if someone *goes missing*?
b Why do people *go red*?
c What happens if someone *goes blind*?
d When does food *go bad*?
e What happens if someone *goes bald*?
f When do people *go grey*?
g Why do people *go berserk*?
h What happens if someone *goes quiet*?

1 Because they feel very angry, and can't control themselves.
2 They can't see.
3 When they are old.
4 Look for them and then contact the police.
5 When it is old and no longer fresh.
6 They stop talking.
7 Because they are embarrassed.
8 They lose their hair.

EXTENSION 1: Colour expressions

Choose the correct colour from the box to complete each sentence. Be careful – there is one extra colour!

black / blue / green / red / white / yellow

a When Paul asked Jackie to marry him, she didn't know what to say – the question came completely out of the _____.
b My brother's just bought a fantastic new car. As you can imagine, I'm absolutely _____ with envy.
c I'll only believe they are giving me the job when I see something in _____ and _____.
d I had a shock this morning. A letter from the bank said I'm over £1000 in the _____! I don't know how I'm going to pay it back.
e "How would you like your coffee?" "_____ please, but not too much milk."

E *Blame* and *fault*

1 Look at these examples of sentences using *blame* or *fault*.

She says it's his fault. = She blames him.
They said everything was my fault. = They blamed me for everything.

2 Rewrite these sentences using *blame* or *fault*.

a I think the accident was John's fault.
b They blamed the government for the disaster.
c Don't say it's my fault.
d I blame Rachel.

F Formal and informal words

Match the formal words **a–f** from the article with the informal equivalents **1–5**.

a *assistance*
b *guarantee*
c *injured*
d *obtain*
e *provide*
f *receive*

1 get
2 give
3 help
4 hurt
5 promise

EXTENSION 2: Meanings of *get*

The verb *get* has many meanings. Which of the meanings in the box does *get* have in sentences **a–f**?

arrive / become / buy / earn / receive / understand

a I'm going into town to *get* some new jeans.
b Sorry, I don't *get* what you mean. Can you tell me again, please?
c Can we go home now? I'm *getting* really tired.
d My sister *got* a CD player for her 18th birthday.
e If we *get* there early, we'll have time for a coffee.
f Dave's fairly well-off – he *gets* over £30,000 in his new job.

G Puzzle

Find the following words in this puzzle. They can be horizontal, vertical or diagonal.

a Two formal words meaning *get*
b A formal word meaning *help*
c A formal word meaning *hurt*
d Two nouns which can follow *make*
e Two nouns which can follow *take*
f Two adjectives which can follow *go*
g A colour connected with envy
h A colour connected with owing money

A	R	P	R	O	F	I	T	E	P
A	S	T	I	L	M	E	G	T	J
W	G	S	I	B	A	L	D	Y	O
L	L	E	I	N	K	E	R	C	K
I	R	E	D	S	J	S	Q	A	E
V	S	E	B	C	T	U	R	U	I
I	S	E	A	R	N	A	R	U	W
N	A	D	V	I	C	E	N	E	L
G	G	R	E	Y	D	T	C	C	D
G	R	E	E	N	E	B	U	Y	E

12 Odd news

A Introduction

1 These words and phrases are from the article below. Try to match them with their meanings.

a	*alternative*	**1**	to make, to get ready
b	*consist of*	**2**	a worker trained in special scientific skills
c	*cosmetics*	**3**	one part of the contents of something (e.g. a cooking recipe)
d	*discovery*	**4**	something that can be used instead of something else
e	*equivalent to*	**5**	something added to something else to improve it
f	*impress*	**6**	something you find out
g	*ingredient*	**7**	different kinds of make-up
h	*prepare*	**8**	to be made up of, to include
i	*supplement*	**9**	to have a favourable effect on, to influence positively
j	*technician*	**10**	having the same value as

2 Check in a dictionary the meaning of any of these words and phrases you do not understand.

B Reading

Read these three short news stories and fill each gap with the correct form of a word or phrase from **A1**.

Odd News Odd News Odd News Odd News

Raspberries help you slim

A Japanese cosmetics company has brought out a slimming pill that uses the power of raspberries to burn unwanted fat. The pleasant-tasting pill has really **(a)** _____ Japanese women who are trying to lose weight.

Each pill is loaded with raspberry ketones, the **(b)** _____ which reduces fat, and is **(c)** _____ to 1,000 fresh raspberries. The **(d)** _____ company claims that 70 per cent of people who took part in a study of the raspberry **(e)** _____ each lost an average of one kilo after taking the pills for a week.

The company also produces an **(f)** _____ to the pills which has the same effect: 'sheets' containing raspberry ketones that can be placed on parts of the body.

The Viennese Vegetable Orchestra

Forget the cello, just listen to that 'cucumberophone'! The First Viennese Vegetable Orchestra, which **(g)** _____ of eight musicians, a sound **(h)** _____ and a cook, plays vegetable instruments they make themselves. Their instruments can produce sounds that cannot easily be made by a normal orchestra. It takes the band about half an hour to make a carrot flute, and under 15 minutes to make a 'cucumberophone'. Other instruments include aubergine cymbals and pumpkin drums.

At the end of a performance, the stage is cleared and the cook uses the instruments to **(i)** _____ a soup for the audience and the musicians. The audience can once again enjoy what they have just heard. 'We employ a real chef,' says the band, 'so the soup is tasty and very special.'

Chocolate is good for you

American scientists have discovered that a group of chemicals found in cocoa beans, from which chocolate is made, can increase the production of nitric oxide, which helps to keep our blood pressure at a safe level. The highest levels of these chemicals are found in cocoa drinks, but are also present in dark, and even milk, chocolate.

Professor Norman Hollenberg, who led the study, said: 'Nitric oxide is very necessary for healthy blood pressure and therefore for keeping the heart in good condition. This **(j)** _____ could be of great importance for public health.'

C Related words

1 Fill the gaps in this chart with words related to the words given. (X = no useful word at this level.)

Noun	Verb	Adjective	Adverb
a _____	discover	X	X
b importance	X	_____	_____
c _____	include	_____	X
d _____	X	necessary	_____
e supplement	_____	_____	X
f _____	prepare	_____	X
g _____	reduce	X	X
h _____	X	safe	_____

2 Fill the gaps in these sentences with words you have added to the chart.

  a There used to be accidents at work every day. Now _____ is taken more seriously.

  b This meal doesn't need a lot of _____ – it'll be ready in about 20 minutes.

  c Motorists are delighted about this week's _____ in the price of petrol.

  d You must vote tomorrow. It's the most _____ election for 20 years.

  e Many people take vitamins to _____ their diet.

  f A television isn't a _____, you know! You don't actually need one!

D Adjective-noun collocations

1 Which nouns in the box can follow these adjectives? One noun goes with two different adjectives.

general   normal   public

> behaviour / day / election / health / holiday / interest / knowledge / opinion / price / relations / rule / way

2 Which collocations from **D1** mean the following?

  a what you usually pay for something

  b the occasion when people vote for a new national government

  c how most people do something

  d what ordinary people think about a subject

  e non-specialised information which people have about all kinds of subjects

  f a day on which most people in a particular country don't go to work

E Nationalities

Which countries do the three news stories relate to? Write them in the correct spaces in the chart. Then complete the rest of the chart.

Country	Nationality
a _____ (Story 1)	_____
b _____ (Story 2)	_____
c _____ (Story 3)	_____
d China	_____
e Egypt	_____
f _____	Canadian
g Sweden	_____
h _____	Spanish
i The Netherlands	_____
j Iraq	_____
k _____	Thai

F Adjectives + prepositions

*Each pill is loaded **with** raspberry ketones.*
Complete each sentence below with one of the prepositions from the box.

> about / at / for / of / to

a Unfortunately he doesn't have the qualifications necessary _____ the job.

b Five British pounds is equivalent _____ about eight Euros.

c Thanks a lot. I'm very grateful _____ the offer.

d Are you available _____ work? If so, you can start on Monday.

e Have you got any good ideas? I'm quite open _____ suggestions.

f Where have you been? I've been so worried _____ you!

g Children are sometimes afraid _____ the dark.

h I am completely opposed _____ the plan to build a new airport near here.

i Fruit and vegetables are good _____ you.

j Julie has always been good _____ languages.

EXTENSION: Adjectives starting with a...

Many English adjectives starting with a... cannot be used immediately before a noun. For example, it is not correct to say: [the afraid child]. We say: The child is afraid or the frightened child.

Make phrases from these sentences using another adjective before each noun.

a The passengers are *asleep*. _____

b The car is *ablaze*. _____

c The creatures are *alive*. _____

d The ship is *afloat*. _____

G Homophones

A homophone is a word which sounds like another word, but has a different spelling and meaning. For example, *no* and *know* are homophones.
Here are some words from the news stories. Can you think of a homophone for each word using the clues?

		Homophone	Clue
a	*weight*	_____	to stay where you are until someone comes
b	*week*	_____	the opposite of *strong*
c	*hour*	_____	belonging to us
d	*cymbal*	_____	a sign or object which represents something else
e	*led*	_____	a heavy metal / the part of a pencil which writes
f	*so*	_____	to make or repair using a needle and thread

H Puzzle

Read the clues and complete the puzzle. All the answers are words from this unit.

a To be made up of = to _____ of.
b Usual, ordinary
c Thankful
d Act, show, entertainment
e Burning
f Someone from the Netherlands is this.
g Someone skilled in practical science
h Decrease (noun)
i A new government is voted for in this kind of election.
j Things like *lipstick* and *mascara*, used to improve your appearance
k Something that is used in cooking

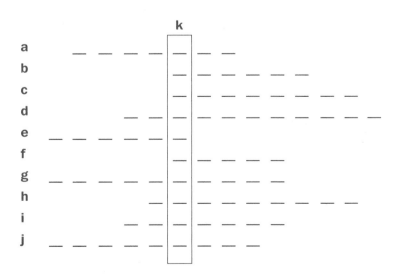

A Introduction

1 These words are from the article below. Try to match them with their meanings.

a	*agriculture*	**1**	strength, power
b	*cage*	**2**	to teach, to instruct
c	*force*	**3**	to look at for a long time
d	*herd*	**4**	farming, the farming business
e	*pet*	**5**	to gather animals together
f	*stare*	**6**	an animal kept at home for pleasure
g	*stubborn*	**7**	to move away from a place
h	*tough*	**8**	a place where animals and birds are kept, often made of wire
i	*train*	**9**	obstinate, refusing to change your mind
j	*wander*	**10**	strong, hard-working

2 Check in a dictionary the meaning of any of these words you do not understand.

B Reading

1 Read the article and fill each gap with the correct form of a word from **A1**. You will need to use one of the words twice.

The shepherd's best friend

When Bob Hooker was a student in Texas, he came across something that astonished him. He was keeping horses at the home of a man who **(a)** _____ border collies.

"The first day I went there, I noticed he had some puppies in a **(b)** _____," says Hooker. "One made a hole in the side and got into an area with chickens. The puppy went around the chickens, gathering them up in the centre, then lay down and watched them. When they started to **(c)** _____ from the centre, he patiently rounded them up again. He did that over and over again. I was amazed." Hooker decided then and there that he wanted to find out more about these dogs and to have one himself. So he went to Britain, the original home of the border collie. Here he found world-class trainers, learned more and bought dogs from them. Now, at the age of 56, he is a trainer himself.

"If you're in **(d)** _____, every animal you own should be able to make money for you," he says. "So, certainly, you can have a dog as a **(e)** _____, but all the better if it can **(f)** _____ animals. But you must have one which is right for the purpose, and there's none better than the border collie. It's a **(g)** _____ dog that can do the work of twenty people."

The border collie lives to work and is ideal with sheep. It doesn't move the animals by

(h) _____, but by the power of its presence and by **(i)** _____ at them intently. Occasionally a **(j)** _____ animal has to be shown who's boss, but the dog works silently, able to work out different situations. It is intelligent, quick, easy to **(k)** _____ and hard-working. In fact, it's unhappy if it's not working, which makes it a good partner for farmers with animals, but not such a good pet, unless you can keep it busy.

2 How much do you remember about the article? Answer these questions, then read the article again to check your answers.

a Where did Bob Hooker first see border collies?
b What did the puppy do which surprised Bob Hooker?
c Where did he go to find out more about border collies?
d What does Bob Hooker do now?
e Why don't border collies make good pets?

C Animals

1 Group the animal words in the box under the headings below. Some animals can belong to more than one group. One example of each is given.

camel / cat / chicken / cow / deer / dog / donkey / duck / elephant / giraffe / horse / lion / monkey / pig / rabbit / sheep / tiger / turkey

Pets	Working animals	Farm animals and birds	Wild animals and birds
rabbit	dog	chicken	giraffe

2 Add any more animals and birds you know to the four groups.

3 Match these animals with their young.

a cat   1 cub
b cow   2 foal
c dog   3 piglet
d horse   4 kitten
e lion   5 lamb
f pig   6 calf
g sheep   7 puppy

57

EXTENSION: Animal idioms

What could you call the people below? Choose the correct idiom from the box.

a Someone who shows no feelings or emotions
b Someone we don't know much about – perhaps they have a secret life
c Someone who gets up at 5 o'clock in the morning and starts work before everyone else
d Someone who is always active, who never stops doing things
e Someone who is used in an experiment, for example to test a new kind of medicine
f Someone who is very important or powerful in an organisation, like a government minister or a managing director

> *an early bird / the top dog / a cold fish / a dark horse / a busy bee / a guinea pig*

D Phrasal verbs

1 Match these phrasal verbs from the article with one or more of meanings **a–f**.

come across   find out   lie down   round up   work out

a gather together
b calculate the answer to a problem, understand something
c find, see or meet by chance
d put yourself into a horizontal position, to rest or sleep
e do physical exercise to make yourself fit
f learn, discover

2 Complete each sentence with the correct form of one of the phrasal verbs from **D1**.

a You're looking incredibly fit. Have you been _____ _____?

b I _____ _____ everything I know about animals from working on a farm in my holidays.

c The children had spent all day on the beach. Eventually their parents _____ them _____ and took them home.

d You look exhausted. You should go and _____ _____.

e While I was tidying the cellar, I _____ _____ a collection of old family photos.

f Can I borrow your calculator? I can't _____ _____ what 25 per cent of £3.50 is.

E Phrasal verbs with *come*

Choose the correct phrasal verb in each of these sentences.

a When we were trying to repair the car, we *came out with / came up against* all kinds of problems.
b A fantastic job has *come up / come round* in London. It's ideal for me so I'm going to apply for it.
c Did you watch the interview with the princess? She *came out with / came up with* some amazing bits of gossip.
d When she *came round / came by* she was in bed holding her baby. Everyone was smiling and congratulating her.
e *Come off / Come on*! If you don't hurry up, we'll be late.
f I'm living in New York now, but I actually *come by / come out of / come from* Scotland.

F 'Seeing' verbs

Complete the sentences with the correct form of one of these 'seeing' verbs. Sometimes more than one answer is possible.

> *gaze at / look at / notice / see / stare at / watch*

a Did you _____ the late film on TV last night?

b I can't _____ properly – I think I need to have my eyes tested.

c Why are you _____ me like that?

d It was their first romantic meal together. They spent the whole evening _____ each other.

e 'Did you _____ the colour of the car she was driving?' 'I'm not sure. I think it was green.'

f _____ that girl over there! She looks exactly like someone I was at school with.

G Puzzle

Read the clues and complete the puzzle. All the answers are words from this unit.

a A kind of horse we don't know much about
b A verb which can mean to look at someone romantically
c Another word for *instructor* or *teacher*
d A *cold* _____ is someone who has no feelings.
e A young lion
f Another word for *obstinate* – like a donkey
g A young cow
h A young cat
i A young dog
j To look at hard without turning your eyes away
k Animals and birds are kept in this in a zoo.
l The business of farming

Freak weather

A Introduction

1 These words are from the article below. Try to match them with their meanings.

a *convinced*	**1** difficult or impossible to believe
b *flabbergasted*	**2** a view of something for a very short time
c *funnel*	**3** to show, to make visible
d *glimpse*	**4** an image of something which is not really there
e *incredible*	**5** extremely surprised, amazed
f *invert*	**6** sure, certain
g *mirage*	**7** to turn upside down
h *reveal*	**8** a metal chimney

2 Choose the correct geographical word or phrase from the box for each label **a–f**.

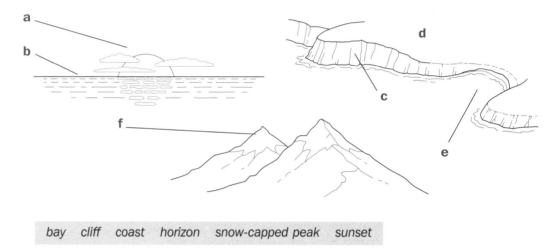

| bay | cliff | coast | horizon | snow-capped peak | sunset |

3 Check in a dictionary the meaning of any of these words you do not understand.

B Reading

1 Read the article and fill each gap with the correct form of a word or phrase from **A1** or **A2**.

Village in the sky

There are no mountains or trains in the Orkney Islands of Scotland. So when the people of Sanday woke up one day to find that snow-capped peaks and a village with a train had appeared at the north end of their tiny island, they were **(a)** _____. They hadn't been there the day before. Yet suddenly there was a large white building with several smaller houses grouped around it. And the ghost village remained on view for several hours before vanishing at **(b)** _____. The islanders were **(c)** _____ that a trick of the light had brought them a **(d)** _____ of Norway, 800 kilometres away. Experts agreed that it was a mirage.

Another **(e)** _____ sight hung in the sky over Hastings on the south coast of England in July 1797. The **(f)** _____ of France suddenly appeared, clear as daylight, as if it was just across a **(g)** _____. Local resident William Latham wrote: "The coast of France could be clearly seen without a telescope. I could see **(h)** _____ on the opposite coast 50 miles distant." Sailors and fishermen could make out places they had visited, and with a telescope they could even see the French fishing boats.

(i) _____ like these are caused by the weather. When conditions are calm, and warm air sits on top of cool air, it creates what is called a _temperature inversion_. The place where the two types of air meet behaves like a mirror, creating amazing images and revealing places hidden under the curve of the earth.

Sometimes the temperature inversions actually **(j)** _____ the images as well. This happened in 1957 when passengers on the ship _Edinburgh Castle_, which was sailing up the English Channel, suddenly saw a line of ships on the **(k)** _____ – upside down, some on top of each other, funnel to funnel.

2 Match each sentence beginning with the correct ending. You may need to check your ideas in the article.

Beginnings	Endings
a The people of Sanday saw mountain peaks ...	**1** if they used a telescope.
b The islanders thought ...	**2** the coast of France.
c In 1797 the people of Hastings clearly saw ...	**3** which were covered in snow.
d They could see fishing boats ...	**4** looked as if they were upside down.
e The ships which the passengers on the _Edinburgh Castle_ saw ...	**5** they had seen a village in Norway.

C People

Find words in the article which mean the following. Someone who ...

a ... goes to sea to catch fish _____

b ... knows a lot about a particular subject _____

c ... lives permanently in a particular place _____

d ... lives on an island _____

e ... travels on a ship, a train or a plane _____

f ... works at sea _____

EXTENSION: More people

Think of words which mean the following. Someone who ...

a ... lives in a village _____

b ... travels by bicycle _____

c ... works in a shop _____

d ... buys things in a shop _____

e ... suffers as a result of a crime _____

f ... works in a library _____

g ... breaks the law _____

h ... works in a garden _____

i ... paints people's houses _____

j ... bets money on the lottery, horse-racing, etc _____

D Near synonyms

1 Find **six** groups of **three** words or phrases from the box which have similar meanings.

> *a few / appear / become visible / calm / cause / clear / come into view / create / disappear / fade / on view / peaceful / produce / quiet / several / some / vanish / visible*

2 Fill the gaps in these sentences with appropriate words and phrases from **D1**. Sometimes more than one word or phrase can be used.

a It is more comfortable to travel by ship when weather conditions are _____.

b When there are no clouds at night, the moon and stars are _____.

c Unusual weather conditions sometimes _____ strange mirages.

d These mirages sometimes last for _____ hours.

e We had been sailing for three hours, when suddenly the fog cleared and the coast of France _____.

f The speedboat roared past us and in a few minutes had _____ over the horizon.

E Phrasal verbs with *make*

1 Choose the best meaning for *make out* in this extract from the article:
*Sailors and fishermen could **make out** places they had visited.*

  a describe
  b manage to see
  c make contact with

2 Match these *make* verbs with one or more of the meanings below.

make for   make off   make up

  a become friends again after an argument
  b produce or invent something from your imagination, e.g. a recipe, a story, an excuse
  c go in the direction of (a place)
  d leave (a place) quickly

3 Complete these sentences with the correct form of one of the verbs from **E2**.

a I never use books when I'm cooking. I prefer to _____ _____ my own recipes.

b The thieves stole £3 million pounds worth of jewels from the shop and _____ _____ in a stolen car.

c They didn't speak to each other for a year after their row, but they eventually _____ _____ and have been the best of friends ever since.

d We set off at seven o'clock and _____ _____ the airport.

e I didn't believe a word of his story. It was obvious he was _____ it all _____ .

F Place prepositions

Fill the gaps in these sentences with suitable prepositions. There are similar sentences in the article.

a Felixstowe is a port _____ the east coast of England.

b The ship sailed _____ the river as far as the capital city.

c There were clouds in the sky _____ London all day long.

d There are lots of trees growing _____ our house.

e It was a clear day so we could easily make out four ships _____ the horizon.

f My grandparents live _____ the south end of the island.

G Puzzle

Find the following words in this puzzle. They can be horizontal, vertical or diagonal.

a Three adjectives which mean *believing strongly that something is true*
b Something you think you can see, but that doesn't actually exist
c The time in the evening when the sun disappears
d Very high rocks on the coast
e The line between the sky and the land or sea
f A very knowledgeable person
g An adjective describing something which it is possible to see
h Two adjectives which mean the same as *peaceful*

V	E	S	U	R	E	O	N	E	M
I	C	H	O	R	I	Z	O	N	I
S	O	C	E	R	T	A	I	N	R
I	N	E	T	S	T	A	Y	C	A
B	V	T	X	H	U	P	E	A	G
L	I	Q	U	P	R	N	L	L	E
E	N	U	G	H	E	L	S	M	N
D	C	I	P	L	E	R	M	E	O
O	E	E	X	I	T	O	T	O	T
G	D	T	H	C	L	I	F	F	S

Old tyres

A Introduction

1 These words and phrases are from the article below. Try to match them with their meanings.

a *ban (on)*		**1**	a place where rubbish (waste) is buried
b *breeding grounds*		**2**	something which is burnt for heat or energy
c *convert*		**3**	against the law, unlawful
d *dispose of*		**4**	to make use of again
e *estimate*		**5**	the top covering or layer of something
f *fuel*		**6**	an official rule prohibiting something
g *landfill site*		**7**	places where animals, fish etc produce their young
h *illegal*		**8**	to throw away, to get rid of
i *recycle*		**9**	to guess, to calculate approximately
j *surface*		**10**	to change something into something else

2 Check in a dictionary the meaning of any of these words or phrases you do not understand.

B Reading

1 Read this article and fill each gap with the correct form of a word or phrase from **A1**.

No more dumping

One of Britain's most serious environmental problems is what to do with millions of used car tyres. 'By their very nature, tyres are difficult to dispose of,' says David Santillo, an environmentalist from Exeter University. 'They are designed not to fall apart while you're driving along the motorway.' The problem will become more serious in the near future when European countries will no longer be allowed to bury tyres in **(a)**_____ .

The problem

• After the **(b)**_____ on the use of landfill sites, new ways will have to be found to dispose of 13 million tyres in Britain every year. By 2021 the number of tyres in use will increase by about 60%.

• Every day, up to 100,000 tyres are taken off cars, vans, trucks, buses and bicycles.

• It is **(c)**_____ that there are now more than 200 million tyres lying around the country.

What to do with old tyres

• The best use of old tyres is to make them into new tyres, but this is expensive, and only 18% are **(d)**_____ in this way.

• 48,500 tonnes are **(e)**_____ into 'crumb rubber', used to make **(f)**_____ for running tracks and children's playgrounds.

• Currently 18% are burnt at high temperatures as **(g)**_____ in the manufacture of cement.

This is becoming the most popular way of disposing of tyres, but it is of increasing concern to environmentalists and scientists.

• Britain sends 26% of its tyres to landfill sites, much less than some other EU countries. France sends almost half, and Spain 58%, but Holland sends none. Britain is now wondering how to **(h)**_____ the extra 13 million tyres once landfill becomes **(i)**_____ .

A new way forward

One new way of re-using old tyres that is being tested around the world is 'tyre reefs'. These are made of old tyres which are tied together and dropped in the sea. It is hoped that they will become successful **(j)**_____ for fish.

2 What do you remember about the article? Answer these questions, then read the article again to check your answers.

    a Which countries will not be allowed to use landfill sites to bury tyres?
    b How many tyres a day are taken off cars and other vehicles in Britain?
    c What percentage of old tyres are made into new tyres?
    d Which country mentioned in the article buries the most tyres in landfill sites?
    e Where are 'tyre reefs' put?

C Related words

1 Fill the gaps in this chart with words related to the words given. Sometimes there are two words in one group. (X = no useful word at this level.)

Noun	Verb	Adjective	Adverb
a concern	_____	_____	X
b environmentalist	X	environmental	_____
c _____	estimate	X	X
d _____	X	expensive	_____
e _____	X	popular	_____
f _____ scientist	X	_____	_____
g _____	_____	successful	_____

2 Fill the gaps in these sentences with the appropriate form of words you have added to the chart.

    a If at first you don't _____, try again.
    b As oil prices have risen, small cars have grown in _____.
    c According to scientists, landfill sites damage the natural _____.
    d What _____ environmentalists is the increase in pollution.
    e You don't have to tell me the exact time you will arrive. A rough _____ will be OK.
    f _____ does not have the answers to all our problems.
    g Elaine must earn a lot. She's always very _____ dressed.

D Phrasal verbs with *fall*

1 Choose the best meaning for *fall apart* in this sentence from the article:
*They are designed not to **fall apart** while you're driving along the motorway.*

    a drop off the car
    b go down, lose air
    c break into pieces

2 Match each of these *fall* verbs with one of the meanings **a–e**.

fall behind   fall down   fall for   fall out   fall through

a fall in love with
b move more slowly, make slower progress than other people
c go wrong (e.g. an arrangement)
d collapse, no longer be standing (e.g. like a tree or a house)
e stop being friendly with someone

3 Complete these sentences with the correct form of one of the verbs from **D2**.

a Unfortunately our plan to have a holiday together has _____ _____.
b Being off school for three weeks meant that I _____ _____ with my work.
c I've always loved you. I _____ _____ you the first time we met.
d After the heavy storms, the bridge was so weak that it _____ _____.
e My brother and I frequently used to _____ _____ with each other, but we were always friends again by the next day.

E Verbs + prepositions

The article says ... *new ways will have to be found to dispose **of** 13 million tyres in Britain every year.*
Fill the gaps in the sentences with one of the prepositions from the box.

> *about / between / from / in / into / of / on / to / with*

a These days most people *believe* _____ recycling waste material if possible.
b The government does not *approve* _____ the use of landfill sites for burying old tyres, and I must say I *agree* _____ them.
c Large old houses in city centres are often *converted* _____ apartments.
d I *object* _____ breathing other people's cigarette smoke.
e Customers should *insist* _____ high standards of service from supermarkets.
f This car *belongs* _____ my father, but I sometimes *borrow* it _____ him.
g If I had to *choose* _____ walking and driving, I'd walk – it's good exercise.
h Most people *know* very little _____ environmental problems.

F Prefixes

1 Prefixes often give clues to the meaning of words. For example the prefix **re-** means 'again' or 'back' , so *to recycle* means 'to use again'. Does **re-** add the meaning 'again' or 'back' to the verbs in these sentences?

a After three weeks I *returned* the books to the library.
b I *reread* the question several times but I still did not understand it.
c After I'd listened to the cassette, I *rewound* it and listened again.
d The teacher was not satisfied with my work, so I had to *redo* it.
e They're having to *rebuild* the houses that were damaged in the flood.

2 Match these verb prefixes with the meanings they add.

a	*anti*	**1**	single, one
b	*bi*	**2**	half
c	*mis*	**3**	not enough
d	*mono*	**4**	later than, after
e	*over*	**5**	against
f	*post*	**6**	twice, two
g	*semi-*	**7**	wrongly, badly
h	*under*	**8**	too much, more than necessary

3 Complete each sentence with a prefix from **F2**.

a Because of the bad weather, they've _____*poned* the match until next week.

b The teacher sent the boy to the head because he had _____*behaved* in class.

c A _____*detached* house is one which is joined to another house on one side.

d If someone is _____*lingual*, they can speak two languages fluently.

e The food in that restaurant is very good, but they often _____*charge* you.

f I'd hate to do a _____*tonous* job where I had to do the same thing every day.

g People sometimes think she's _____*social*, but actually she's just very shy.

h These potatoes are _____*cooked*. They need to be boiled for at least five more minutes.

EXTENSION

Answer the questions with appropriate nouns from the box below.

a What do you call a word like *you*, *book* or *leave* (but not *fuel*, or *bury*)?
b What do you call someone who is illegally married to two people at the same time?
c What does PS at the end of a letter stand for?
d What is another word for bad luck?
e What should you take if you have been bitten by a poisonous snake?

antidote / bigamist / misfortune / monosyllable / postscript

G Practice

Read this short article about the use of tyres as fuel. Fill the gaps with the correct form of words from the box. There are two words you do not need to use.

convert / dispose of / environment / fuel / oil / recycle / smoke / surface / temperature / tyre

Blue Circle, Britain's largest cement maker, uses old **(a)** _____ as a replacement **(b)** _____. The company says that this is a 'win-win' situation for the environment: less **(c)** _____ and coal are used and the tyres are **(d)** _____ instead of being **(e)** _____ in landfill sites. Blue Circle also gains because the 4 million tyres it burns every year save the company about £6 million.

Their own experiments have shown that burning tyres reduces the damage to the local **(f)** _____ by 27%. Tyres which are burned at a very high **(g)** _____ do not produce black **(h)** _____ or an unpleasant smell.

16 Volcanoes

A Introduction

1 These words and phrases are from the article below. Try to match them with their meanings.

a	*active*	1	probable
b	*climate*	2	to stop something continuing in the normal way
c	*disrupt*	3	in danger
d	*erupt*	4	to say what will happen in the future
e	*flow*	5	weather conditions
f	*fragment*	6	not dead, likely to erupt
g	*likely*	7	to watch and check regularly
h	*liquid*	8	a small piece
i	*monitor*	9	to burst or explode
j	*predict*	10	to move smoothly in one direction
k	*at risk*	11	like water, oil, milk, etc, not solid

2 Check in a dictionary the meaning of any of these words you do not understand.

B Reading

1 Read the article and fill each gap with the correct form of a word or phrase from A1.

Predicting eruptions

Today there are many (**a**)_____ volcanoes worldwide and, as the world's population grows, more and more people are living in dangerous volcanic areas. South of Mexico City, Popocatépetl has begun to come to life again, putting a million people (**b**)_____. Another million people living near Naples are threatened by Mount Vesuvius.

What are volcanoes?

Deep inside the Earth, between the (**c**)_____ core and the thin crust at the surface, there is solid rock called the mantle. When rock from the mantle melts, moves to the surface, and releases gases, volcanoes erupt. When we think of a volcanic eruption, we usually imagine red-hot lava (**d**)_____ down a volcano. But falling ash is another problem. In an explosive eruption the liquid rock, 'magma', which has risen to the surface, bursts from the volcano

in a column of ash and fiery (**e**)_____. In a large-scale eruption, the cooled ash and fragments that fall back to Earth can cover vast areas with a thick layer. Severe eruptions can even affect the (**f**)_____, as happened in the case of Mount St Helens in the USA which erupted in 1980 and (**g**)_____ normal weather conditions for months.

Warning signs

Trying to (**h**)_____ when a volcano will (**i**)_____, scientists study what is left behind from past eruptions. They are also skilled at recognising the warning signs. Before an eruption, magma moves nearer the surface and releases gases, which can be measured for changes in quantity and make-up. Volcanologists are becoming very skilled at predicting how (**j**)_____ an eruption is, but it is still very difficult for them to say exactly when it will happen. Monitoring possible eruptions is expensive and, with many volcanoes erupting only every few hundred or thousand years, it is not practical to (**k**)_____ every site.

2 Read the article again and find **one** word to complete each label on this diagram.

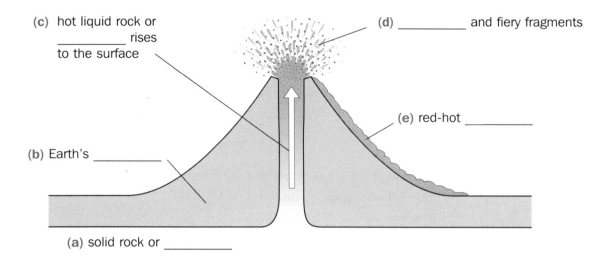

(c) hot liquid rock or _____ rises to the surface

(d) _____ and fiery fragments

(e) red-hot _____

(b) Earth's _____

(a) solid rock or _____

C Related words

1 Fill the gaps in this chart with words related to the words given. Sometimes there are two words in one group. (X = no useful word at this level.)

Noun	Verb	Adjective	Adverb
a _____ _____	_____	active	_____
b _____	disrupt	_____	X
c _____	erupt	X	X
d _____	_____	explosive	_____
e _____	predict	_____	_____
f _____	X	severe	_____
g _____	threaten	_____	_____
h _____	X	_____	violently
i volcano	X	_____	X

2 Fill the gaps in these sentences with the correct forms of words you have added to the chart.

a The bad weather caused severe _____ to the train services.

b Police and politicians are worried about the recent rise in crimes of _____ .

c Soon after the car caught fire, the petrol tank _____ .

d When business is bad, employees face the _____ of losing their jobs.

e Volcanoes are not _____ . We don't know when they are going to erupt.

f The _____ of the storm surprised even the weather experts.

D Adjectives and their opposites

1 Match these adjectives from the article with words that have the opposite meaning.

a *active (volcano)*	1 small
b *normal*	2 solid
c *dangerous*	3 dormant
d *likely*	4 unusual
e *liquid*	5 mild
f *severe*	6 inexperienced
g *skilled*	7 safe
h *vast*	8 improbable

2 Add one of the following prefixes to form the opposite of each adjective.

im-   in-   non-   un-

a *active* _____   e *predictable* _____

b *usual* _____   g *expensive* _____

c *likely* _____   f *possible* _____

d *violent* _____   h *practical* _____

3 Use some of the words you have just formed to complete these sentences.

a Theft and shoplifting are examples of _____ crimes.

b At the moment the weather is completely _____ – today it's sunny and yesterday it rained.

c I'm afraid that's a(n) _____ suggestion. We haven't got enough money.

d It's _____ that he'll come now. He's already two hours late.

e They're night birds. It's quite _____ to see them during the day.

f Compared to driving a car, cycling is a(n) _____ way to travel.

E Collocations: 'Size' adjectives + nouns

1 Which nouns in the box can follow these 'size' adjectives?

deep   small   thick   thin   vast

area / book / business / change / country / feeling / hair / hole / layer / line / majority / number / pullover / shirt / water

2 Which collocations from **E1** mean approximately the same as the following?

a strongly-felt emotion   d coins
b something to wear in warm weather   e something to wear in cold weather
c a very large proportion   f a company which employs only a few workers

EXTENSION: Idioms with 'size' adjectives

Match the idioms in these sentences with meanings **1–5**.

a If you're late for work again, you'll be *in deep water*.
b We were up until *the small hours* – that's why we're so tired.
c Nothing you say will worry him. He's very *thick-skinned*.
d She wasn't here a minute ago. She just appeared *out of thin air*.
e I'm very grateful to my parents. They've helped me *through thick and thin*.

1 very early in the morning or very late at night
2 in good times and bad times
3 from nowhere
4 in serious trouble
5 not worried by criticism

F Plurals of nouns ending in -o

1 Read these rules. Can you think of any more examples for each group?

   a The plural of some common nouns ending in a consonant + -o is **-oes**:

     volcano → volcanoes, tomato → tomatoes

   b Some exceptions to this rule are abbreviations, foreign words and words ending in a vowel + -o:

     photo → photos, peso → pesos, radio → radios

2 For each of these definitions write down the correct word ending in **-oes** or **-os**.

   a Famous men everyone admires
   b Places where artists and photographers work
   c Abbreviation for kilograms
   d Cassettes which we can watch films or TV programmes on
   e Places where people go to dance to modern music, usually at night

G Practice

Read this short article about planning for the future and fill the gaps with words from the box. There are **two** words you do not need to use.

dangers / eruption / impossible / lava / measure / practical / predict / prevent / safer / severe / volcanic / volcano

Planning for the future

Obviously, it is (**a**)_____ to stop a volcanic (**b**)_____, but there are certain (**c**)_____ steps we can take to reduce the effects. For example, we can make buildings stronger and build protective walls to stop or redirect (**d**)_____ flows. Such efforts can be successful, although they may not help much in the case of a large-scale eruption.

By contrast, protecting future buildings from (**e**)_____ hazards is a simpler task. Before building, we should (**f**)_____ the risk, and if it seems too great, we should try to find a (**g**)_____ place to build.

When a (**h**)_____ comes to life, a few weeks may not be enough time to (**i**)_____ a tragedy. Planning is the key to saving lives. Well before the warning signs occur, people must be educated about the (**j**)_____ of volcanic eruptions.

17 New carrots

A Introduction

1 These words and phrases are from the article below. Try to match them with their meanings.

a	*artificial*	**1**	to affect the way someone thinks or behaves
b	*bunch*	**2**	available to buy in the shops
c	*commercial*	**3**	to cover a bigger area than before
d	*influence*	**4**	normal, not artificial
e	*on sale*	**5**	economic, connected with business and finance
f	*original*	**6**	a small round thing from which new plants grow
g	*seed*	**7**	not real, not natural
h	*spread*	**8**	eyesight, the ability to see
i	*natural*	**9**	first, what something was like in the beginning
j	*vision*	**10**	a collection or group of similar things, e.g. flowers, vegetables

2 Check in a dictionary the meaning of any of these words or phrases you do not understand.

B Reading

1 Read this article and fill each gap with the correct form of a word or phrase from **A1**.

The future is purple

Five years after a frozen food company tried to encourage children to eat vegetables by covering their carrots in chocolate, supermarkets are now reintroducing carrots in one of their (**a**) _____ colours: purple.

Purple carrots – dark on the outside, orange on the inside – are already (**b**) _____ in shops, while green, yellow, red, white and black varieties may follow. Growers say this change of colour is entirely (**c**) _____, as carrots occurred in many different colours before the Dutch produced an orange variety in the 16th century that became a massive (**d**) _____ success. Temple drawings show that over 4000 years ago the Egyptians had purple-coloured plants thought to be carrots, and researchers have discovered that by the 1300s, purple and yellow varieties of carrot had (**e**) _____ from Afghanistan to Europe and China. Red and white carrots were also grown.

Orange carrots contain high levels of betacarotene, which is a form of vitamin A that improves (**f**) _____ in dim light. Purple carrots also contain anthocyanin, which may help prevent heart disease. The supermarket giant Sainsbury's, which is selling the carrots called Purple Haze, say they are thinking about introducing a rainbow-coloured (**g**) _____ soon.

According to a report in 1999, less than 20% of the vegetable (**h**) _____ available in the early 20th century were commercially grown 100 years later. Over 90% of carrot varieties have been lost. In 1903 there were 287 varieties of carrots being grown, but 80 years later there were only 21 types of carrot seed in the US national seed storage laboratory.

Sainsbury's are hoping for a small change in people's eating habits. A spokesman said: "Hopefully this unusual colour will (**i**) _____ children to eat more vegetables, while parents can be sure that there is nothing (**j**) _____ about the carrots."

2 Decide whether these statements about the information in the article are true (**T**) or false (**F**). Then read the article again to check your answers.

a	Carrots have always been orange.	T / F
b	Purple carrots are purple in the middle and on the outside.	T / F
c	Betacarotene helps to prevent heart disease.	T / F
d	Purple and yellow carrots came from Afghanistan.	T / F
e	You can buy more types of carrots now than you could 100 years ago.	T / F

C Related words

1 Fill the gaps in this chart with words related to the words given. (X = no useful word at this level.)

Noun	Verb	Adjective	Adverb
a _____	encourage	_____	X
b X	X	_____	entirely
c _____	influence	_____	X
d _____ _____	_____	original	_____
e _____	prevent	_____ _____	X
f storage	_____	X	X
g variety	X	_____ _____	X

2 Fill each gap in these sentences with the correct form of a word you have added to the chart.

a When the company closes, the _____ workforce will be made redundant, even the top managers.

b A healthy diet plays an important part in the _____ of disease.

c Employees work best when they get _____ from their boss and their colleagues.

d There are _____ reasons why people prefer orange carrots.

e One of the main _____ in my childhood was my older sister. She was more important to me than my parents.

f I live in France now, but I come from Scotland _____.

g It isn't necessary to _____ carrots in the fridge.

D Vegetables and colours

1 Check the meaning of any of these vegetables you do not understand.

aubergine / bean / broccoli / cabbage / carrot / cauliflower / courgette / garlic / onion / pea / potato / mushroom

2 What colours are the vegetables in **D1**? Use words from this box.

> black / blue / brown / green / grey / orange / purple / red / yellow / white

Example: *Carrots are usually orange.*

E Adjective-noun collocations

1 Match these three adjectives with one or more of meanings **a–g** below:

dark   dim   dull

a boring
b not pale or light in colour
c not clear (e.g. something you see or remember)
d not bright (e.g. a light)
e not sharp (e.g. a headache)
f unintelligent, not clever
g with no light (e.g. a room)

2 Which nouns in the box can follow these adjectives?

dark   dim   dull

> colour / eyes / glasses / hair / light / memory / pain / story / student / weather

3 Fill each gap in these sentences with the correct form of a collocation from **E2**.

a I can remember my first day at school quite clearly, but I have very _____ _____ of my life before that.

b The dentist took one of my teeth out yesterday. It's almost better, but I can still feel a _____ _____.

c At first she thought everyone was asleep but then she saw a _____ _____ coming from one of the bedrooms.

d I hope the sun shines when we're on holiday. The _____ has been _____ and wet for the last three weeks.

e Most Japanese and Chinese people have _____ _____ and _____.

f He thought no one would recognise him because he was wearing _____ _____.

4 Replace the words *dark*, *dim* and *dull* in phrases **a–g** with one of these words with the opposite meaning. Some words have more than one possible opposite.

> bright / clear / fair / interesting / light / sharp

a a dull afternoon _____
b dim headlights _____
c a dull pain _____
d dark hair _____
e a dull newspaper _____
f dark green _____
g a dim memory _____

F Numbers and words

These numbers are from the article. Write them in words.

a 4000 _____

b the 1300s _____

c 1999 _____

d 20% _____

e the 20th century _____

f 1903 _____

g 287 _____

EXTENSION: Words and numbers

Read the words and write the numbers.

a twenty-seven point five per cent

b seventeen sixty-two (year)

c fourteen thousand nine hundred and eleven

d three-quarters

e eight-two-oh-double-four-five (phone number)

f six forty-five (time)

g the thirteenth of June (date)

h one point seven five

G Puzzle

Read the clues and complete the puzzle. All the answers are words from this unit.

a A large, round, green and white vegetable

b Intelligent; opposite of *dim* light

c A period of a hundred years

d A noun related to the adverb *originally*

e The noun related to *influential*

f Not clear – like something you cannot remember well

g A group or collection, e.g. flowers, grapes, carrots

h An adjective related to *variety*

i Small round green vegetables

j The opposite of *bright* and *interesting*

k Not real, not natural

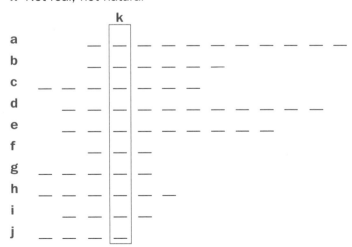

A Introduction

1 These words and phrases are from the story below. Try to match them with their meanings.

a *background*	1 energetic, enthusiastic, showing interest
b *click*	2 to give something in return for something else
c *distant*	3 uncivilised, simple
d *entertain*	4 far away
e *exchange*	5 information about people, places and situations which helps readers to understand a story
f *inhabitant*	6 a short stop or break
g *lively*	7 to become
h *pause*	8 a small noise, like a light being switched on or off
i *primitive*	9 someone who lives in a particular place
j *turn into*	10 to amuse or interest

2 Use your dictionary to check the meaning of any of these words or phrases you do not understand.

B Reading

1 Read this story and fill each gap with the correct form of a word or phrase from **A1**.

Science fiction?

Every month the writers all met to (a) _____ stories and to discuss life as a writer. Their conversations usually (b) _____ storytelling sessions where every writer tried to (c) _____ the others.

Tonight was one of these nights. Laughter and (d) _____ talk filled the warm room. It was getting late, and most of the writers had already told their story. After a brief (e) _____ in the conversation and to everyone's surprise, John started talking. John was a science fiction writer who usually just listened and watched the others, but never participated. This evening, he began his story. Everyone listened.

"I used to live in a house in the country with my family," he began. "One day I started thinking about a new novel, and decided to write the (f) _____ to the story."

"I described a world in a (g) _____ galaxy, with details of the dangerous plants and animals, and suddenly I felt or heard something like a (h) _____, a feeling as if what I wrote had become real. It was a very strange, but very real feeling. Then I filled this world with half-intelligent, savage creatures who were always fighting terrible wars. I also put strange diseases in many parts of my new world. Again I experienced the 'click', and I was sure that somewhere, very far away, what I wrote had become real."

The listeners leaned closer. "What happened then?", a woman asked. John went on: "I decided to write about myself as one of the (i) _____ of this peculiar world. I described every detail of the life of the new 'me'. I suddenly felt a 'click' which was much stronger than before, and I found myself in my new world."

He paused, and sipped his drink. "In this world I was also a writer. I wrote about my own life and the half-intelligent, (j) _____ people in the world seemed to find what I wrote interesting. They even paid me for it. In this way I managed to earn my living."

The woman smiled and asked: "Well, how did you get back?"

"I didn't get back," he replied. "I'm still here."

2 What do you remember about the story? Make true sentences by matching each beginning with the correct ending.

Beginnings	Endings
a Every month the writers met…	1 science fiction writer.
b John was a …	2 primitive.
c John didn't usually …	3 very interested in John's story.
d The people in John's story were …	4 for writing stories.
e The other writers were …	5 to tell each other stories.
f In his story, John was paid …	6 say anything to the other writers.

C Related words

1 Fill the gaps in this chart with words related to the words given. Sometimes there are two words in one group. (X = no useful word at this level.)

Noun	Verb	Adjective	Adverb
a creature _____ *	_____	_____	_____
b _____	describe	_____	X
c _____	X	distant	_____
d _____ _____ *	entertain	_____	_____
e inhabitant*	_____	_____ _____ (opposite)	X
f _____	X	intelligent _____ (opposite)	_____
g laughter	_____	X	X

These words refer to people.

2 Fill the gaps in these sentences with the appropriate form of words you have added to the chart.

a Films, music and sport are three forms of _____.

b When he finished his story, nobody _____. They didn't think it was funny.

c As far as anyone knows, there is no life on Mars. It is a(n) _____ planet.

d Science fiction writers _____ new worlds from their imagination.

e On a clear day you can see the mountains in the _____. They are actually over 100 kilometres away.

f The police gave a full _____ of the missing person.

D Verb-noun collocations

1 Which nouns in the box can follow these verbs?

earn   gain   win

experience / your living / the lottery / money / a prize / a race / wages / weight

2 Complete these sentences using verb-noun collocations from **D1**.

a My friend has _____ _____! She got all six numbers right.

b I ate lots of nice food on holiday. That's why I've _____ so much _____ recently.

c I play the saxophone in my spare time, but I _____ my _____ as an accountant.

d When he was at school he _____ several _____ for doing well at sports.

e Nurses work long hours and don't _____ very high _____.

f While she was a teacher she _____ valuable _____ in working with young children.

EXTENSION: Countable and uncountable nouns

1 The nouns experience and weight can be countable or uncountable.
In each of these sentences, decide whether experience or weight is countable (C) or uncountable (U).

a I'm trying to lose weight.
b Be careful when you're lifting heavy weights.
c That job interview was a most unpleasant experience.
d You need experience for this job.

2 Match the countable and uncountable forms of these words with their meanings.

a a lamb (C)   **1** substance used for making furniture
b lamb (U)   **2** stuff for writing on
c a glass (C)   **3** large group of trees
d glass (U)   **4** something you read to find out the news
e a wood (C)   **5** substance used for making windows
f wood (U)   **6** meat from a young sheep
g a paper (C)   **7** something to drink from
h paper (U)   **8** young sheep

E Onomatopoeic words

Onomatopoeic words are words that sound like the noise they are describing.
Example: a click is a small noise, like a light being switched on or off.

Complete the sentences with appropriate onomatopoeic words from the box.

crash / creak / growl / jingle / splash / whisper

Note: All these words can be verbs or nouns.

a The children jumped into the swimming pool together, making a great _____.

b The dog _____ and then barked, but it didn't attack me.

c They were _____, so I couldn't hear what they were saying.

d There was a loud _____ as the two cars went into each other.

e The heavy wooden door _____ as she pushed it slowly open.

f As he ran past, you could hear the coins _____ in his pocket.

F Phrasal verbs with *go*

This sentence is in the story: *He **went on**: 'I decided to write about myself...'*
Here *went on* means *continued talking after an interruption*. These are some more
phrasal verbs with *go* and their meanings:

go by	pass
go down with	catch (an illness)
go off	become bad or rotten (food or drink)
go through	experience something unpleasant
go without	manage without something you need or want

Now fill the gaps in these sentences with one of the *go* verbs above.

a I know this exam is very important, but you should stop work now and go to
bed. It's bad for you to _____ sleep.

b If you leave food out of the fridge in hot weather, it soon _____.

c As a family they've _____ a terrible time. Paul lost his job and they've had
to sell their car.

d I feel terrible. I hope I'm not _____ something.

e As the train _____, I thought I saw one of my friends at the window.

G Puzzle

Find the following words in the puzzle. They can be horizontal, vertical or diagonal.

a Water can make this noise.
b A large group of trees
c A short break, stop or hesitation
d To get heavier = to _____ weight.
e Enthusiastic and energetic
f The verb related to *creative* and *creature*
g A person who lives in a place
h The sound of a light switch

O	L	C	R	E	A	T	E	F	I
C	L	I	M	A	T	W	O	O	N
C	H	I	V	E	R	O	O	M	H
W	H	A	V	E	T	O	A	R	A
P	L	I	T	I	L	D	O	R	B
A	R	M	S	C	I	Y	P	M	I
U	N	D	E	R	L	N	N	O	T
S	E	G	A	I	N	I	G	N	A
E	X	P	E	R	I	E	C	E	N
R	E	S	P	L	A	S	H	K	T

An unusual suggestion

A Introduction

1 These words and phrases are from the story below. Try to match them with their meanings.

a	*by mistake*	1	the part of a jacket, shirt etc that covers your arm
b	*denim*	2	easy to see, clear, noticeable
c	*charity shop*	3	without meaning to, accidentally
d	*crowded*	4	an enclosed area of shops where no cars are allowed
e	*panic*	5	a shop owned by a charity, which sells things, especially clothes, which people have given
f	*scruffy*	6	to have a sudden strong feeling of fear
g	*obvious*	7	dirty and untidy
h	*scared*	8	thick cloth that jeans are usually made of
i	*shopping mall*	9	frightened
j	*sleeve*	10	busy, full of people

2 Use your dictionary to check the meaning of any of these words or phrases you do not understand.

B Reading

1 Read the story and fill each gap with the correct form of a word or phrase from **A1**.

The **Big** Blue Shirt

The boy sat there in the **(a)**_____ café, sipping his drink, making it last. His face was sad and thin. Bits of his long brown curly hair were sticking out from under his **(b)**_____ old baseball cap. But it was his big blue **(c)**_____ shirt that really caught my attention.

I was afraid to take my eyes off him in case he disappeared outside into the busy **(d)**_____. I'd never find him again if he did. I had to be sure. Sitting opposite him, I tried not to stare, so that my watching him would not be **(e)**_____. Had he been warned not to speak to strangers? Would he **(f)**_____ if I asked the question I needed to ask?

Suddenly he looked up and I caught his eye. This was my chance. "Excuse me, son. That shirt you're wearing ... did you get it at the **(g)**_____ round the corner?" He suddenly looked **(h)**_____, as if I was a policeman who might arrest him for not being at school. But before he could jump up and run away, I went on: "It was mine, you see. It was my favourite. You can see my name Steve on the **(i)**_____. My wife gave it to the charity shop **(j)**_____. I'd really like to buy it back."

2 What do you remember? Answer these questions, without looking back at the story. Then read the story again to check your answers.

    a What colour was the boy's hair?
    b What was he wearing on his head?
    c Where was the café?
    d What did the man ask the boy?
    e What was the man's name?
    f Where was his name written on the shirt?
    g What did the man want to do about the shirt?

C Clothes and parts of clothes

1 Match the correct words from the box with pictures **A–F**.

> *baseball cap / jacket / shirt / socks / trainers / trousers*

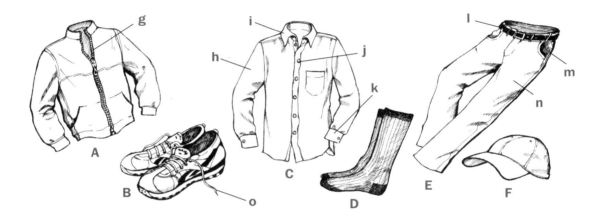

2 Now use these words to label **g–o** above.

> *belt / button / collar / cuff / lace / leg / pocket / sleeve / zip*

D Idioms with *eye*

1 There are two idioms in the story which include the word **eye**. Find them and match them with the correct meanings **a–c**. One meaning does not fit either of the idioms.

    a stop looking at someone for a short time
    b watch someone for a long time
    c make someone notice you

2 Here are some more idioms with the word **eye**. Match them with meanings **1–5** below.

    a *keep your eye on* someone / something
    b *see eye to eye* (with someone)
    c *turn a blind eye to* something
    d *be up to your eyes in* something
    e *pull the wool over someone's eyes*

    1 ignore something / pretend not to notice something
    2 be very busy, usually with work of some kind
    3 watch or take care of someone / something
    4 deceive trick someone
    5 have the same opinion as someone

3 Complete these sentences with the appropriate form of one of the **eye** idioms.

a He and his brother have completely different ideas about things. They never

_____ with each other.

b Sorry, but I can't come to your party – I'm _____ in work this week.

c My boss knows we email our friends at work, but he _____ to it.

d You can't _____. She knows what you're saying is not true.

e Would you mind _____ the children for half an hour while I go out?

EXTENSION: More things you can wear

Label the picture with words from the box.

bracelet / earring / glasses / lipstick / nail varnish / necklace / ring / watch

E Adjective order

1 These three phrases are from the story, but only one of them has the words in the correct order. Which one? Rewrite the other phrases in the correct order then check in the story.

a *long brown curly hair*
b *old baseball scruffy cap*
c *denim blue big shirt*

2 Some of the phrases in italics in these sentences are in the wrong order. Rewrite them in the correct order.

    a I love your *bright red silk blouse*.
    b She was wearing *pear-shaped silver beautiful earrings*.
    c He's got *dark short straight hair*.
    d I've bought some *wonderful French new trainers*.
    e They found a *black leather small bag*.

F Meanings of *look*

1 The verb *look* has many meanings. Match the expressions with *look* in these sentences with meanings **1–6** below.

    a The boy *looked up*.
    b She *looked like* my sister.
    c Don't worry. Try to *look on the bright side*.
    d He suddenly *looked* scared.
    e *Look out*!
    f If you're not sure, *look it up* on the Internet.

    1 be careful
    2 appear, seem
    3 try to find information about
    4 be optimistic
    5 resemble
    6 raise your eyes

2 Rewrite these sentences, replacing the words in italics with the appropriate form of one of the expressions from **F1**.

    a There's a car coming! *Be careful!*
    b People say I *resemble* my father.
    c I didn't know what the word 'scared' meant, so I *tried to find the information* in a dictionary.
    d My mother *appeared* older than when I last saw her.
    e I know it's been a bad year for you, but try to *be optimistic* – you're starting a new job next week.

G Practice

Read this short version of *The Big Blue Shirt* and fill the gaps with words from sections **A–F** above.

In the story, the writer's wife had given his favourite (**a**)_____ (*2 words*) shirt to a (**b**)_____ (*2 words*) by (**c**)_____. While he was in a (**d**)_____ in town, the writer saw a young (**e**)_____ wearing his shirt. He didn't speak to him at first because he thought the boy might (**f**)_____ and run (**g**)_____. When he finally asked him about the shirt, the boy was (**h**)_____ because he thought the man was a policeman who was going to (**i**)_____ him.

Random acts of kindness

A Introduction

1 These words and phrases are from the article below. Try to match them with their meanings.

a	*fare*	1	a place where you pay money to travel on a road, a bridge, a tunnel, etc
b	*frail*	2	in poor condition, in need of decoration (used to describe buildings and places)
c	*impulse*	3	a stick with cloth on the end, which is used for washing floors
d	*mop*	4	to notice, to see by chance
e	*jot down*	5	a sudden feeling which makes you want to do something
f	*random*	6	done or happening by chance, not according to a plan
g	*rundown*	7	money you pay for a journey
h	*spot*	8	to write quickly
i	*tollbooth*	9	weak, fragile (used to describe people)

2 Use your dictionary to check the meaning of any of these words or phrases you do not understand.

B Reading

1 Read this article and fill each gap with the correct form of a word or phrase from **A1**.

Kindness is spreading

It's a cold winter day in San Francisco. A woman in a red Honda drives up to the Bay Bridge **(a)**_____. "I'm paying for myself, and for the six cars behind me," she says with a smile, handing over money for seven tickets. One after another, the next six drivers arrive at the booth, dollars in hand, and are told, "Some lady up ahead already paid your **(b)**_____. Have a nice day."

The woman in the Honda, it turned out, had read a message on a friend's fridge: "Practice **(c)**_____ acts of kindness." The phrase impressed her so much that she copied it down.

Judy Foreman **(d)**_____ the same phrase spray-painted on a wall a hundred miles from her home. "I thought it was so inspiring," she said, "that I now write it at the bottom of all my letters." Her husband Frank liked the phrase so much that he put it up on the wall for his seventh-graders, one of whom was the daughter of a local journalist. The journalist put it in her newspaper. Two days later, she heard from Anne Herbert who had read the phrase in her newspaper and **(e)**_____ it _____.

In Portland, Oregon, a man might plunk a coin into a stranger's parking meter just in time. In Patterson, New Jersey, a dozen people with pails and **(f)**_____ might arrive at a **(g)**_____ house and clean it from top to bottom while the **(h)**_____ elderly owners look on, dazed and smiling! In Chicago, a teenage boy may be shovelling snow off the driveway when he feels the same **(i)**_____. "Nobody's looking," he thinks, and clears the snow off the neighbor's driveway too.

A woman in Boston writes "Merry Christmas!" to the tellers on the back of her checks. A man in St Louis, whose car has just been rear-ended by a young woman, waves her away, saying. "It's only a scratch. Don't worry."

Now the phrase is spreading, on bumper stickers, on walls, at the bottom of letters and business cards. As Anne Herbert says: "Kindness can build on itself as much as violence can."

2 The article you have just read is about the idea behind this phrase: *'Practice random acts of kindness.'* What does this phrase mean? Choose one of these meanings.

    a *Don't plan what you do. Just do what you feel like.*
    b *Behave generously towards other people with no plan in mind.*
    c *Try to shock and surprise people by doing unexpected things.*

3 What do you remember about the article? Make true sentences by matching each beginning with the correct ending.

Beginnings	Endings
a The woman in San Francisco …	1 to prevent someone from getting a parking fine.
b One of the children in Frank Foreman's class …	2 didn't want people to see him helping his neighbours.
c The Portland man wanted …	3 when people came and cleaned their house for them.
d The old people in New Jersey were surprised …	4 was driving a red car.
e The teenager in Chicago …	5 was the daughter of a journalist.

C Word groups

1 In the following groups of words, one word is a general word and the others are examples of this general word.

Example: *coffee / **drink** / tea / water*

Which are the general words in these groups?

    a *bus / car / lorry / vehicle*
    b *language / phrase / sentence / word*
    c *bed / chair / furniture / table*
    d *instrument / piano / trumpet / violin*
    e *rose / flower / poppy / tulip*

2 Add two more words to each group in **C1**.

D American English

1 The article you have read is written in American English. Match these words from the article with the correct meaning and with the British English equivalent if there is one.

American English	Meaning	British English
a *driveway*	1 a water container	*plonk*
b *pail*	2 to put in or down heavily without taking care	*year seven pupil*
c *plunk*	3 to drive into the back of the car in front of you	*drive*
d *rear-end*	4 a child in the seventh year of education	*cashier*
e *seventh-grader*	5 a bank employee who accepts or pays out money	*bucket*
f *teller*	6 a wide path beside your house where you can park your car	no equivalent word

2 How are these two American words from the article spelled in British English?

    a *a check*
    b *to practice*

E Describing periods of time

The first *random act of kindness* in the article took place on a *cold winter day*. Three-word phrases like this are often used to describe periods of time. Make up a three-word phrase to describe each of the following.

a It's 2 p.m. The weather is warm and it's summer. It's a _____

b The evening is cool and the season is autumn. It's a _____

c It's spring. The sun is shining brightly and it's 8 a.m. It's a _____

d Our holiday in the summer lasts a long time this year. We're having a

_____

e It's cold. It's 11 p.m. The month is December. It's a _____

F Phrasal verbs with *hand*

1 The article tells us that the woman in the red car **handed over** money for seven tickets. Match each of these *hand* verbs with one of the meanings **a–d**.

hand back   **hand in**   **hand out**   **hand over**

    a give something to somebody so that it belongs to them
    b give things to everybody in a group
    c give a piece of work to a teacher to be marked or corrected
    d return something you have borrowed from someone

2 Now fill the gaps in these sentences with the correct form of one of the *hand* verbs from **F1**.

    a The students have got to _____ _____ their homework on Thursday morning.

    b She looked closely at the photograph the police officer had given her and then

        _____ it _____.

    c The teacher asked David to _____ _____ the papers.

    d The bank robbers told the cashier to _____ _____ the money.

EXTENSION: Idioms with *hand*

1 Match each idiom with the correct meaning **1–4**.

    a *Hands off!*
    b *have your hands full*
    c *out of hand*
    d *lend someone a hand*

    1 to help someone
    2 difficult to control
    3 to be very busy, to have a lot of work to do
    4 Don't touch!

2 Complete these sentences with the correct form of one of the *hand* idioms.

    a The children soon get _____ if you don't watch them.

    b You look terribly busy. Can I _____ you _____?

    c _____ the food! I'll let you know when it's time for lunch!

    d I'm afraid I can't help you at the moment. I've got _____ looking after the visitors.

G Puzzle

Read the clues and complete the puzzle. All the answers are words from this unit.

a Something we use to carry water in

b A *tulip* is a kind of _____.

c A sudden desire to do something

d The American English word for a cashier in a bank

e To *hand* _____ means to return something you have borrowed.

f Not according to a plan, by chance

g To _____ *down* means to write something quickly.

h To notice or see

i Cars and buses are two different kinds of _____.

j Drivers pay money to use a bridge at a _____.

j

a   _ _ _ _ _ _

b   _ _ _ _ _ _

c   _ _ _ _ _ _ _

d   _ _ _ _ _ _

e   _ _ _ _

f   _ _ _ _ _ _

g   _ _ _

h   _ _ _ _

i   _ _ _ _ _ _ _ _

Review 1 (Units 1–4)

1 Related words

Fill each gap with a word related to the word in capitals. The first one has been done for you.

a Many people find TV soap operas _addictive_. They can't stop watching them. ADDICT

b Even the most well-known celebrities need their _____ from time to time. PRIVATE

c Last year there was a two per cent _____ in the population. GROW

d Millions of _____ come to Britain every year. VISIT

e Holidays are my favourite way of escaping from _____. REAL

f As he started to speak, there was complete _____ in the room. SILENT

g Alex is training to be an _____ . ELECTRIC

h The house was full of _____ antique furniture and paintings. VALUE

2 Verb-noun collocations

Complete the sentences with the correct form of one of these verbs. You will need to use one of the verbs twice.

hold / keep / lose / save / spend / waste / win

a I know I should have been more careful, but don't _____ your temper!

b Instead of walking, why don't we _____ time and take a taxi?

c When they close the factory, the employees all expect to _____ their jobs.

d Don't _____ time watching TV – you should be revising for your exam.

e Email is one of the cheapest ways of _____ in contact with people in other countries.

f Do you know where tomorrow's meeting is being _____?

g Can you lend me some money? I've _____ all mine.

h The Democratic Party were very lucky to _____ the election.

3 Make and do

Complete the sentences with the correct form of make or do.

a He finished the whole exam in thirty minutes and _____ no mistakes.

b Stop _____ so much noise – I'm on the phone.

c Is it my turn to _____ the cooking tonight?

d Are you going to be long? I've got three phone calls to _____.

e I'll _____ my best to persuade him not to leave.

f Excuse me, can I _____ a suggestion?

g You can't have it both ways – you've just got to _____ a decision.

4 Adjectives

Choose the correct adjectives in these sentences.

a We're going to buy a new electric / electrical cooker.

b I love going to the theatre but I'm afraid I can't afford expensive / valuable seats.

c Walking is certainly the most economic / economical way of travelling.

d Her coat was made of cheap / free imitation leather.

e It was very irrelevant / irresponsible of you to drive through a red light.

5 Adjective opposites

Add prefixes to these adjectives to make their opposites.

a attractive
b polite
c mature

d legal
e intentional

6 Odd one out

Which word or phrase is the odd one out in each group? Why? The first one is done as an example.

a apple / banana / (carrot) / orange (The others are **fruits**.)

b keys / ring tone / piano / screen

c folk / jazz / rock / track

d band / cassette / CD / mini-disc

e amazing / angry / surprising / unexpected

f cellphone / highway / number plate / trash

Review 2 (Units 5–8)

1 Verb-noun collocations

Make phrases to match definitions a–f below. Use one of these verbs and a noun or phrase from the box.

cut   find   have

> breakfast / someone guilty / prices / a shower / taxes / your way

a A jury in a court of law can decide to do this.
b You manage to get to the place you want to go to.
c What a shopkeeper can do if things in his / her shop are too expensive.
d You do this if you are hungry when you get up in the morning.
e A government can do this if it wants to be more popular with people.
f You might do this after a hot, tiring day at work.

2 Adjective-noun collocations

Choose the best adjective in each of these sentences.

a David Bellamy is one of the world's *leading / natural / positive* experts on conservation.
b The police are sure he committed the crime, but they can't arrest him because they have no *natural / concrete / mental* evidence.
c That's a(n) *enthusiastic / brilliant / leading* idea! Let's do it!
d These days many sports are played at night under *natural / physical / artificial* light.
e Old people often have an excellent *short-term / mental / long-term* memory, but can't remember what they did yesterday.
f He's such a(n) *enthusiastic / leading / inspiring* politician that thousands of people come to hear him speak.

3 Phrasal verbs

Complete the sentences with the correct form of a phrasal verb from the box.

> carry on / carry out / come up with / put up with / set off / set up

a What time shall we _____ tomorrow? We have to be there by lunchtime.
b Is that really the best idea you can _____?
c Don't blame me. I'm just _____ the instructions my boss gave me.
d I'll have to see the dentist. I can't _____ this toothache any longer.
e The government has _____ a new committee to look into the rise in crime.
f Shall I stop now or shall I _____ until I've finished?

4 Related words

Fill each gap with a word related to the word in capitals.

a The character Indiana Jones is an archaeologist and _____. EXPLORE
b I was quite good at practical subjects at school, but I didn't understand some of the _____ background. THEORY
c The better the working conditions, the higher the workers' _____. PRODUCE
d I can't study if there's any noise – it interferes with my _____. CONCENTRATE
e People recognised Mozart's _____ when he was a young child. BRILLIANT

5 Prepositions

Complete the sentences with prepositions from the box. You will need to use some prepositions twice.

> for / from / in / of / on / with

a You can't rely _____ warm weather, so you'd better take a coat.
b The children went out into the garden and filled their pockets _____ apples.
c I hope you succeed _____ getting the job you want.
d After finishing the marathon he collapsed – he was suffering _____ exhaustion.
e Thank you _____ inviting me to your party.
f Her letters always smelt _____ expensive perfume.
g He should have passed the exam. He has no explanation _____ his failure.
h They have no interest _____ music of any kind.

Review 3 (Units 9–12)

1 Related words

Fill each gap with a word related to the word in capitals.

a Environmental groups are trying to prevent the _____ of the rainforests. DESTROY

b Taxi drivers should have detailed _____ of the area they work in. KNOW

c The young Japanese violinist gave a brilliant _____. PERFORM

d John's parents watched _____ as their son received his prize. PRIDE

e There's been a 10% _____ in the price of petrol this year. REDUCE

f The man was kept at the police station overnight for his own _____. SAFE

2 Adjective-noun collocations

Match adjectives from box **A** with nouns from box **B**. Then use the pairs of words to complete the sentences.

> **A** common / hard / heavy / lasting / normal / public / sharp / strong

> **B** behaviour / coffee / effect / increase / luck / opinion / rain / sight

a If I'm feeling sleepy in the morning, I have a cup of _____ _____ to wake me up.

b There's been a _____ _____ in compensation claims.

c Politicians are quite unpopular at the moment. It's because they don't listen to _____ _____.

d Young children with mobile phones are a _____ _____ these days.

e I don't care what you say: standing in the middle of the road and screaming is not _____ _____.

f Seeing that terrible accident had a _____ _____ on Debbie.

g The match had to be postponed because of the _____ _____. It was _____ _____ on people who had already bought tickets.

3 Verb-noun collocations

Fill each gap with a verb from the box.

> catch / drive / make / miss / pay / ride / take / travel

a I ran as fast as I could because I thought I was going to _____ the bus.

b Photographers can _____ a very good living by selling pictures of famous people to the newspapers.

c I just wish you'd _____ the doctor's advice and stop smoking.

d If you leave now, you could _____ the half-past eight train.

e If I'm going somewhere on business, I prefer to _____ by plane.

f I learned to _____ a bike when I was six years old.

g I have to _____ the rent every Friday evening.

4 Choose the correct word

Choose the correct words in these sentences.

a My sister was really *annoyed / annoying* when she found out that I'd been reading her email.

b The weather was terrible, so she was really grateful *for / to* the offer of a lift.

c I've just won £25,000 on the lottery – my friends are *green / red* with envy.

d Don't be afraid *for / of* the dog – he won't hurt you.

e It's nobody's *blame / fault*. It was just an accident.

f This coffee's terribly *weak / week*.

g Don't *blame / fault* me. I wasn't even there.

5 Compound adjectives

Which compound adjectives can be used to describe these people and things? The first one has been done for you.

a Someone who writes with their *right hand*.
   right-handed

b A person who has *short hair*.

c A meal that you *cook* at *home*.

d A person who *looks healthy*.

e A person with *blue eyes*.

f Something which is the same *shape* as a *heart*.

Review 4 (Units 13–16)

1 Phrasal verbs

Choose the correct phrasal verb in each sentence.

a That's a really difficult problem. I'll need more time to *round up* / *work out* the answer.

b It was difficult to *make off* / *make out* the road signs because of the fog.

c The excuse he *made for* / *made up* was impossible to believe.

d I always get on well with my parents. We've never *fallen out* / *fallen behind*.

e The old cottage *fell down* / *fell through* after the heavy lorry crashed into it.

2 More phrasal verbs

Complete each sentence with the correct form of a phrasal verb from the box.

> come from / come out with / come round /
> come up / come up against / come up with

a You're not American, are you? Where do you _____?

b Some old friends will be here tomorrow. Why don't you _____ and see them?

c You know that problem we've got? Well, I've _____ the perfect solution.

d Everything was going well until I _____ a difficulty I hadn't expected.

e I can't stay long. Something important has just _____ at work.

3 Related words

Fill each gap with a word related to the word in capitals.

a You could hear the _____ 50 kilometres away. EXPLODE

b The overnight rain has caused flooding and general _____. DISRUPT

c If you receive a _____ letter you should inform the police immediately. THREAT

d The weekend sport has been _____ affected by the bad weather. SEVERE

e In recent years organic food has gained in _____. POPULAR

f United are definitely going to win the cup. That's my _____. PREDICT

g Dumping rubbish can cause serious _____ damage. ENVIRONMENT

h The _____ of the volcano came as a complete surprise. ERUPT

4 Prepositions

Choose the correct prepositions in these sentences.

a Does this book belong *to* / *with* you?

b My parents don't approve *about* / *of* me smoking.

c I'd love to live *in* / *on* the coast.

d I object *about* / *to* people using their mobile phones while they're driving.

e I'm sorry but I can't agree *to* / *with* you – I think you're quite wrong.

f Look! There's a helicopter *over* / *up* the house!

5 True or false?

Decide if each sentence is true (**T**) or false (**F**).

a A *cold fish* is someone who has a secret life.

b A *guinea pig* is someone who never stops doing things.

c A young lion is called a *cub*.

d A young horse is called a *lamb*.

e A *resident* is someone who lives in a particular place.

f If someone is *bilingual* it means they are fluent in three languages.

g If something is *overcooked*, it hasn't been cooked enough.

h The plural of *radio* is *radioes*.

i The opposite of an *active* volcano is a *non-active* volcano.

j The opposite of *expensive* is *inexpensive*.

6 Confusing words

Choose the correct words in these sentences.

a I saw Emma arrive but I didn't *notice* / *stare at* what she was wearing.

b That's a really *deep* / *thick* book – it would take weeks to read it.

c Is a twenty-pound note okay? I'm afraid I haven't got any *small* / *thin* change.

d Did you *notice* / *see* the news on TV yesterday?

e The *thick* / *vast* majority of the population are hooked on soap operas.

f I know he has a strange hairstyle, but don't *stare* / *watch* – it's rude.

Review 5 (Units 17-20)

1 Related words

Fill each gap with a word related to the word in capitals.

a He's one of the most _____ people I've ever met. CREATE

b We could hear _____ coming from the classroom as the teacher told the class a story. LAUGH

c The oldest _____ in the village will be 100 next month. INHABIT

d Most children do well at school if they get _____ from their parents and teachers. ENCOURAGE

e This year the police are concentrating on crime _____. PREVENT

f Can you give me a _____ of the man you saw coming out of the bank? DESCRIBE

g Bill Clinton was one of the most _____ politicians of the 1990s. INFLUENCE

h The latest CD by the New Symphony Orchestra shows great _____. ORIGIN

i I've always enjoyed live _____ far more than films or television. ENTERTAIN

2 Phrasal verbs

Make phrasal verbs with **go** and **hand** and words from the box to complete the sentences.

> back / by / down / in / off / out / over / through / without

a There was no coffee left, so we had to
   _____ _____.

b The teacher asked me to _____ _____ the new textbooks to the class.

c I saw the bus _____ _____, but I didn't recognise any of the passengers on it.

d The child admitted he'd taken the chocolate and reluctantly _____ it _____ to his mother.

e I feel okay, but half of my class has _____ _____ with flu.

f I'm sorry you've lost your job, but I know what you're _____ _____ – the same thing happened to me three years ago.

g How old is this milk? I think it's _____ _____.

3 Adjective-noun collocations

Choose the correct adjectives in these sentences.

a Why are you wearing those *dark / dim* glasses? It isn't sunny.

b I've had a *dim / dull* pain in my leg since I fell over last week.

c I can hardly remember my first day at school. It's just a *dark / dim* memory.

d That was a really *dim / dull* film. I nearly fell asleep halfway through.

e My sister has got *dark / dim* brown hair.

4 Adjective order

Put the adjectives in italics in these sentences into the correct order.

a My brother has a(n) *American fantastic silver-grey* car.

b I've just bought a(n) *green glass tall* vase.

c My mother's got *dark curly short* hair.

d She'll probably be wearing a(n) *old woollen brown* pullover.

e He usually wears a(n) *incredible gold large* ring.

5 True or false?

Decide if each sentence is true (**T**) or false (**F**).

a To *whisper* means to speak very quietly.

b If you drop something heavy into water, it makes a *crash*.

c Some animals *growl* when they are angry.

d If you *pull the wool over someone's eyes*, it means you pretend not to notice them.

e If you *see eye to eye with someone*, it means you trick or deceive them.

f The British English for *driveway* is *motorway*.

g The American English for *cashier* is *teller*.

h A *lorry* is a kind of *vehicle*.

i You can play a *trumpet*.

j A *collar* is something you find on a shoe.

Adjective collocations

Numbers are unit numbers.

artificial	light **5**
bright	afternoon / headlights / green **17**
brilliant	expert / idea / politician / teacher **6**
cheap	fare / gift / holiday / imitation / newspaper / seat / ticket **2**
clear	afternoon / memory **17**
common	effect / flower / name / sight **10**
concrete	effect / evidence / solution **7**
dark	colour / eyes / glasses / hair **17**
deep	feeling / hole / water **16**
dim	light / memory / student **17**
dull	colour / hair / pain / story / student / weather **17**
enthusiastic	expert / politician / teacher / worker **6**
expensive	fare / gift / holiday / mistake / newspaper / seat / ticket **2**
fair	hair **17**
free	fare / gift / holiday / information / newspaper / seat / ticket **2**
general	election / interest / knowledge / rule **12**
hard	decision / drugs / luck / work **9**
heavy	rain / smoker / traffic / work **9**
inspiring	idea / meeting / politician / teacher **6**
interesting	afternoon / newspaper **17**
lasting	effect / impression / relationship **10**
leading	expert / politician **6**
light	hair / green **17**
long-term	effect / memory **5**
mental	ability **5**
natural	ability / effect / light **5**
negative	effect **5**
normal	behaviour / day / price / relations / way **12**
physical	ability / effect / evidence **5**
positive	effect / evidence **5**
productive	meeting / worker **6**
public	health / holiday / interest / knowledge / opinion / relations **12**
sharp	bend / contrast / increase / knife / teeth **10**
	pain **17**
short-term	effect / memory **5**
small	area / book / business / change / country / hole / majority / number **16**
strong	coffee / leader / opinion / taste / wind **9**
thick	book / hair / layer / line / pullover / shirt **16**
thin	book / hair / layer / line / pullover / shirt **16**
valuable	experience / gift / information **2**
vast	area / country / majority / number **16**

afraid of **12**	**loaded** with **12**
available for **12**	**necessary** for **12**
equivalent to **12**	**open** to **12**
good at / for **12**	**opposed** to **12**
grateful for **12**	**worried** about **12**

Verb collocations

Numbers are unit numbers.

catch	someone's attention / a bus / a coach / a criminal / flu / a plane / what someone says / someone doing something / a train **10**
change	(TV) channels / your clothes / currency / jobs / your mind / the subject / trains **1**
cut	bread / costs / prices / a scene from a film / taxes **8**
do	your best / business with someone / the cooking / a crossword / damage / exercises / housework / a job / a painting / the shopping **4**
drive	a bus / a car / a coach / a taxi / a train **10**
earn	your living / money / wages **18**
exchange	glances / greetings / ideas / information / phone numbers **1**
find	the answer to a question / a cure for a disease / the solution to a problem / your way **8**
gain	experience / weight **18**
go for	a bicycle ride / a drink / a drive / a picnic / a run / a swim **1**
have	a bath / a break / breakfast / dinner / a holiday / a rest / a shower **8**
hold	a conversation / an election / a meeting / an opinion **1**
keep	in contact with / your job / your temper **1**
kill	someone / time **3**
lose	contact with someone / an election / interest in / your job / sight of / your temper / your way **1**
make	a decision / an effort / a mistake / a noise / someone an offer / a phone call / progress / room for / a suggestion / trouble **4**
	fun of / a joke / money / notes / a profit **11**
	a scene **19**
miss	a boat / a bus / a coach / a plane / a train **10**
offer	advice / someone a drink / an explanation / information / someone a lift / an opinion **1**
pay	fees / money / rent / tax(es) **11**
play	a CD / chess / football / the piano / a trick on someone **3**
press	a button / a key / a switch **3**
ride	a bicycle / a horse / a motorbike **10**
save	energy / food / money / someone / time **3**
send	a letter / a message / money / a present / a signal **3**
spend	energy / your life / money / time **3**
take	advice / care / an exam / a joke / medicine / notes / responsibility for **11**
travel by	bicycle / boat / bus / car / coach / motorbike / plane / taxi / train **10**
waste	energy / food / your life / money / time **3**
win	an election **1**
	the lottery / money / a prize / a race / a war **18**

agree with **15**	**fill** with **7**
approve of **15**	**focus** on **6**
associate with **5**	**insist** on **15**
believe in **15**	**know** about **15**
belong to **15**	**object** to **15**
blame for **11**	**pay** for **7**
borrow from **15**	**protest** against **4**
choose between **15**	**rely** on **7**
consist of **12**	**smell** of **7**
convert into **15**	**succeed** in **7**
depend on **7**	**suffer** from **7**
dispose of **15**	**thank** someone for **7**

Index

Numbers are unit numbers.

Key

1 A day without the Internet

A Introduction
1
a 9
b 6
c 1
d 10
e 2
f 4
g 5
h 3
i 8
j 7

B Reading
a virtual
b junk
c isolates
d big business
e researchers
f mouse
g event
h risky
i controversial
j passively

C Related words
1
a reality, really
b addiction, addict
c damage, damaging
d communication, communicative, communicatively
e contact
f visit, visit
g perfection, perfect, perfectly
h excitement, excite, excited
i risk, risk, riskily
2
a addict
b risk
c visit
d communicative
e damage
f contact
g excited

D The suffix -free
alcohol-free: drink / lager / wine
duty-free: cigarettes / drink / goods / lager / petrol / wine
fat-free: yoghurt
lead-free: paint / petrol
rent-free: accommodation / holiday
trouble-free: holiday / journey

EXTENSION 1
1 Addictions
A chocoholic is addicted to eating chocolate.
A shopaholic is addicted to shopping.
A workaholic is addicted to working.
2 *Go for*
We can go for: a bicycle ride / a drink / a picnic / a run / a swim

E Verb-noun collocations
1 **exchange**: glances / greetings / ideas / information / phone numbers
hold: a conversation / an election / a meeting / an opinion
lose: contact with / an election / interest in / your job / sight of / your temper / your way
offer: advice / someone a drink / an explanation / information / someone a lift / an opinion
2
a 4, offered
b 8, holding
c 1, lose
d 3, lost
e 7, offer
f 2, exchange
g 6, holding
h 5, offers

EXTENSION 2
1 Opposites of *lose*
a keep
b find
c keep
d keep
e win
2 Collocations with *change*
a trains
b your clothes
c currency
d your mind
e the subject
f jobs
g channels

F Phrasal verbs with *turn*
1
a turn up
b turn up
c turn off
d turn on
e turn off
f turn down
g turn down
2
a turn it down
b turn off
c turned up
d turn the heater on / up
e turned him down

G Practice
a addicted
b virtual
c workaholic
d put down
e turn off
f contact
g event
h real
i going for
j risky

2 The future of music

A Introduction
1
a 8
b 6
c 7
d 10
e 2
f 9
g 1
h 5
i 4
j 3

B Reading
1
a duplicate
b tunes
c flexible
d consumers
e mass
f value
g accessible
h luxury
i download
j select
2
a F It was invented in the 19th century.
b F It made it less flexible – it fixed it.
c F Analog copies were cheap, but digital copies are free.

d T '... the only truly valuable things are those which cannot be copied.'

e F 'Music will continue to be sold, because it will be easier to buy music you really like than to find it for free.'

C Related words

1 a access, access
b electrician
c industry, industrialise, industrialised
d luxurious
e performer, perform
f repetition, repetitive
g selection, selective
h technologist, technological
i transformation
j value

2 a industry
b performed
c luxurious
d electric
e selection
f repetitive

EXTENSION: Adjective pairs

a economical
b historic
c electric
d economic
e electrical
f historical

D Adjective-noun collocations

1 cheap: fares / gift / holiday / imitation / newspaper / seat / ticket

expensive: fare / gift / holiday / mistake / newspaper / seat / ticket

free: fares / gift / holiday / information / newspaper / seat / ticket

valuable: experience / gift / information / (ticket)

2 a free gift
b cheap imitation
c valuable information
d expensive mistake
e free newspapers
f valuable experience
g cheap seats / tickets
h expensive holiday

E Music words

1 Kinds of music: *jazz, opera, pop, rock*
People: *band, composer, orchestra, singer*
Words connected with recordings: *cassette, mini-disc, studio, track*
Other words: *performance, rhythm, song, tune*

3 Other possible words
Kinds of music: *classical, country, reggae, world music*
People: *drummer, guitarist, musician, pianist, player*
Words connected with recordings: *CD cover / case, recording, sound engineer*
Other words: *melody, words / lyrics*

F Word groups

a *Energy* is the general word. *Electricity, gas, nuclear power and solar power* are different kinds of energy.

b *Entertainment* is the general word. *Cinema, theatre and television* are different kinds of entertainment.

c *Meal* is the general word. *Breakfast, dinner, lunch and supper* are different meals.

d *Time* is the general word. *Century, month, week and year* are different lengths of time.

e *Recording* is the general word. *Cassette, CD, DVD and mini-disc* are different kinds of recording.

G Puzzle

a expensive, cheap
b consumer
c select
d folk
e flexible
f technologist, electrician
g tune
h economic
i repetition
j luxurious
k supper
l video

3 Mobile phones

A Introduction

1 a A watch does not have a screen. It has a *face* or a *digital display*.
b A video recorder does not have *keys*. It has *buttons*.

2 a peaktime
b emergencies
c communicating
d rings
e compose
f text
g characters
h companies
i Pre-paid

B Reading

a emergencies
b text
c communicate
d companies
e pre-paid
f peaktime
g characters
h ring
i keys
j compose
k screens

C Verb-noun collocations

1 play: a CD / chess / football / the piano / a trick on someone

press: a button / a key / a switch

send: a CD / a letter / a message / money / a present / a signal

spend: energy / money / time

2 a 4 press
b 8 've spent
c 1 playing

d 7 play
e 2 sent
f 6 press
g 5 played
h 3 spent

EXTENSION 1

The following words should be ticked:

kill: a person
save: energy, food, a person, money
spend: energy, your life, money
waste: energy, food, your life, money

D Compound nouns

1 *mobile phone* adjective + noun
street corner noun + noun
text messaging noun + *-ing*
school classroom noun + noun + noun
phone companies noun + noun
phone calls noun + noun
under-18s preposition + noun
picture message noun + noun
pop songs noun + noun, or adjective + noun (if *pop* is seen as short for *popular*)

2 a a phone conversation
b the over-30s
c a ring tone
d a public phone box
e an answerphone message

E Related words

1 a mobility / mobile (phone), immobile
b imagination, imaginary / imaginative, unimaginative
c intend, intentional, unintentional
d growth, grow
e attract, attractive, unattractive
f silence, silence
g secret / secrecy
h privacy
i immediacy
2 a intentional
b growth
c attract
d silence
e imaginary
f privacy

EXTENSION 2: Adjectives and their opposites

Some adjectives which begin with *m* add *im-*, e.g.
mobile / mature / moral / modest
Some adjectives which begin with *l* add *il-*, e.g.
legal / legible / logical
Some adjectives which begin with *r* add *ir-*, e.g.
responsible / rational / regular
Some adjectives which begin with *p* add *im-*, e.g.
polite / patient / possible / personal / practical

a irregular
b impatient
c illegible
d immature
e irrelevant

F Practice

a growth
b under
c attractive
d communicate / communicating
e phoning
f sending
g messages
h spending

4 Camera rage in Hawaii

A Introduction

1 a 3 **b** 9 **c** 6 **d** 10
e 7 **f** 1 **g** 8 **h** 4
i 2 **j** 5

B Reading

1 a are protesting against
b unmarked
c speed
d furious
e gestures
f major
g residential
h drops
i packs
j rage
2 a In unmarked vans
b Morning radio shows
c 55 mph
d They cover their license plates; they drive in packs

(close to each other, so that the cameras cannot see their plates).
e Nearly 1,300

C Strong adjectives

1 a irritated / angry / furious
b cool / cold / freezing
c satisfactory / good / excellent
d sleepy / tired / exhausted
e unexpected / surprising / amazing
2 a exhausted
b freezing
c amazing
d furious
e excellent

EXTENSION 1: Related words

a amazement
b coolness
c excellence
d fury
e goodness
f irritation
g satisfaction
h surprise

D American English

1 a 5
b 3
c 6
d 1
e 4
f 2
2 b centre
c humor
d licence
e catalog
f travelled

E Verb-noun collocations: *Make* and *do*

1 make: a decision / an effort / a mistake / a noise / someone an offer / a phone call / progress / room for / a suggestion / trouble
do: your best / business with someone / the cooking / a crossword / damage / exercises / housework / a job / a painting / the shopping
2 a do the shopping
b ('ve) made a terrible mistake
c make a much bigger effort

d did / has done a lot of damage
e make room for
f make a suggestion
g made so much noise

EXTENSION 2: Meanings of *make* and *do*
a earn
b travel
c spend
d come to / equal
e come to
f cut or style

F Verb-adverb collocations
1 drive: carefully / carelessly / dangerously / fast / quickly / slowly
sleep: heavily / lightly / well
speak: carefully / carelessly / clearly / fast / loudly / noisily / quickly / slowly
walk: briskly / carefully / carelessly / fast / heavily / lightly / loudly / noisily / quickly / slowly
work: carefully / carelessly / fast / hard / loudly / noisily / quickly / slowly
2 a speak more clearly / slowly
b walk / drive a little more quickly
c driving fast / dangerously / carelessly
d sleeps heavily / well
e works hard / fast / quickly / carefully
3 a a careful driver
b a clear speaker
c a light sleeper
d a good worker
e a slow walker

G Puzzle

```
                 k
a        R E S I D E N T I A L
b              R A G E
c            T R A S H
d        F U R I O U S
e        G E S T U R E
f              C A R E F U L L Y
g E X C E L L E N T
h            A M A Z I N G
i        C A T A L O G
j        C E L L P H O N E
```

5 Is chewing gum good for you?

A Introduction
1 a 3
b 6
c 8
d 2
e 7
f 1
g 4
h 5

B Reading
1 a F
b T
c F
d T
e F
2 a associated
b mental
c imitation
d assessment
e exploring
f theories
g evidence
h concentration

C Related words
1 a assessor, assess
b concentrate, concentrated
c evident, evidently
d exploration, explorer, explorative
e imitator, imitate, imitative
f association
g mentality, mentally
h theoretical, theoretically
2 a explorer
b imitate
c evidently
d concentrate
e Theoretically
f mentally

D Adjective-noun collocations
1 a 5
b 4
c 1
d 3
e 2
2 mental / physical / natural / *ability*
long-term / short-term / natural / physical / positive / negative *effects*
physical / positive / concrete *evidence*
natural / artificial *light*
long-term / short-term *memory*

3 a natural ability
b concrete evidence
c positive effects
d short-term memory
e artificial light

EXTENSION: 'Memory' verbs
1 a 4
b 3
c 5
d 2
e 1
2 a recognise
b memorising
c reminds
d recall
e remind

E Phrasal verbs with *carry*
a carrying out
b carry through
c carry on
d carried it off
e carried away

F Nouns + prepositions
a in
b on
c to
d between
e in
f on
g for
h into, between
i for

G Practice
a memory
b recognise
c remember
d short-term
e remember / recall
f recall / remember
g improvement
h concentrate
i mental

6 Job stress in Sweden

A Introduction
1 a 7
b 8
c 6
d 10
e 2
f 1

g 4
h 9
i 5
j 3

B Reading
  a burned out
  b casualties
  c experience
  d experts
  e clinic
  f high-pressure
  g campaigns
  h focus on
  i sick
  j productive

C Adjective-noun collocations
1 brilliant: expert / idea / politician / teacher
enthusiastic: expert / politician / teacher / worker
inspiring: idea / meeting / politician / teacher
leading: expert / politician
2 a leading experts
  b brilliant idea
  c inspiring teacher
  d leading politicians
  e enthusiastic workers

D Related words
  a brilliance, brilliantly
  b enthusiasm / enthusiast, enthuse, enthusiastically
  c inspiration, inspire
  d leader, lead
  e product / productivity / producer, produce, productively

EXTENSION 1: *High- / Low-*
  a high-speed car
  b low-fat food
  c high-risk sports
  d low-cost housing
  e high-class hotel
  f high-level meeting
  g low-lying land

E Phrasal verbs with *out*
  a run out
  b tires me out
  c knocked out
  d dying out
  e blew out
  f sold out

EXTENSION 2
  a 2
  b 4

c 1
d 3

F Three-part phrasal verbs
  a 5
  b 3
  c 2
  d 1
  e 4
  f 6

G Confusing words
  a *effect* This is a noun. *Affect* is a verb = *to have an effect on*.
  b *experiments* This means tests. *Experiences* = things that happen to people.
  c *home* Home is the place you live. *A house* is a particular kind of building.
  d *sensitive* This means delicate or tender. *Sensible* = reasonable / practical.
  e *worthless* This means having no value. *Priceless* = very valuable.
  f *alone* This means on your own, by yourself. *Lonely* = feeling unhappy because you are alone.

H Practice
  a effect
  b productive
  c idea
  d enthusiasm
  e came up with
  f employees
  g Experiments
  h expert

7 A short history of frozen food

A Introduction
1 a crystal / to defrost / to freeze / freezer / freezing / frozen / to thaw out
  b They contain the letters *fr-*.
  c 1 freezer
    2 crystal
    3 to freeze
    4 to defrost / thaw out
    5 frozen
    6 freezing

d 1 crammed
  2 to stuff
  3 to preserve
  4 naturalist
  5 mushy
  6 to keep

B Reading
1 a The Chinese
  b In the Canadian Arctic
  c It goes mushy. Slow-freezing forms large ice crystals which break up the flesh of the fish.
  d 26 different kinds of frozen food were sold (to the public) from a freezer in a shop in Massachusetts.
2 a stuffing
  b frozen
  c naturalist
  d preserve
  e thawed out (defrosted *is possible*)
  f froze
  g mushy
  h crystals
  i freezing
  j freezer
  k crammed
  l defrosted (*or* thawed out)

C Verbs + prepositions
  a of (to smell *of*)
  b in (to succeed *in* doing something)
  c with (to fill something *with* something)
  d on (to rely *on* something / someone)
  e on (to depend *on* something / someone)
  f for (to thank someone *for* (doing) something)
  g for (to pay (money) *for* something)
  h from (to suffer *from* an illness)

D Near synonyms
1 *appalling / awful / horrible* (= very bad)
appetising / delicious / tasty (= tasting good)
to fill / to pack / to stuff (= to put a lot of things into)
heaps / loads / piles (= large numbers, quantities of)
microscopic / minute / tiny (= very small)

2 a awful / appalling / horrible
  b tiny / microscopic / minute
  c stuffed / packed (You cannot *fill* clothes *into* something. You *fill* something *with* clothes.)
  d loads / piles / heaps
  e delicious / appetising / tasty

EXTENSION: Word stress
  a con'tent
  b 'desert
  c ob'ject
  d 'permit
  e pre'sent
  f 'refuse

E Materials
  a Shoes: leather (and rubber?)
  b Car wheel: metal and rubber (and plastic?)
  c Jug: pottery
  d Mirror: glass and wood
  e Sunglasses: metal or plastic (frames) and glass or plastic (lenses)
  f Trousers: cloth / material
  g Notebook: paper and metal or plastic

F Occupations
  a music**ian**
  b guitar**ist**
  c window clean**er**
  d act**or**
  e biolog**ist**
  f politic**ian**
  g econom**ist**
  h direct**or**
  i company manag**er**
  j computer operat**or**

G Puzzle
  a defrost, freezer
  b tiny, minute
  c appalling, awful
  d content, desert
  e glass, plastic
  f actor
  g guitarist

8 Emails home

A Introduction
1 a 5
  b 7
  c 8
  d 6
  e 2
  f 1
  g 3
  h 9
  i 4
2 *Possible answers*:
  a I'm going to hire a bike and explore the area.
  b There is sand on the beach. / The beach is made of lovely golden sand.
  c We took sleeping bags and a tent so that we could camp.

B Reading
  a hectic
  b recovering
  c impressive
  d body clocks
  e harbour
  f hire
  g spa
  h cut costs
  i backpackers

C Verb-noun collocations
1 cut: bread / costs / prices / a scene from a film / taxes
  find: the answer to a question / a cure for a disease / the solution to a problem / your way (somewhere)
  have: the answer / a bath / a break / breakfast / dinner / a holiday / a rest / a shower
2 a have a break
  b cut several scenes
  c find a cure

  d find my way
  e had a holiday
  f find the answer
  g cut their prices

EXTENSION 1: Idioms with *cut*
  a 3
  b 2
  c 5
  d 1
  e 4

D Phrasal verbs with *set*
  a set up
  b set about
  c set off
  d set back
  e setting down

E 1 Adverbs meaning 'completely'
  a fast asleep
  b wide open
  c dead easy
  d flat broke (*broke* = having no money)
  e dead quiet

F Comparative adjectives
  a busier
  b more exhausted
  c better
  d happier
  e hotter
  f more impressive
  g lovelier
  h newer
  i safer
  j more special
  k stranger
  l tireder / more tired

G Practice
  a wonderful / amazing
  b exhausted
  c body clock
  d hire
  e area
  f camp
  g sleeping bag
  h tent
  i beach
  j amazing / wonderful

9 Rowing across the Atlantic

A Introduction
1 a 10
  b 1
  c 6

d 3
e 8
f 7
g 4
h 5
i 2
j 9

B Reading
a completed
b reception
c sensation
d developed
e phobia
f pulled out
g rowing
h ups and downs
i loneliness
j misery

C Related words
1 a beautiful, beautifully
b destroy, destructive, destructively
c instruct, instructive
d know, knowledgeable, knowledgeably
e lonely
f miserable, miserably
g peaceful, peacefully
h sense, sensational, sensationally
2 a instructive
b knowledgeable
c sensational
d peaceful
e miserable
f destructive
g beautiful
h lonely

D Adjective-noun collocations
1 hard: decision / drugs / luck / work
heavy: rain / smoker / traffic / work
strong: coffee / leader / opinion / taste / wind
2 a heavy smoker
b taste, strong
c hard decision
d hard luck
e traffic, heavier
f strong leader

EXTENSION: Adjectives ending in -ed and -ing
1 a excited
b amazing

2 *Bored* is how you feel. *Boring* describes something (or somebody) that gives you this feeling.
3 a interesting
b relaxed
c tiring
d annoying
e depressed

E Phrasal verbs
a pulled out
b carry on
c get up
d ran (her) down
e going on

F Phrasal verbs with *pull*
1 a pull down
b pull off
c pull out
d pull in
e pull through
f pull off
g pull out
2 a pulled off
b (has) pulled through
c pulled down
d pull out
e pulled out

G People
a 5
b 7
c 6
d 8
e 10
f 4
g 9
h 2
i 3
j 1

H Puzzle

```
                  k
a          P H O B I A
b          D E S T R O Y
c      H A R D
d          P E A C E
e          R E S I D E N T
f  R E C E P T I O N
g          S T R O N G
h          M I S E R Y
i          H E A V Y
j          A N N O Y E D
```

10 A journey to remember

A Introduction
1 a 7

b 10
c 1
d 6
e 9
f 4
g 2
h 5
i 8
j 3

B Reading
a deserted
b timidly
c confidently
d honked
e proudly
f founded
g Tragically
h destroyed
i contrast
j purchased

C Related words
1 a confident, confidence
b desperate, desperation
c fluent, fluency
d frequent, frequency
e particular
f proud, pride
g timid, timidity
h tragic, tragedy
2 a desperate
b tragedy
c timidity, confidence
d particular
e fluent
f frequent
g proud

D Adjective-noun collocations
1 common: effect / flower / name / sight
lasting: effect / impression / relationship
sharp: bend / contrast / increase / knife / teeth
2 a a common flower
b a lasting relationship
c a common name
d a sharp bend

EXTENSION 1: Verbs ending in -en
a shorten
b straighten
c widen
d tighten
e sweeten
f loosen

103

E Verb-noun collocations

1 catch: a bus / a coach / a plane / a train

drive: a bus / a car / a coach / a taxi / a train

miss: a boat / a bus / a coach / a plane / a train

ride: a bicycle / a horse / a motorbike

travel by: bicycle / boat / bus / car / coach / motorbike / plane / taxi / train

Note: *travel on horseback, take a taxi*

2 a 5, miss
b 3, travel
c 1, bicycle
d 6, catch
e 2, drive
f 4, ride

Extension 2: Expressions with *catch*

a got
b attract / get
c captured
d hear
e found

F Travel nouns

a airport, plane, pilot
b port, boat, sailor
c bus station, bus, driver
d railway station, train, driver

G Compound adjectives

1 a handmade / hand-woven
b fast-moving / strong-looking
c curly-haired / long-legged

2 a government-financed
b egg-shaped
c warm-hearted
d slow-moving
e sweet-smelling
f left-handed

H Practice

a fluently
b railway
c missed
d train
e deserted
f catch
g dark
h attention
i timidly
j driver

11 Claiming compensation

A Introduction

1 a 5
b 8
c 10
d 1
e 9
f 3
g 4
h 2
i 6
j 7

B Reading

1 a entitled
b legal
c injuries
d claim
e fees
f blaming
g pavements
h fault
i compensation
j rise

2 a They may be able to *claim compensation*.
b They are offering *legal assistance*.
c If they *lose their claim*.
d They *blame the school*.
e To *make money*.
f The customers of *insurance companies* usually pay the money.

C Verb-noun collocations

1 make: fun of someone / a joke / money / notes / a profit

pay: fees / money / rent / tax(es)

take: advice / care / an exam / a joke / medicine / notes / responsibility (for)

2 a takes advice
b medicine to take
c made a small profit
d make fun, take a joke
e pay rent
f Take care

D Expressions with *go* + adjective

a 4
b 7
c 2
d 5

e 8
f 3
g 1
h 6

EXTENSION 1: Colour expressions

a blue
b green
c black (and) white
d red
e White

E *Blame* and *fault*

2 a I blame John for the accident.
b They said the disaster was the government's fault.
c Don't blame me.
d (I think) it's Rachel's fault / it was Rachel's fault.

F Formal and informal words

a 3
b 5
c 4
d 1
e 2
f 1

Extension 2: Meanings of *get*

a buy
b understand
c become
d receive
e arrive
f earn

G Puzzle

a earn, buy
b assistance
c injure
d profit, living
e joke, advice
f bald, grey
g green
h red

12 Odd news

A Introduction
1 a 4
   b 8
   c 7
   d 6
   e 10
   f 9
   g 3
   h 1
   i 5
   j 2

B Reading
   a impressed
   b ingredient
   c equivalent
   d cosmetics
   e alternative
   f consists
   g technician
   h performance
   i prepare
   j discovery

C Related words
1 a discovery
   b important, importantly
   c inclusion, inclusive
   d necessity, necessarily
   e supplement, supplementary
   f preparation, prepared
   g reduction
   h safety, safely
2 a safety
   b preparation
   c reduction
   d important
   e supplement
   f necessity

D Adjective-noun collocations
1 **general**: election / interest / knowledge / rule
   normal: behaviour / day / price / relations / way
   public: health / holiday / interest / knowledge / opinion / relations
2 a the normal price
   b a general election
   c the normal way
   d public opinion
   e general knowledge
   f a public holiday

E Nationalities
   a Japan, Japanese
   b Austria, Austrian
   c America / the United States, American
   d Chinese
   e Egyptian
   f Canada
   g Swedish
   h Spain
   i Dutch
   j Iraqi
   k Thailand

F Adjectives + prepositions
   a for
   b to
   c for
   d for
   e to
   f about
   g of
   h to
   i for
   j at

EXTENSION: Adjectives starting with *a...*
   a the sleeping passengers
   b the burning / blazing car
   c The living creatures
   d The floating ship

G Homophones
   a wait
   b weak
   c our
   d symbol
   e lead
   f sew

H Puzzle
```
                k
a    C O N S I S T
b          N O R M A L
c          G R A T E F U L
d      P E R F O R M A N C E
e    A B L A Z E
f          D U T C H
g    T E C H N I C I A N
h          R E D U C T I O N
i        G E N E R A L
j    C O S M E T I C S
```

13 The ideal sheepdog

A Introduction
1 a 4
   b 8
   c 1
   d 5
   e 6
   f 3
   g 9
   h 10
   i 2
   j 7

B Reading
1 a trained
   b cage
   c wander
   d agriculture
   e pet
   f herd
   g tough
   h force
   i staring
   j stubborn
   k train
2 a In Texas at the home of a trainer
   b It gathered chickens together and kept them in one place.
   c England and Scotland
   d He is a dog trainer. / He trains border collies.
   e They like to work all the time.

C Animals
1 **Pets**: cat / dog / horse / monkey (?) / rabbit
   Working animals: camel / dog / donkey / elephant / horse
   Farm animals and birds: chicken / cow / deer / duck / pig / sheep / turkey
   Wild animals and birds: camel / deer / dog / duck / elephant / giraffe / horse / lion / monkey / rabbit / tiger / turkey
3 a cat / kitten
   b cow / calf
   c dog / puppy
   d horse / foal
   e lion / cub
   f pig / piglet
   g sheep / lamb

EXTENSION: Animal idioms
a a cold fish
b a dark horse
c an early bird
d a busy bee
e a guinea pig
f the top dog

D Phrasal verbs
1 a round up
b work out
c come across
d lie down
e work out
f find out
2 a working out
b found out
c rounded (them) up
d lie down
e came across
f work out

E Phrasal verbs with *come*
a came up against
b come up
c came out with
d came round
e Come on!
f come from

F 'Seeing' verbs
a see / watch
b see
c staring at / looking at
d gazing
e notice / see
f Look at

G Puzzle

```
              I
a        D A R K
b        G A Z E
c      T R A I N E R
d        F I S H
e          C U B
f    S T U B B O R N
g      C A L F
h      K I T T E N
i          P U P P Y
j    S T A R E
k    C A G E
```

14 Freak weather

A Introduction
1 a 6
b 5
c 8
d 2
e 1

f 7
g 4
h 3
2 a sunset
b horizon
c cliff
d coast
e bay
f snow-capped peak

B Reading
1 a flabbergasted
b sunset
c convinced
d glimpse
e incredible
f coast
g bay
h cliffs
i Mirages
j invert
k horizon
2 a 3
b 5
c 2
d 1
e 4

C People
a fisherman
b expert
c resident
d islander
e passenger
f sailor

EXTENSION: More people
a villager
b cyclist
c shop assistant
d customer / shopper
e victim
f librarian
g criminal / law-breaker
h gardener
i decorator / painter
j gambler

D Near synonyms
1 a few / several / some
appear / become visible /
come into view
calm / peaceful / quiet
cause / create / produce
clear / on view / visible
disappear / fade / vanish
2 a calm (peaceful *and* quiet
are also possible)
b visible
c cause / create / produce

d a few / several (some *is
also possible*)
e appeared / became
visible / came into view
f disappeared / vanished

E Phrasal verbs with *make*
1 Meaning **b** is correct.
2 a make up
b make up
c make for
d make off
3 a make up
b made off
c made up
d made for
e making it all up

F Place prepositions
a on
b up / down
c in, over
d around / close to / near /
in front of / behind
e on
f at / on

G Puzzle
a sure, certain, convinced
b mirage
c sunset
d cliffs
e horizon
f expert
g visible
h quiet, calm

15 Old tyres

A Introduction
1 a 6
b 7
c 10
d 8
e 9
f 2
g 1
h 3
i 4
j 5

B Reading

1 a landfill sites
b ban
c estimated
d recycled
e converted
f surfaces
g fuel
h dispose of
i illegal
j breeding grounds
2 a European countries
b up to 100,000
c 18 per cent
d Spain
e in the sea

C Related words

1 a concern, concerned
b environment, environmentally
c estimate
d expense, expensively
e popularity, popularly
f science, scientific, scientifically
g success, succeed, successfully
2 a succeed
b popularity
c environment
d concerns
e estimate
f Science
g expensively

D Phrasal verbs with *fall*

1 Meaning **c**
2 a fall for
b fall behind
c fall through
d fall down
e fall out
3 a fallen through
b fell behind
c fell for
d fell down
e fall out

E Verbs + prepositions

1 a believe in
b approve of, agree with
c converted into
d object to
e insist on
f belongs to, borrow it from
g choose between
h know very little about

F Prefixes

1 a return: take back
b reread: read again
c rewound: wound back
d redo: do again
e rebuild: build again
2 a 5
b 6
c 7
d 1
e 8
f 4
g 2
h 3
3 a postponed
b misbehaved
c semi-detached
d bilingual
e overcharge
f monotonous
g antisocial
h undercooked

EXTENSION

a a monosyllable
b a bigamist
c postscript
d misfortune
e an antidote

G Practice

a tyres
b fuel
c oil
d recycled
e disposed of
f environment
g temperature
h smoke

16 Volcanoes

A Introduction

1 a 6
b 5
c 2
d 9
e 10
f 8
g 1
h 11
i 7
j 4
k 3

B Reading

1 a active
b at risk
c erupt
d liquid
e flowing
f fragments
g climate
h disrupted
i predict
j likely
k monitor
2 a mantle
b crust
c magma
d ash
e lava

C Related words

1 a action / activity, act, actively
b disruption, disruptive
c eruption
d explosion, explode, explosively
e prediction, predictable, predictably
f severity, severely
g threat, threatening, threateningly
h violence, violent
i volcanic
2 a disruption
b violence
c exploded
d threat
e predictable
f severity

D Adjectives and their opposites

1 a 3
b 4
c 7
d 8
e 2
f 5
g 6
h 1
2 a inactive
b unusual
c unlikely
d non-violent
e unpredictable
f impossible
g inexpensive
h impractical
3 a non-violent
b unpredictable
c impractical
d unlikely
e unusual
f inexpensive

E Collocations: 'Size' adjectives + nouns

1 deep: feeling / hole / water
small: area / book / business / change / country / hole / majority / number
thick: book / hair / layer / line / pullover / shirt
thin: book / hair / layer / line / pullover / shirt
vast: area / country / majority / number

2 a deep feeling
b a thin shirt
c the vast majority
d small change
e a thick pullover
f a small business

EXTENSION: Idioms with 'size' adjectives

a 4
b 1
c 5
d 3
e 2

F Plural of nouns ending in -o

1 a Other examples: *cargoes, echoes, potatoes*
b Other examples: *euros, memos, pianos, rhinos*

2 a heroes
b studios
c kilos
d videos
e discos

G Practice

a impossible
b eruption
c practical
d lava
e volcanic
f measure
g safer
h volcano
i prevent
j dangers

17 New carrots

A Introduction

1 a 7
b 10
c 5
d 1
e 2

f 9
g 6
h 3
i 4
j 8

B Reading

1 a original
b on sale
c natural
d commercial
e spread
f vision
g bunch
h seeds
i influence
j artificial

2 a F There were many different colours in the past.
b F They are orange on the inside.
c F Betacarotene improves vision in dim light. (*Anthocyanin* may help prevent heart disease.)
d T
e F Over 90% of carrot varieties have been lost.

C Related words

1 a encouragement, encouraging
b entire
c influence, influential
d origin / originality, originate, originally
e prevention, preventable / preventive (*or* preventative)
f store
g various / varied

2 a entire
b prevention
c encouragement
d various
e influences
f originally
g store

D Vegetables and colours

2 *Aubergines* are usually purple.
Beans can be many different colours.
Broccoli is green, or green and purple.
Cabbage is green or purple.
Cauliflower is white.

Courgettes are green or yellow.
Garlic is white.
Onions are white, or red and white.
Peas are green.
Potatoes are white on the inside and brown on the outside.
Mushrooms are white.

E Adjective-noun collocations

1 dark: b, g
dim: c, d, f
dull: a, e, f

2 dark: colour / eyes / glasses / hair
dim: light / memory / student
dull: colour / hair / pain / story / student / weather

3 a dim memories
b dull pain
c dim light
d weather, dull
e dark hair and eyes
f dark glasses

4 a bright / clear / interesting
b bright
c sharp
d fair / light
e interesting
f light / bright
g clear

F Numbers and words

a four thousand
b the thirteen hundreds
c nineteen ninety-nine
d twenty per cent
e the twentieth century
f nineteen oh three
g two hundred and eighty-seven

EXTENSION: Words and numbers

a 27.5%
b 1762
c 14,911
d $^3/_4$
e 820445
f 6.45
g 13th June
h 1.75

G Puzzle

```
                k
a        C A U L I F L O W E R
b        B R I G H T
c      C E N T U R Y
d        O R I G I N
e        I N F L U E N C E
f          D I M
g      B U N C H
h      V A R I E D
i          P E A S
j      D U L L
```

18 The writer

A Introduction

1 a 5
  b 8
  c 4
  d 10
  e 2
  f 9
  g 1
  h 6
  i 3
  j 7

B Reading

1 a exchange
  b turned into
  c entertain
  d lively
  e pause
  f background
  g distant
  h click
  i inhabitants
  j primitive
2 a 5
  b 1
  c 6
  d 2
  e 3
  f 4

C Related words

1 a creator, create, creative, creatively
  b description, descriptive
  c distance, distantly
  d entertainment, entertainer, entertaining, entertainingly
  e inhabit, inhabited, uninhabited
  f intelligence, unintelligent, intelligently
  g laugh
2 a entertainment

  b laughed
  c uninhabited
  d create
  e distance
  f description

D Verb-noun collocations

1 **earn**: a living / money / wages
  gain: experience / weight
  win: the lottery / money / a prize / a race / a war
2 a won the lottery
  b gained (so much) weight
  c earn (my) living
  d won (several) prizes
  e earn (very high) wages
  f gained (valuable) experience

EXTENSION: Countable and uncountable nouns

1 a U
  b C
  c C
  d U
2 a 8
  b 6
  c 7
  d 5
  e 3
  f 1
  g 4
  h 2

E Onomatopoeic words

  a splash
  b growled
  c whispering
  d crash
  e creaked
  f jingling

F Phrasal verbs with *go*

  a go without
  b goes off
  c gone / been through
  d going down with
  e went by

G Puzzle

  a splash
  b wood
  c pause
  d gain
  e lively
  f create
  g inhabitant
  h click

```
O L C R E A T E F I
C L I M A T W O O N
C H I V E R O O M H
W H A V E T O O A A
P L I T I L D O R B
A R M S C I Y P M I
U N D E R L B N O T
S E G A I N G N A A
E X P E R I E C E N
  S P L A S H K T
```

19 An unusual suggestion

A Introduction

1 a 3
  b 8
  c 5
  d 10
  e 6
  f 7
  g 2
  h 9
  i 4
  j 1

B Reading

1 a crowded
  b scruffy
  c denim
  d shopping mall
  e obvious
  f panic
  g charity shop
  h scared
  i sleeve
  j by mistake
2 a brown
  b a (scruffy old) baseball cap
  c in a shopping mall
  d He asked him if he had got / bought the shirt at a charity shop.
  e Steve
  f on the sleeve
  g He wanted to buy it back from the boy.

C Clothes and parts of clothes

1 A jacket
  B trainers
  C shirt
  D socks
  E trousers
  F baseball cap

2 g zip
 h sleeve
 i collar
 j button
 k cuff
 l belt
 m pocket
 n leg
 o lace

D Idioms with *eye*

1 *I was afraid to take my eyes off him ...* Meaning **a**
I caught his eye ... Meaning **c**

2 a 3
 b 5
 c 1
 d 2
 e 4

3 a see eye to eye
 b up to my eyes
 c turns a blind eye
 d pull the wool over her eyes
 e keeping your eye on

EXTENSION: More things you can wear

 a glasses
 b ring
 c bracelet
 d nail varnish
 e earring
 f lipstick
 g necklace
 h watch

E Adjective order

1 a ✔
 b scruffy old baseball cap
 c big blue denim shirt

2 a ✔
 b beautiful pear-shaped silver earrings
 c short dark straight hair
 d wonderful new French trainers
 e small black leather bag

F Meanings of *look*

1 a 6
 b 5
 c 4
 d 2
 e 1
 f 3

2 a Look out!
 b look like
 c looked it up

 d looked
 e look on the bright side

G Practice

 a blue denim
 b charity shop
 c mistake
 d café
 e boy
 f panic
 g away
 h scared
 i arrest

20 Random acts of kindness

A Introduction

1 a 7
 b 9
 c 5
 d 3
 e 8
 f 6
 g 2
 h 4
 i 1

B Reading

1 a tollbooth
 b fare
 c random
 d spotted
 e jotted (it) down
 f mops
 g rundown
 h frail
 i impulse

2 Meaning **b** is correct.

3 a 4
 b 5
 c 1
 d 3
 e 2

C Word groups

1 a vehicle
 b language
 c furniture
 d instrument
 e flower

2 *Other possible examples:*
 a motorbike, van, tractor, truck, coach
 b accent, punctuation, grammar, vocabulary
 c desk, bookshelf, wardrobe, chest of drawers
 d guitar, saxophone,

clarinet, flute
 e daffodil, carnation, lily, orchid

D American English

1 a 6, drive
 b 1, bucket
 c 2, plonk
 d 3, *no equivalent word*
 e 4, year seven pupil
 f 5, cashier

2 a a check
 b to practise (in British English *practice* is the noun)

E Describing periods of time

 a warm summer afternoon
 b cool autumn evening
 c bright / sunny spring morning
 d long summer holiday
 e cold December night

F Phrasal verbs with *hand*

1 a hand over
 b hand out
 c hand in
 d hand back

2 a hand in
 b handed it back
 c hand out
 d hand over

EXTENSION: Idioms with *hand*

1 a 4
 b 3
 c 2
 d 1

2 a out of hand
 b lend you a hand
 c Hands off
 d my hands full

G Puzzle

```
                        j
a    B U C K E T
b            F L O W E R
c    I M P U L S E
d          T E L L E R
e              B A C K
f    R A N D O M
g            J O T
h    S P O T
i        V E H I C L E S
```

Review 1

1 Related words
b privacy
c growth
d visitors
e reality
f silence
g electrician
h valuable

2 Verb-noun collocations
a lose
b save
c lose
d waste
e keeping
f held
g spent
h win

3 *Make* and *do*
a made
b making
c do
d make
e do
f make
g make

4 Adjectives
a electric
b expensive
c economical
d cheap
e irresponsible

5 Adjective opposites
a unattractive
b impolite
c immature
d illegal
e unintentional

6 Odd one out
b piano *The other words are parts of a mobile phone.*
c track *The other words are types of music.*
d band *The other words are types of recordings.*
e angry *The other words have similar meanings.*
f number plate *The others are American English words.*

Review 2

1 Verb-noun collocations
a find someone guilty
b find your way
c cut prices
d have breakfast
e cut taxes
f have a shower

2 Adjective-noun collocations
a leading
b concrete
c brilliant
d artificial
e long-term
f inspiring

3 Phrasal verbs
a set off
b come up with
c carrying out
d put up with
e set up
f carry on

4 Related words
a explorer
b theoretical
c productivity
d concentration
e brilliance

5 Prepositions
a on
b with
c in
d from
e for
f of
g for
h in

Review 3

1 Related words
a destruction
b knowledge
c performance
d proudly
e reduction
f safety

2 Adjective-noun collocations
a strong coffee
b sharp increase
c public opinion
d common sight
e normal behaviour

f lasting effect
g heavy rain, hard luck

3 Verb-noun collocations
a miss
b make
c take
d catch
e travel
f ride
g pay

4 Choose the correct word
a annoyed
b for
c green
d of
e fault
f weak
g blame

5 Compound adjectives
b short-haired
c home-cooked
d healthy-looking
e blue-eyed
f heart-shaped

Review 4

1 Phrasal verbs
a work out
b make out
c made up
d fallen out
e fell down

2 More phrasal verbs
a come from
b come round
c come up with
d came up against
e come up

3 Related words
a explosion
b disruption
c threatening
d severely
e popularity
f prediction
g environmental
h eruption

4 Prepositions
a belong to
b approve of
c on the coast
d object to
e agree with
f over the house

5 True or false?

a F A *cold fish* is someone who shows no feelings. Someone who has a secret life is called a *dark horse*.

b F A *guinea pig* is someone who is used in an experiment. Someone who never stops doing things is called a *busy bee*.

c T

d F A young horse is a *foal*. A *lamb* is a young sheep.

e T

f F They can speak two languages.

g F It has been cooked too much.

h F *radios*

i F a *dormant* volcano

j T

6 Confusing words

a notice

b thick

c small

d see

e vast

f stare

Review 5

1 Related words

a creative

b laughter

c inhabitant

d encouragement

e prevention

f description

g influential

h originality

i entertainment

2 Phrasal verbs

a go without

b hand out

c go by

d handed it back

e gone down

f going through

g gone off

3 Adjective-noun collocations

a dark (glasses)

b dull (pain)

c dim (memory)

d dull (film)

e dark (brown hair)

4 Adjective order

a a fantastic, silver-grey American car

b a tall green glass vase

c short dark curly hair

d an old brown woollen pullover

e an incredible large gold ring

5 True or false?

a T

b F It makes a *splash*.

c T

d F *To pull the wool over someone's eyes* means to deceive them.

e F *To see eye to eye with someone* means to agree with them.

f F The British English for *driveway* is *drive*.

g T

h T

i T

j F A *collar* is part of a shirt, blouse, dress, jacket or coat. It is the part that goes round your neck.

Chris Morphew was born in Sydney in 1985. He spent his childhood drawing comic books and writing stories about dinosaurs and time machines. After school, Chris did a short stint as a primary school teacher – which he thinks is the second-best job in the world – and then started writing for kids and young adults. He lives in Australia.

Follow Chris on Twitter @ChrisMorphew

"THE PHOENIX FILES absolutely blew me away"
Michael Grant, author of *GONE*

FALLOUT

Chris Morphew

THE PHOENIX FILES

SCHOLASTIC

First published in the UK in 2012 by Scholastic Children's Books
An imprint of Scholastic Ltd
Euston House, 24 Eversholt Street
London, NW1 1DB, UK
Registered office: Westfield Road, Southam, Warwickshire, CV47 0RA
SCHOLASTIC and associated logos are trademarks
and/or registered trademarks of Scholastic Inc.

Text © Chris Morphew, 2012
This edition published by arrangement with
Hardie Grant Egmont Publishers, Australia.
The right of Chris Morphew to be identified as
the author of this work has been asserted by him.

ISBN 978 1407 13120 7

Printed by CPI Group (UK) Ltd, Croydon, CR0 4YY
Papers used by Scholastic Children's Books are made
from wood grown in sustainable forests.

1 3 5 7 9 10 8 6 4 2

www.scholastic.co.uk/zone

To my family at
Abbotsford Presbyterian Church.
May we shine like stars.

Chapter 1

Phoenix in a spiral. Eventually, far out of sight, it bypassed the warehouse and petered out, dead-ending into the trees just short of the towering wall that sealed us off from the outside world.

The road was a lie, like almost everything else in this place. But those lies were starting to unravel.

It had been three weeks since Shackleton gave up the benevolent-leader act and turned the town centre into a concentration camp. Three weeks of scouring hijacked surveillance feeds, of searching the bushland for anything or anyone that might be able to put a dent in the Co-operative's plans, of watching the days slip out from under us.

And now our food was running out.

There were thirteen of us down in the Vattel Complex, getting by on food supplies originally meant for two, and things had only got worse when Kara's hydroponics bay finally bit the dust. Watered-down soup might trick the eyes, but it didn't trick the stomach, and it seemed like a waste to die of starvation when there were so many other, more interesting threats to my life – like getting gunned down by a Co-operative security officer, or disappearing into one of my visions of the past or future, either of which might happen at any minute.

I shivered, hugging myself through the same crusty jumper I'd been wearing for five days straight. It was one of Luke's, although we didn't really think like that any more. It had been a long time since I'd worn anything properly clean or entirely mine.

The wind picked up and I glanced over to the side of the road. It was impossible to tell through the jostling leaves whether anyone was out there.

Mind on the job, Jordan, I ordered myself. *No time to start jumping at—*

My eyes snapped forward again as the low hum of an engine cut through the noise of the bush. I took a breath, steeling myself.

The rumbling grew louder, and a black supply truck crested the rise in front of me. I held my ground in the middle of the road, fists clenched at my sides. The driver jolted in surprise and slammed on the brakes, screeching to a stop about five metres short of me.

The passenger door flew open. A black-uniformed security officer jumped out, raising the semi-automatic rifle that was apparently standard-issue now.

It was Officer Cohen. Formerly just *Mr* Cohen, the school cleaner.

"Down on the ground," he ordered. His voice was hard, but his eyes flashed back and forth, like he already suspected he was being set up.

"Mr Cohen, please," I said, refusing to let the nerves spill into my voice. "You don't want to shoot me."

"No," he said, fingers tensing. "No, Jordan, I don't. But I will if I have to."

I glanced into the bush, opening my hands and

3

slowly raising them into the air.

"Down on the ground," Mr Cohen repeated, "or I promise you, I will—'

There was a crash. A figure flew from the bushes, impossibly fast, hair streaming behind her like black fire. The figure collided with Mr Cohen. I heard a split second of his startled shout before it was drowned in gunfire. I dived to the asphalt, rolling clear of the torrent of bullets.

Mr Cohen fell to the ground, rifle slipping from his grip, putting an end to the firing. The black-haired figure – Amy – landed on top of him. She grabbed the rifle and jumped up, stumbling off again, and spun her gaze to the trees. "Get out here!" she yelled in her weird, too-fast voice. "Hurry!"

Luke and his dad burst out from their hiding places, wielding a rusty bit of pipe and one of Kara's pickaxes. Soren swept in from the other side of the road, carrying a rifle identical to Mr Cohen's. All three of them were as dirty and underfed as I was. They looked like a pack of survivors from a zombie movie.

I got up, ears still ringing from the blast of the gun. No way had they missed that, back at the warehouse.

We had maybe five minutes before more trouble arrived.

Luke's dad bent down to disarm Mr Cohen. "Nice work, girls."

"Thanks," I said, looking up at the driver, frozen in his seat. "Hey, you! Get out here!"

The driver nodded shakily and cut the engine. He clambered down from the truck, and I recognized him as one of the old delivery guys from back when Phoenix was still a town. He glanced out at the bush, like he'd love to make a break for it, but he came around to kneel next to Mr Cohen.

"Please," Mr Cohen whimpered, as Luke's dad stood up with his rifle. "Shackleton – he'll kill me."

"I will do it for him if you don't keep your mouth shut!" Soren snarled.

"No, you won't," I said, wishing I'd fought harder to keep him from coming with us. "And Shackleton won't either. Just let us pick up a few supplies and we'll be out of your hair."

"Where are the keys?" asked Luke. The driver cocked his head in the direction of the truck, and Luke went to pull them from the ignition. I followed after him, leaving the others to handle the guard duty.

As soon as we got around the back of the truck, Luke dragged me into a hug. "That was ridiculous. I thought he was going to—"

"We've done worse," I said, squeezing him back, still dizzy with adrenalin.

"Yeah, but usually I don't have to sit there and *watch* it."

"Good thing this is a one-off then," I said. No way would we get away with it again.

Luke turned his attention to the truck. I watched him cycle through the keys, dirty fingers fumbling in the cold, and the low-grade dread I carried everywhere with me swirled up to the surface again, clawing holes in my stomach.

He was going to die.

If that old surveillance video of Kara's was to be believed, he'd *already* died.

Sometime in the next two weeks, Luke was going to find himself thrown twenty years into the past. We had no idea how that was even possible, but neither of us doubted for a second that it was going to happen – unless we did something about it.

And we *were* going to do something about it.

Because Luke wasn't the only one going back. According to the video, Peter was going to follow him back there, stab him to death in a blind rage, and return to the present again.

And then came the final piece of the puzzle: as he bled out on the floor, Luke was going to deliver – had already delivered – a message.

Take Tobias to the release station.

Tobias. The anti-Tabitha. The cure for the end of the world. The answer we'd been waiting so long, so desperately for. At least, that's what we were hoping it was. But for all our talking and searching and tying ourselves up in knots about it, we were still no closer to knowing what Tobias even *was*.

"Got it," said Luke, popping open the padlock and heaving the roller door into the air to reveal mountains of neatly labelled boxes. A month ago, we might've found pretty much anything in here – office stuff, school uniforms, magazines – everything a town needed to keep believing it was still connected to the outside world. Now it just looked like food and a few other basics. Exactly what we were after.

"All right," I said, climbing into the back of the

truck, stomach grumbling in anticipation. "Let's go shopping."

My hands landed on the nearest box, and it took all my self-control not to tear it open and start gorging myself.

Focus, I thought, hauling the box down to Luke. I dropped a second box on top of the first, and he ran them around to the front of the truck.

I could hear Soren threatening Mr Cohen again, shouting at him in the weird, stilted voice he'd picked up over a lifetime in isolation.

"Everything OK back there?" I asked as Luke returned.

"Hard to say," said Luke. He grunted as I dumped a giant bag of rice into his arms. "Shackleton's guys aren't giving us any trouble. Soren might be a different story, though."

I gritted my teeth and ducked back into the truck. Theoretically, we were all on the same side now, but that didn't make Soren any less unstable. Sooner or later, he was going to become a real problem.

I heaved a box of soup tins down from the top of a pile, then froze as I heard the growl of another engine coming up behind us.

Luke jogged back. "Already?"

"Yeah," I said, passing the soup down to him. "Time to go." I grabbed one last box, and we raced to rejoin the others.

Amy and Mr Hunter were loaded up, ready to run. Soren's box was still at his feet. He was standing over Mr Cohen and the driver, waving his gun around like a crazy person. Luke tossed the keys out into the bush and looked down at the two men. "Just stay where you are until your mates get here, OK?"

The driver nodded.

"I don't trust him," said Soren, pointing the rifle in the driver's face.

The driver lurched. "No! You can't!"

"Tell me about Tobias," said Soren. "Tell me where Tobias is being kept and I may let you live."

"I don't know!" the driver moaned. "I swear – please – I don't even know who that *is!*"

"Soren," I snapped, over the growing engine noise behind us. "Put it down. We're going."

"Please," said Mr Cohen. "Please, just go."

"Shut up," Soren grunted. He pulled the trigger.

Click.

The men on the ground shrieked and reeled out of the way, not registering at first that the weapon hadn't fired. Soren squeezed the trigger a few more times, shaking the rifle like that was going to fix it.

Click, click, click.

He shot me a furious look. "You did this!"

Soren let the rifle drop to his waist. He growled in frustration and kicked the truck driver in the face, knocking him to the ground. Then he snatched up the box at his feet and followed the rest of us into the bush.

Chapter 2

**Thursday 30 July
14 days**

Soren lashed out at me as soon as the entrance to the Vattel Complex rolled shut above our heads. "Never do that again!"

"Won't be an issue," I muttered, moving ahead of him down the decaying stairs, fingernails digging into the box in my hands.

Soren swore. "What is that supposed to mean?"

"Trust me," I said, "that's the last time you're going up with us."

Soren charged into the hallway behind me. He dropped his box, grabbed me with both hands and shoved me up against the wall, sending my own box flying. I felt the rifle hanging between us,

11

pressing into my stomach.

"Do not pretend you are in charge here," he said. "You do not decide—"

"You would have killed them!" I shouted. "You would have *murdered* two people who weren't any threat to us!"

"Hey!" said Luke's dad, coming up behind us and grabbing Soren's shoulder. "That's enough."

Soren shrugged the hand off. "Do you expect me to apologize? They are the enemy, Jordan! If you are not willing to do what is necessary—"

"You know what, Soren?" I said. "You don't exactly have a brilliant track record of figuring out who the enemy is. How about you let someone else decide what's necessary?"

Soren opened his mouth and closed it again. He stormed off to the surveillance room, throwing his rifle to the ground.

"Yeah, that's right," I said under my breath, "go and have a whinge to your mum."

A thin face framed by matted black hair appeared in a doorway off the corridor, peering at Soren as he passed. Mike. Soren scowled at him and he shrank back inside.

Luke glanced sideways at me, checking if I was OK. "Come on," he said, grunting under the weight of the box in his hands, "let's get this stuff to the kitchen."

We headed up the corridor and I shoved past Mike into Kara and Soren's old lounge room, which was now set up as one of our main sleeping areas. Theoretically it was the boys" room, but I'd moved my bed in here too. I didn't care how "safe" Peter was, locked in his cell at the other end of the Complex. I wasn't taking any chances when it came to keeping Luke alive.

"You should speak to Soren with more respect," hissed Mike, following along behind us.

I glanced back at him, but didn't respond. Not worth the energy.

We'd picked up him and Cathryn about a week ago. Luke and I had been out past the eastern end of town, setting up a fake campsite to keep security looking for us on the surface, when the two of them burst out of the bushes, half-starved and begging us to take them in.

Turned out Kara had warned them. Two days before Shackleton took the rest of the town captive, she'd written to Mike, Cathryn and Tank, telling them to get out. A gesture of goodwill, I guess, after everything she and Soren had put them through.

She'd come clean with them about all of it. Who she and Soren really were. The whole elaborate deception they'd used to lure Mike and the others into kidnapping Peter. But one letter wasn't going to undo all the wrong that had been done – and it wasn't going to bring Mike's fingers back either.

He'd been badly injured when we found him, hand torn up by a bullet wound from a run-in with security a few nights earlier. They were separated from Tank that same night, and he hadn't been seen since. Kara did what she could for Mike, but the infection had already set in. His left thumb and forefinger ended up getting left behind on the operating table.

"Everyone OK?" asked Luke's mum, already waiting when we arrived in the kitchen.

Soren's furious voice echoed across the corridor. Luke raised an eyebrow. "More or less."

He dropped his box on the floor and gave his mum a hug. He seemed to be feeling a bit more sympathetic towards her these days, after what had happened to Dr

Montag. Luke had hated his mum's new boyfriend all along, but that didn't make his murder any easier to stomach.

Managing the food supply was kind of Ms Hunter's thing now. Luke said it was good for her, that she needed something like this to help her deal with everything. He said she'd be fine with the end of the world, so long as she had a project to be in charge of.

Cathryn was in here too, sitting on the bench, picking the dirt out of her nails. She smiled at us as we piled into the room.

Amy squeezed in after us, deliberately slow again now that we were back underground. She glanced around anxiously. "Hey, Ms Hunter? Um, could you…?"

Luke's mum nodded. She unlocked the cupboard above her head, pulled out two chocolate bars, and passed them down to Amy. My stomach growled again.

"Thanks," Amy breathed, turning to leave.

Mike grabbed her with his good hand. "Hey. Wait."

"Problem, Mike?" I said, before he had time to do something stupid.

He ignored me, turning to Luke's mum. "Seriously? *Two?*"

"You know she's entitled to extra rations," Ms Hunter said evenly.

"That's crap. She doesn't need all that."

"Mike," I said. "Let her go."

Ms Hunter stared down at him. "Would you like me to give her your dinner as well?"

Mike muttered under his breath. He threw down Amy's arm and pushed his way out of the room.

"Not your fault," I told Amy, catching the look on her face.

"Yeah," she sighed, and slipped off to her bedroom.

Cathryn dropped down from the bench and went after her. The two of them had struck up a bit of a friendship this past week. Something to fill the void for Cathryn now that she and Mike were barely speaking.

Luke's dad put his box down where Cathryn had been sitting. Ms Hunter tore it open and looked inside. "What's this?"

"Cereal," said Luke's dad, pointing to the label on the box.

"Does this look like cereal to you, Jack?" She

pulled a smaller box out of the big one. It was a video camera. One of those little handheld ones, about as big as a phone. Ms Hunter stared at her ex-husband, pursing her lips like it was his fault the box had been mislabelled.

"Sorry," said Luke, moving quickly to head off another argument, "should've checked inside before we took it." He pulled another camera out of the box. "It's not like the Co-operative to stuff up like this."

"I'm going to have a shower," said Luke's dad stiffly, walking out.

Too many people down here, I thought, not for the first time. Too many people and not enough space. Things had never exactly been friendly in this place, but now it was like you couldn't open a door without walking in on someone else's argument.

Luke stared at the ground, turning the camera box over in his hands. I felt a flicker of recognition, but the thought was pushed out of my mind as my mum appeared in the doorway. She walked into the kitchen, bleary-eyed, with Georgia trailing behind her.

"Oh, thank goodness," said Mum, putting an arm around me. Her stomach bulged out in front of her, pushing up her shirt. We'd done our best to make sure everyone had enough clothes, but maternity wear options were pretty limited down here. "Sorry, I didn't mean to fall asleep. I was just—"

"Mum, it's fine," I said, crouching to put my hands on her stomach. "How's she going in there?"

"She?" said Mum.

"Yeah, I changed my mind," I said. "I'm going with girl."

Mum sighed, resting her hands on mine. "Believe me, I will be only too happy whenever this kid decides to come out and settle it for us."

According to Kara, that could happen any day now. But given that Mum was carrying an almost full-term baby after less than three months of pregnancy, it wasn't much more than guesswork.

"We just have to ask him to come out," said Georgia, nudging me aside and grabbing hold of Mum. "Hey baby!" she shouted. "Get out of there! We want to talk to you!" She collapsed against Mum's stomach, giggling.

"Hey, Georgia," said Luke, holding a bright pink camera he'd pulled from the box. "We got you a present."

Georgia's face lit up. "Cool!" She grabbed the camera and gave him a lung-collapsing hug. "Thanks!"

"No worries," Luke coughed.

"Thank you," mouthed Mum, looking even more grateful than Georgia. It hadn't been easy keeping a six-year-old entertained in this place.

Georgia loosened her grip on Luke. She looked up, face twisted in concentration.

"What's wrong?" he asked.

Georgia frowned. "You're trying to be happy, but you're not."

Luke stepped away from her, suddenly uncomfortable, knowing as well as I did that this was beyond the scope of a normal six-year-old's perception skills. "I'm fine," he said. "It was a bit scary going out to get the food, but I'm OK now."

Georgia shook her head. "I don't believe you."

My stomach turned. We'd been protecting Georgia as much as we could from all the horrors of this place, but how are you supposed to keep anything from a kid who can read your mind?

"I'm going to go check on Kara and Soren," said Luke, heading for the door.

"Yeah," I said. "I'll come with you."

"You should kiss my sister some more!" Georgia shouted as we left the room. "That's what makes you feel happy!"

She burst into another round of giggles, and I felt a smile creep across my face. I saw Cathryn re-emerging from the girls" bedroom and quickly wiped it away again. "She OK?" I asked.

Cathryn shrugged. "She said she just needs to rest."

I didn't know what to do for Amy. She never complained about life down here, or about what was happening to her, but I could see she was struggling. And her body's need for extra food wasn't exactly helping her fit in.

Kara had done a few tests, trying to figure out what exactly was happening to Amy. The closest she could get was that the fallout had somehow "sped her up". Amy's whole body – heartbeat, nervous system, even her *mind* – was running three or four times faster than normal.

It should've killed her. That was Kara's diagnosis. But then, I could fill a warehouse with all the things in Phoenix that *should* have been true.

With practice, Amy was getting better at slowing

her movement and her speech down to normal, but it was a big effort for her. It didn't surprise me that she was choosing to spend a lot of her time alone.

"You OK?" asked Luke, nodding at the surveillance room. "You sure you want to go in there?"

"Don't worry," I said, pushing the door open, "I won't hurt him."

Kara and Soren were across the room, setting up a row of computers along the wall that, until recently, had been covered in photos of Peter, Luke and me. Kara had been in here all afternoon, rearranging things.

Soren was lying under the table, plugging something in. Kara moved along the row, hitting the power buttons, and the laptops whirred to life.

"I'd like to apologize for my son's outburst," she said, turning around.

Soren's head snapped up. "It was not an *outburst*. I have nothing to—"

Kara stared at him over the top of her glasses. "I am not interested in having this discussion again."

Soren's hands twitched, like his first impulse was to throttle her. But whatever else he might be capable of, Soren was still not in the habit of standing up to his mum.

"Fine," he growled. He got up and walked back out of the room. Kara pursed her lips, but let him go.

"Anything new in town?" I asked, turning to the main circle of surveillance computers in the middle of the room.

"There was another altercation at one of the meal tables a little while ago," said Kara. "The men involved were disciplined."

"Nothing unusual there," said Luke, leaning in behind me as I sat down at a laptop looking in on the Shackleton Building. I punched the right arrow, cycling through the different camera angles.

By now, Shackleton's concentration camp was running with typical Phoenix precision. Everyone in town had been assigned their own seat in the town hall to sleep on. They even played movies on the big screen to keep the kids from getting too out of hand.

Outside, in the giant, sparkling foyer area that had once been Shackleton's "welcome centre", security had set up a food line and a row of portable showers and toilets. They'd also erected a circle of razor-wire fence on the main street, stretching from the front doors of the Shackleton Building to the fountain in the centre of town, so that the prisoners could get out into the sun.

People seemed to be allowed to move freely around the camp, but there was no escaping the eye of security. Dozens of officers, all armed with rifles and capsicum spray, patrolled the building around the clock, quickly stamping out any hint of misbehaviour.

The whole thing was just a bit too clean for something the Co-operative had come up with on the fly. It seemed to be a contingency plan they'd had up their sleeves all along.

I kept scanning through the surveillance images, hammering the button more quickly now, nerves starting to get the better of me. *"Where are you?"*

"There!" said Luke. I backtracked through a couple of images, hand freezing over the keyboard as I spotted him at a table in the welcome centre, hunched over an empty dinner plate. Dad.

He was deep in conversation with Peter's parents. It was hard to tell from this distance, but it didn't seem like anything too awful had happened to them while we were out. Maybe Calvin really had given up on them.

After they were captured, Calvin had dragged the three of them to the security centre every day for interrogation, trying to figure out where the rest of us were hiding. And every day I'd sat here, glued to the screen, watching. It had been horrible. Excruciating. At one point, Luke and his dad had needed to physically hold me back from running out there in a suicidal attempt to put an end to it. But no matter what Calvin did to them, Dad and the others never gave us up.

And now, it seemed like Calvin might have finally put an end to it himself. Today made it a full week since their last trip to the security centre.

Dad glanced up as a security officer approached the table. The officer jerked his head in the direction of the hall. Dad and the Weirs got up without arguing and joined the crowd that had started milling towards the doors.

Bedtime. They were shutting everyone in for the night.

Kara walked up behind us. "Soren is still working on a way to circumvent the new restrictions on the surveillance network," she said, in the closest she ever came to a sympathetic tone. "Once we've established a way to disable—"

I rolled my eyes. "No offense, Kara, but if Peter hasn't been able to figure that out, why on earth would you think Soren had any chance of…?"

I stopped talking, distracted by the grainy surveillance image that had just flashed into view in front of me. Kara's new row of computers – which I now realized were just the old surveillance monitors from the storeroom – had finished loading and were now relaying footage of the Complex's research module, or at least the few rooms that hadn't been blown up or concreted over.

Crazy Bill lay strapped to a bed in the room where I'd been held prisoner the night we first came down here. In the three weeks since we'd rescued him from the medical centre, Kara had kept him alive with an old I.V. unit that Soren had repaired and a feeding tube thing. She'd done everything she could think of to bring Bill around, but he hadn't even moved since we'd put him there. Hadn't even opened his eyes.

At least, not until about five seconds ago.

Chapter 3

We bolted into the corridor. Soren had just emerged from the toilet. He doubled back to follow us, guessing that something was up.

Mike had been waiting outside for him. "Hey, boss—"

"Not now!" snapped Soren, shooing him away, and we raced through to the old research building, down a half-destroyed corridor strewn with debris.

"Have you been down to see him?" Luke glanced back at Kara. "While we were up on the surface, did you do anything?" He ducked just in time to avoid smashing into a bit of pipe sticking out of the concrete.

"No," said Kara, ducking under the pipe after him,

"no-one has gone near him." And it was a sign of how far we'd come that I actually believed her.

The corridor opened up for a minute, and we shot past Peter's room, still barricaded from the outside. His face appeared behind the little hole in his door.

"Jordan! Jordan, get over here!"

"In a minute!" I called back.

We kept running, snaking past abandoned research stations half-drowned in concrete. The destruction got steadily worse as we went along, closing in on the site of the explosion that had brought this place down.

I stopped as we reached a block in our path: a rusty old bookcase, pinned to the wall by two heavy lengths of pipe we'd wedged across the corridor. I kicked the bits of metal loose and they clattered to the ground, freeing the bookcase.

Luke pulled it aside, revealing a misshapen gap in the wall – the remains of an old doorway, leading into the remains of an old laboratory.

Kara slipped inside and I ducked in after her. I could still hear Peter shouting behind us. I tried to tune it out, tried not to let it get to me, but the dull dread was already creeping back into my stomach.

He was right here. Luke's future murderer, *right here* under our roof, and getting more unstable by the day. It was insane. An accident waiting to happen. But what choice did we have? We weren't about to kill Peter, couldn't let him loose on the outside, and didn't have enough sedatives to keep him knocked out for more than a few days. Our only option was to keep him here, keep him as calm as possible, and try to avoid giving the past any reason to repeat itself.

Not that *reason* was much of a priority for Peter any more.

Bill's bed sat in the middle of the room, on the one bit of ground that still resembled a flat surface. Steel chairs littered the floor, cemented in at weird angles. I guessed this had been a meeting room back before the explosion. But given that my first experience of this place had been waking up strapped to one of those chairs, it was hard to picture it as anything other than a prison.

I crossed to the bed. Bill wasn't moving. His hair and beard had grown back a bit, and Kara had found a gown for him to wear, but apart from that he looked exactly the same as when we'd brought him down here.

"Who *are* you?" I whispered, staring down at his closed eyes.

Bill had been a piece of this puzzle since the very beginning. It had been *him* who'd dragged us into this fight. He knew – or *seemed* to know – more about what was going on in Phoenix than practically anyone. But since he'd spent most of the last few months either imprisoned or unconscious or both, we knew almost nothing more about him than the day we'd first met.

Kara frowned and reached down to take Bill's pulse.

"You saw it, right?" I said. "You saw him moving on the monitor."

Bill let out a groan, twisting away from her. Kara's hand snapped back. We'd warned her what Bill was capable of.

"I certainly saw *that*," she said, as Bill settled back down. He didn't open his eyes again, but there was something different about the rhythm of his breathing. He seemed less comatose and more like he was just sleeping.

"Bill?" I said, ignoring the nervous shiver that ran up my spine as I leant over him. "Bill, can you hear me?"

No response. I put a hand on his shoulder.

"Careful," said Luke.

"Yeah," I whispered. But if Bill knew something about Tobias, we couldn't afford not to know too. I bent down to try again. "Bill. It's Jordan. Are you—?"

"Jordan," Bill croaked.

I straightened up again, giving him space. Giving *myself* space, in case he decided to lash out or something. "Yeah, that's right," I said. "Are you ready to wake up now, Bill?"

His mouth opened again. He murmured something but I couldn't make it out, especially not with Peter still yelling from up the corridor. I threw a frustrated glance behind me.

"I'll go and see what he wants," said Luke.

"No," I said reflexively, wishing I hadn't let my irritation show. "Leave him. Wait until—"

"Jordan, I'll be fine."

"Soren, why don't you go with him?" Kara suggested.

"No," said Soren and I at the same time.

"Don't worry," said Luke, "I won't open the door."

He'll be OK, I told myself. But it was like this every

time I wasn't with him. Because that was the thing that kept bugging me about the surveillance video Kara and Soren had shown us: I wasn't in it.

Where was I when Luke was getting stabbed to death?

I pushed the thought aside and bent over the bed again. "Bill? Are you still there?"

If he was, he showed no sign of it.

"Waste of time," Soren muttered under his breath. He grabbed Bill by the shoulders and started shaking him. "Hey! Wake up!"

"Stop that!" I shoved him away and he staggered on the uneven concrete, almost knocking over the I.V.

Soren grabbed the back of a chair, finding his footing again. "I am not afraid of—"

"*Soren,*" said Kara, silencing him. "Why don't you take a seat, and I'll tell you if I need your assistance?"

"Mum, you cannot just—"

"Take a seat, Soren."

Soren glared at her, but did what he was told. I circled around the bed to avoid having my back to him.

Outside, Peter's shouting came to a sudden stop.

I tried to convince myself that meant he was calming down.

Bill was flat on his back again, like nothing had happened. Kara crouched down and opened the battered kit she kept under the bed. "My kingdom for fifteen minutes in that medical centre," she said under her breath, bobbing back up with a torch and a silver sedative pen. "Only use it if you have to," she said, handing me the pen. "They're not going to last for ever."

She eased one of Bill's eyes open and flashed the torch inside. The pupil shrank a bit under the light. Kara let go of him and the eye snapped shut again.

"Is that good?" I asked, as she reached across to check the other one.

"It means he's alive," said Kara. "But given I have no idea what that 'machine' you found him in was doing…" She trailed off as Luke reappeared in the doorway.

"Is Peter OK?" I asked.

Luke shrugged, rolling his eyes. "He only wants to talk to you."

"Of course he does." I sighed, looking to Kara.

32

"What's the story here?"

"He might wake up at any moment," Kara told me, in a voice that said my guess was probably as good as hers, "or he might never wake up at all. I'll send Soren for you if anything changes."

"Don't worry," said Luke. "If Bill does wake up, I'm sure he'll let *everyone* know about it."

By the time Luke and I got to his room, Peter was back to yelling again. "JORDAN! JORD—!"

"Yeah," I said, crossing to his door. "I'm here. What's up?"

"Jordan! Quick, come in," said Peter. "I need to show you something."

"Not now," I said. "Luke and I are—" I faltered, catching the flicker in Peter's eyes at the mention of Luke's name. "It's Crazy Bill. Kara thinks he might be about to come around."

"Oh," said Peter. "Crap. What are you going to do if he wakes up, you know, *crazy*?"

"Good question," I said, mind already drawing up contingencies to get Mum and Georgia to safety. "But that's why we need to get back there. What did you want to tell me?"

"Right," said Peter. He grabbed his laptop from the bed. "Thought you might want to know about this."

Peter held the screen up in front of the gap in the door. It was a surveillance feed. The entrance above our heads. The sun had gone down on our way back from the supply truck, but I could still make out the dark form moving low across the ground.

There was someone up there, and they were trying to get in.

Chapter 4

The figure moved again, shifting through the grass on hands and knees. It was impossible to see much more than an outline, but there weren't many people in Phoenix with a silhouette that size.

"Tank," I said.

"Alive," Luke commented.

No-one had seen Tank since Mike and Cathryn lost him in that skirmish with security. All we'd known for sure was that he hadn't reappeared back in town. But then, neither had a bunch of others. There were at least thirty people who hadn't shown up on our feeds.

"Jordan!" said Peter. "If you let me out, I can go up there and—"

"He's digging," breathed Luke, as though Peter hadn't spoken. "Look. He's trying to find the entrance."

A shiver raced up my back. "We need to get him down here."

"Whoa, hang on, are you sure that's—?"

"Before someone *sees* him!" I said, running for the entrance.

Luke came sprinting up the corridor behind me. "What if it's a trap?"

"A trap?" I said, ducking under a half-collapsed beam. "If Shackleton knew we were here, you really think he'd send *Tank*?"

"That would be the 'trap' part," said Luke. "Like in your vision. You *saw* security coming down here."

"Yeah, but…" I trailed off, realizing I had no end to that sentence.

We shot out of the research module and up the hall through the living area. I poked my head into the lounge room on my way past. Mr Hunter was sitting on his bed, drying his hair with a towel. Mum and Georgia were still in the kitchen, helping Ms Hunter pack away the food.

"Get ready to run," I said.

"Why?" said Mum, grabbing Georgia's hand. "What's going on?"

"Probably nothing," I said. "But get ready."

Way down in the bowels of the Complex, I'd set up a panic room to hide Mum and Georgia whenever my vision came true and Shackleton finally worked out where we were.

Not today, I thought. *Please don't let it be today.*

Luke's dad followed us into the surveillance room. "What's happening?"

"Tank," said Luke. "He's up at the entrance."

Mr Hunter glanced at the same feed Peter had shown us. "We need to get him down here before someone sees him."

Luke threw up his hands like we were staging a mutiny.

I stopped at the control panel, fingers hovering over the button that would open the trapdoor. I could see the anxiety on Luke's face, and suddenly I wasn't so sure he was wrong. "Are we doing this?" I asked.

Luke took another look at the feed. Tank was still clawing at the ground. How long before he hit concrete?

"All right," said Luke, shaking his head. "Yeah. Open—"

"Wait!" said Mr Hunter.

I jerked back from the control panel. "What?"

Then I saw it. A second shadowy figure, shifting into view behind Tank. It turned slowly, peering around at the bush, sweeping a long, dark shape through the air at chest height.

"He's got a rifle," said Mr Hunter.

"See?" said Luke, his face drained of colour.

Mr Hunter rubbed his face. "Get the others. Get them as deep into the Complex as you can."

"What? No! I'm not just going to leave you out here to get—"

"Hang on," I said, watching the screen. The man with the gun crouched next to Tank. I moved closer, scrutinizing the man's ragged outline. "Look at him. Look at his clothes. I don't think – does that look like a security officer to you?"

Neither of them answered. My eyes stayed fixed on the monitor. Something about this didn't add up. Either way, the image of security storming in and gutting this place was too fresh in my mind for me to feel sure of anything.

Finally, Mr Hunter turned and headed for the corridor. "Whatever this is, we need to deal with it. Open the door."

Luke started to answer, but his dad had disappeared.

I pushed the button. On the laptop screen, Tank and the other man scrambled out of the way as the ground opened up under them.

They knelt over the entrance, staring down into the blackness.

"What are you waiting for?" I hissed, hand resting on the control panel, ready to close the trapdoor as soon as they got inside. But still they didn't move.

I gave up waiting and dashed out after Luke's dad.

I could hear Tank calling down the stairs. "Hello?"

"Shh!" I hissed. Even if this wasn't a trap, Tank was going to bring the whole Co-operative down on top of us if he didn't shut up.

Mr Hunter was standing at the bottom of the stairs, shoving a clip into the rifle Soren had abandoned before.

"Tank!" I snapped, cutting him off as he started calling out again. "Get down here!"

Silence. Then: "Jordan?"

"Hurry up! And tell your friend to put his gun down."

My heart pounded. I heard a shuffling noise, feet on concrete, and then a dull hiss as Luke sealed the entrance.

"It's closing!" Tank panicked.

"Just get down here." I said. My eyes flickered to Mr Hunter, kneeling to take aim up the stairs. "Wait. The gun. Throw the gun down first."

"No way!" said Tank. "You think we're—?"

But he was drowned out by a sudden, noisy clattering as the other man did what I'd asked. I jumped out of the way as the rifle rocketed off the stairs and skittered across the floor.

"All yours, Jordan," called a second voice, warm and familiar. "But how about you let me come down and say hi before you start shooting?"

Relief exploded in my chest. Mr Hunter stood up, lowering his rifle. A huge smile broke across my face as the mysterious gunman slowly descended the last few steps, hands above his head, grinning. I ran forward and hugged him. "Reeve!"

"Good to see you, kid," he said, lowering his arms and patting me on the back.

"Reeve, where have you—? You're so *thin,*" I said, feeling the bumps of his spine poking up through his clothes. I stood back from him. He was wearing a tattered old hospital gown, the one he'd had on the night we'd rescued him from the medical centre. It was belted together with a bit of rope over a pair of jeans that might once have been the right size for him, but were now hanging off him like clown pants.

"Yeah," said Reeve, bending to pick up his gun again. "It's been a rough few weeks." He smiled again as Luke emerged from the surveillance room. "Hey, mate."

Tank came down the steps behind Reeve, mouth hanging open, dressed in the school uniform he must have been wearing the night Shackleton rounded everyone up. It was filthy, not much more than rags by now. His face was covered in patchy stubble.

A high-pitched shriek cut through the corridor behind me, and I almost jumped out of my skin. Cathryn came hurtling out of the girls" bedroom and threw herself at Tank.

"Guys," said Luke urgently, over the sound of her sobbing. "Did anyone—?"

But he was silenced mid-sentence as Mike came shoving past. "What the *crap*, man?" he laughed, punching Tank in the arm. "Where have you *been?* We thought you were—"

"HEY!" Luke boomed.

And it was such a shock to hear him demanding their attention that they all turned and gave it to him.

"Everyone, please, just shut up for a second," said Luke. He turned to Reeve. "Did anyone see you come down here?"

Reeve scratched at his ragged beard. "No," he said after a minute. "No, I don't think so."

Luke let out a long breath. "OK. Good."

Tank was gazing around at the corridor again. "What is this place?"

"This is *their* place," said Mike. "The overseers. This is where they live."

And at that moment, like he'd been waiting for an introduction, Soren came tearing in from the other end of the corridor. "Jordan! My mother says you have to come back—" He skidded to a stop, taking in the sudden crowd in the corridor. "Why are they here?"

Tank strode towards him. "You."

"Stop!" Soren ordered. "Stop right there!"

Tank kept walking. "Screw you."

"You should do what he says, man," said Mike, weirdly nervous.

"No," said Tank.

Huh, I thought, a smirk pulling at my lips. Since when did Tank start having independent thoughts?

"On your knees!" said Soren, glancing at Luke and me, like he expected us to back him up. "Now!"

"You're not even real," said Tank, closing in. "Where's Peter? Tell me or I'll smash you."

Soren turned and ran. Tank went to chase him, and I was tempted to let him go, but the last thing we needed down here was another fight.

"Tank, wait!" I called. "Just stop for a second."

Tank hesitated long enough for me to come over and grab his arm. "Where's Peter?" he demanded again.

"He's here," said Cathryn. "Pete's here, but…"

"Trust me," said Mike, "you don't want to see him."

After everything they'd put him through, Peter

43

hadn't exactly welcomed Mike and Cathryn with open arms. Even with Phoenix's accelerated healing power, they'd only just lost the bruises from their last visit to Peter, and we'd kept them well away since.

"I'll take you to him," said Cathryn.

"*I'll* take you to him," I said. Better to keep Tank with me for now than to leave him here with these guys. "But don't expect him to be happy to see you. And if you do anything stupid, I'll—"

"What's going on out here?" asked Luke's mum, appearing in the doorway.

"Nothing," I said. "Sorry, false alarm."

"Who are they?" she asked.

"Friends," said Luke, which was true of Reeve at least. "Just give us a minute, all right?"

He turned back to his dad, cocking his head at Mike and Cathryn. "Can you keep an eye on things out here?"

Mike scowled.

"Hey…" said Tank, eyes dropping to Mike's right hand, taking in his missing fingers for the first time. "Mate… What happ—?"

"Go and see Pete," said Mike, sticking the hand into his pocket.

"C'mon," I said, nodding at Reeve to come too.

Luke and I guided the two of them deeper into the Complex, leaving Mr Hunter to hold the fort.

"They didn't tell us about any of this," said Tank, awed.

"Yeah," I said. "There's a lot your overseers didn't tell you."

Tank grunted, squeezing down the hall with more difficulty than Luke and me. "They're not my overseers."

"OK, Peter's just through here," said Luke, as a battered leather couch came into view up ahead. "But listen, he's kind of sick. It doesn't take much to get him angry. You might want to keep your distance."

"I just want to see him," said Tank.

Peter was still standing at his little window.

"Pete?" Tank stopped a few metres short of him, eyeing the bars over his doorway. "Mate, what are you doing in there?"

Peter's eyes went dark. "Open the door."

"Not a good idea," said Luke in an undertone.

"Jordan!" said Peter. "Bring him in here!"

"Hang on," I said, keeping my voice level, suddenly

remembering why we'd been down here before Tank and Reeve had arrived. "Wait until we've checked on Bill, and then we'll work something out."

"He kidnapped me out of my freaking *bed!*" Peter yelled. "He held me down so Mike could beat the freaking crap out of me!"

"Settle down, mate," said Tank. "Let me—"

"BRING HIM IN HERE!"

WHAM!

Tank shot through the air, slamming into Peter's door like he'd been magnetized. He crumpled against the barricades, grunting as the impact knocked the wind out of him, then dropped to the floor in a heap.

Reeve gasped behind me.

Peter shouted and bashed his fists against the other side of the door.

Tank scrambled away from him. "What—?" He stood up, wiping his nose, smearing blood across his face. "What was *that?*"

"Wait over there," I said, pointing Tank across the room and walking over to deal with Peter.

"Jordan, come on," said Peter, eyes darting around. "He should have just done what I said!"

"Listen," I told him, "this isn't how things get fixed. Just relax, OK? Give us time to deal with this properly."

"But—" Peter glanced from Tank to his own hands, then back to me again, like he was struggling to figure out what had happened. His expression softened and his eyes dropped to the floor. "Yeah."

"All right. Good. I'll come and see you tomorrow, OK?" I started back to Bill's room, picking up Luke, Reeve and Tank on my way past. Moving on to the next thing, as though I hadn't just watched someone get levitated across a room.

"I think we might have a bit of catching up to do," said Reeve, looking out the way we'd come.

Soren was waiting for us in the doorway. He ducked back inside as we approached.

Bill looked just the same as we'd left him.

"How is he?" I asked Kara, weaving between the chairs to the bed.

But her attention was fixed on Tank. He stopped in the doorway, like he was thinking about making a run for it. I couldn't figure out the expression on Kara's face, but it was the first time I'd seen her look at him like he was an actual human being.

47

"My letter. You saw it too?"

"Yeah," said Tank, wiping his nose again, "we got it."

"Who's this?" asked Kara, eyeing Reeve with her usual cold scepticism.

Luke was looking at him too. "Hey. You were with Bill in the medical centre. What were they doing to him? Did you ever see them wake him up?"

"Mate," said Reeve, shaking his head at the bizarreness of it all – this weird huddle of people standing around a homeless guy's bed in a secret underground hide-out. "I've got no bloody idea about *any* of—"

There was a groan from the bed.

Bill's eyes snapped open. He rose up from the mattress to look at me, arms tugging at his restraints. He snorted absently as the feeding tube moved in his nose, face breaking into a smile filled with swelling gums and mangled teeth.

And then suddenly, his expression shifted. "NO!" he snarled. "No, no, no! You're not right! You are not mine!"

"It's OK," I said, backing off a bit. "Bill, listen to

me. Just take it slow, all right?"

"No! I need… Please…" He mouthed soundlessly, seeming to lose his train of thought. He gazed around the room and his face lit up again. "We're here," he said breathlessly. "We are here. Yes, yes, it's almost—" He turned to Luke. "How many days?"

"Until Tabitha?" said Luke.

"HOW MANY DAYS?"

"Fourteen," I said. "We've got two weeks left. Bill, what do you know about Tobias? Do you know what—?"

"It's time!" he shouted, falling back against the mattress. "Almost. Almost time." He was crying, ecstatic, head rolling from side to side.

"Almost time for *what?*" snapped Soren, getting tired of it. But if Bill heard him, he didn't show it.

"Bill…?" I said.

"Almost time," he repeated, over and over, eyes drifting shut, tears still rolling down his face. "Almost time… Almost…"

His head slowly rocked to a stop, and then he was gone again.

Chapter 5

"So you guys are, what, scientists or something?" said Reeve the next morning, scraping up the last of the soup Luke's mum had allocated him for breakfast.

"Something like that," said Kara.

Reeve glanced up at Luke and me. "And they're on our side now? Even after what they did to Tank and his mates? And to you guys?"

"It's complicated," I said, standing to collect the empty bowls.

"Yeah," said Reeve. "I got that."

We were sitting around on the beds in the boys' room. Reeve and Tank had spent the night here on the spare bunks and woke up talking as if those springy old mattresses were the best things they'd ever slept on.

"Is there more?" Tank asked.

"Yeah," I said, taking his bowl away from him. "At dinner."

Ms Hunter had already given Tank and Reeve twice as much breakfast as anybody else, a decision which almost brought her and Soren to blows. Kara had broken it up, and Soren had stomped off to his room, where he was probably having a good long whinge to Mike about it.

"I'm still hungry," Tank grumbled.

"Join the club," I told him, taking the bowls through to the kitchen.

"What about you guys?" Luke asked. "Where have you been all this time?"

When we'd last seen Reeve, he was running blindly into the bush, drawing a pair of armed guards away from the rest of us so we could escape from the medical centre.

"Well," said Reeve, leaning back against the wall, "at first it was just me. And for a good while after you kids busted me out, I spent most of my energy just surviving. Hanging around the outskirts of town, trying to get my head around what was going on. Trying to find out where my wife and my kid were. Then, about a week back, I was out at – there's a lake not far from here, and I was out there grabbing a drink, and I spotted this cave in the side of the rock face."

"Yeah," I said, sitting down next to Luke again. "We've been there."

"Course you have," said Reeve. "Anyway, I swam across and climbed up into the cave, and suddenly here was this kid –" He jerked a thumb at Tank. "– standing over me, ready to smash my head open with a rock."

Tank smirked. "Sorry."

"It took a bit of work, but I was able to convince him that I wasn't going to hurt him. I filled him in on what was going on in town, and he explained how these overseers of his had warned him and his mates to get out."

"They're not my overseers," said Tank again, running a hand over his right shoulder, where Kara and Soren had branded him with a tattoo.

"No," said Kara. "We are not. That is why I sent you that last letter. I wanted to offer an explanation for our behaviour. I wanted to apologize."

"No, you didn't, said Tank bitterly. "You never said sorry. You said you *had* to do all that to us."

Typical Kara, I thought. She might have softened since we first met her, but some things never changed.

Kara rubbed her eyes. "You need to believe that everything we asked of you was motivated by the best of intentions."

"Because nothing says 'best intentions' like luring innocent bystanders into a secret kidnapping cult," I muttered, buried anger rising to the surface again. "Who would've thought *that* would turn out—?" I broke off as Luke's fingers brushed over my hand. A gentle suggestion that rehashing this old argument might not be the greatest use of our time.

Tank's eyes widened. "Whoa. You guys are together now? Does Pete know about this?"

I let go of Luke's hand. No, Peter didn't know about it.

"Because, you know," said Tank, "he's totally into you."

"Yeah," I said, "I kind of picked up on that. Can we please focus?"

"We think there's a way to stop Tabitha," said Luke, finally landing on the point I'd been wanting to get to all morning. "Something called Tobias."

"What?" Reeve jolted forward. "What is it?"

"We don't know," said Luke, voice registering the same dull thud of disappointment that had landed in my own stomach. "We were sort of hoping you would."

Reeve scratched at his beard again. His face was half hidden in the shadow of the bunk above his head, but I could still see the network of tiny, faint scars crisscrossing his skin, lingering reminders of his last encounter with Tabitha.

"Tobias," said Reeve, brow furrowed. "Where did you hear that name?"

I glanced over at Kara. "That's complicated too."

We'd filled the others in on the warning about Tobias, but we hadn't told anyone *how* we heard it. Not even Luke's parents. He said he didn't want to worry them. I'd told him he was being dumb, but let it drop after he pointed out that I was acting exactly the same way about my visions.

"Kara told us we had to take Tobias to the release

station," said Luke, not quite managing to keep his expression neutral. "But she heard it from – someone else. She's got no more about Tobias than we do."

"Brilliant." Reeve leant forward, hands pressed together in front of his face. Then he sat up again. "Hang on. Release station. I reckon I might know where that is. At least—" He stared into space, picturing something. "There's a bunker, a little way out past the boundary wall. Only a few of us knew about it, and none of us ever got told what was inside, but they sent us out in the vans to do regular sweeps of the area."

"*That's* what you were doing," I said. "The night we went out there. When you caught us climbing over the wall."

"Yeah," said Reeve. "I had no idea what I was guarding back then, obviously. But it makes sense, doesn't it? What else would they be hiding *outside* the wall?"

Kara frowned. "That still doesn't bring us any closer to—"

She stopped and hurried to her feet as Cathryn's voice rang out in the corridor. "Get away from me, you little freak!"

Luke and I jumped up too, and a second later Georgia tore into the room. She crashed into me, clinging to my waist, tears streaming.

"Hey," I said, hoisting her into my arms. "What's up? Where's Mum?"

"Sleeping," Georgia sniffed. "The baby makes her sleepy."

I carried her out into the corridor where Cathryn stood, red-faced, looking like she didn't know whether to run away or start shouting again. "You got a problem, Cat?"

"She was going to sneak out there and give Peter some of my muesli bars," said Georgia, pointing down the hall.

"I was not, you stupid little liar."

"She *was*," said Georgia, tearing up again. "I'm not lying! She was going to steal the kitchen keys off Luke's mum. She told me!"

"Even if I was, like I'd tell you about it," Cathryn snapped.

"Not with your mouth," said Georgia. "You told me in your head."

Cathryn glared, confirming that Georgia was

telling the truth, and I felt myself ratcheting up from frustration to rage. "You *don't go down there*," I said, closing the gap between us. "What, you don't remember the beating he gave you last time?"

"He's sick!" said Cathryn angrily.

"And you think you can fix him? You think he beat you up because he was *hungry?*"

"She's still in love with him, that's why," Georgia said matter-of-factly.

A second flash of sparks behind Cathryn's eyes told me Georgia was right. Cathryn turned and walked away, almost running into Mr Hunter as he came out of Kara and Soren's room.

"Sorry, Jordan," he said wearily. "I *was* watching her. But then I heard Soren yelling in his room and I thought I should check it out."

"Not your fault," I said, hugging Georgia and passing her across to him. "Just too many children down here. What was he yelling about?"

Mr Hunter shrugged. "The breakfast thing, I think. He and Mike both shut up pretty quick after I got in there." He looked down at Georgia. "You two OK?"

"Yeah," I said. "I think so."

"You're a good boy," said Georgia, patting him on the shoulder.

"Thanks," he smiled. "Come on, let's go have a look at that new video camera of yours."

Luke's dad took Georgia away and I sank back against the wall of the corridor, rubbing my eyes, listening to Cathryn muttering in the next room. She'd always been a bit emotionally volatile, but things had only got worse since she arrived down here.

The morning after we brought her and Mike in, she'd spotted her mum on the surveillance feeds and discovered something the rest of us had known for ages: Mrs Hawking was one of the original members of the Shackleton Co-operative. For days afterwards, Cathryn had just sat in the bedroom, crying on Amy's shoulder.

But as tragic as all that was, it was kind of hard to stay sympathetic when she was taking it out on a six-year-old.

I straightened up again, trying to put it out of my mind, and returned to the bedroom, where Tank had apparently latched on to the idea of Reeve being outside the wall in a van.

"Look," said Reeve, "there's only one exit in Phoenix, and you can't just walk up and open the door."

"But if we *could* get through," Tank pressed, "we could steal one of those vans and drive out and get the army or whatever. Come on, boss. We have to try, at least!"

Boss. The word stuck in my head. Mike had started calling Soren the same thing.

"You OK?" Luke whispered as I sat down.

I sighed. "People keep asking me that."

"Mate, you know I love your enthusiasm," Reeve told Tank. "But we wouldn't get a mile out before Shackleton blew us to pieces. If we're going to take these guys down, we'll have to do it from here."

He turned to the rest of us. "I don't know what to tell you about this Tobias of yours. But I've been working on some plans of my own these past few weeks. Keeping an eye on the security patrols. Intercepting them when I can. Those guys know me. A lot of them were friends, back when I was still working for Calvin. And this end-of-the-world business isn't what any of us signed up for. Some of them are still loyal to Officer Barnett, but a lot are just—"

"To Barnett?" said Luke. "What's he got to do with it?"

Reeve raised an eyebrow. "You kids haven't heard? Calvin went off the map about a week ago. No-one seems to know where he's disappeared to, but it looks like Barnett's in charge until he gets back."

Calvin gone. That explained why he'd suddenly stopped interrogating my dad.

"Not exactly an improvement," said Luke. Next to Calvin, Barnett was the most sadistic, trigger-happy maniac the Co-operative had. "Anyway, sorry, you were saying…?"

"A coup," I said, switching back on to what Reeve was saying and feeling a rush of excitement at the idea. "You want to take the Co-operative down from the inside. Convince security to change sides."

"Some of them, anyway," Reeve said. "I won't lie to you, though, it's slow going. Even the guys that hate Shackleton are terrified of defying him."

"What can we do?" I asked, suddenly bursting with energy. "How can we help?"

"Well, for a start," said Reeve, getting to his feet, "I'd love to get a proper look at this surveillance room of yours. I have a few sets of eyes in town, but nothing like what you guys have got."

"Of course," said Kara, standing too. "Anything you need."

"More food?" said Tank hopefully.

Kara pursed her lips. "Don't push it."

"Tank and I have something to take care of tonight," said Reeve. "We're going to need to head back up to the surface." He looked down at Luke and me. "You kids feel like taking a walk?"

"Absolutely," I said.

"Where are we going?" asked Luke, like he was pretty sure he was going to regret asking.

Reeve smiled grimly. "My tombstone," he said. "There's someone I'd like you to meet."

Chapter 6

Friday 31 July
13 days

I spent most of the day putting off my promised visit to Peter's room, convincing myself that I had other, more important things to deal with. But after washing up from breakfast, giving Reeve a painstakingly detailed overview of the surveillance room, finding clean sets of clothes for him and Tank, and convincing Luke and his dad to help me scrub the bathroom, I had to admit I was just stalling.

After dinner, I told myself. We weren't heading up to the surface with Reeve until midnight. Still plenty of time to see Peter.

We ate around the circle of tables in the surveillance room. Luke's mum sat in the corner, hunched over a notepad, reworking her meal schedule to accommodate our two new arrivals. Amy had offered to help, but Ms Hunter had shooed her away after only a couple of minutes, saying Amy was slowing her down. In reality, I think it was the opposite. With her accelerated brain, Amy could run all the numbers at triple speed, leaving Ms Hunter with nothing much to do. And I was beginning to see that Luke was right: his mum *needed* that job. She needed there to be at least some tiny shred of her life that was still under her control.

I took my time cleaning up after dinner. Eventually, Luke came and found me. "Hey," he said, knocking on the open door. "You ready to go?"

I sighed, draping a grotty tea towel over the edge of the sink. I really didn't want Luke coming down there with me, but I knew he wouldn't let me talk him out of it. "Yeah. Come on."

I heard Georgia's voice from the girls' room as we reached the hall. She walked out with the video camera Luke had given her. "And here's the stinky hallway," she said, panning around the walls, obviously over being upset about her run-in with Cathryn. "And here's my sister and her *boyfriend*. Kiss for the camera, Jordan!"

"Not now, Georgia," I said, brushing past her.

Georgia flipped the camera around, pointing it at herself. "OK, now this is a song I wrote for them: *I know a boy, his name was Luke. He kissed Jordan on – the – cheek!*" she chanted, barely getting the second line out before she doubled over in hysterics.

I stopped at the end of the hall. "You need to stay here, OK? Go find Mum."

Georgia ignored me. She spun the camera around again. "*I know a boy, his name was Luke. He kissed Jordan on the LIPS!*"

"Georgia," said Mum, coming after her, a towel clutched in her hand. "Shower. Now."

Georgia's smile disappeared. "I *hate* the shower," she said. "It's *cold*."

The stern look on Mum's face softened a bit. "I know it is, sweetheart. Just a quick one, and then you can go in and say goodnight to Dad."

"OK," said Georgia wearily. She turned and trudged after Mum.

We mostly tried to keep Georgia out of the surveillance room during the day. No way of predicting what she might see in there. But each night before bed,

Mum took Georgia in to watch Dad on the monitors for a while. It upset her a bit sometimes, but she kept going back. And it was important, I think. Georgia had as much right as any of us to know that he was OK.

"Maybe that camera wasn't such a good idea after all," said Luke, smirking over his shoulder as we headed down to Peter's.

"I think I've seen it before," I said, taking his hand in mine. We'd had too much insanity in the last twenty-four hours for me to dwell on it, but I'd definitely recognized Georgia's camera when Luke pulled it out of the box. "In one of my visions. Two weeks ago, remember? I flashed – forward, it must have been – to the empty bedroom, and we couldn't figure out why. But that camera was sitting on Georgia's bed. Maybe that's the reason I was there. Maybe that camera is going to be important."

"Important," repeated Luke. I knew he wasn't a hundred percent sold on the idea that there even *was* a reason for my visions.

"*Why*, though?" I wondered out loud. "I mean, what are we supposed to do? Film what's going on in town?"

"What's the point of doing that if we can't get the video *out* to anyone?" Luke asked. "You heard Reeve. No point trying to get out in a van. And as far as we know, the only other way to reach the outside is from the communications room in the Shackleton Building. Which, unfortunately, is *in the Shackleton Building*."

He stopped walking, and I guess he must have seen the frustration on my face because he said, "Sorry, I'm not – I would *love* to believe that this video camera could be some kind of solution, but … I don't know. I just don't see it."

"I don't see it either," I said. "Yet. But that doesn't mean it's not true."

Luke put his arms around me, resting his head against my shoulder. "The end of the world gives me a headache."

We stood there for a minute, holding each other in the debris, and I couldn't remember the last time we'd been this quiet or still or alone.

"Are you sure you want to do this?" Luke asked finally. "You don't *have* to go down there."

"Yes, I do," I said. "I have to keep treating him like a person."

I didn't know if there was any way to reverse the path that Peter was on. But if there was, we weren't going to do it by cutting him out of our lives. And in the meantime, I'd come up with a way to keep Luke out of the line of fire, at least for a while.

"I was thinking," I said, as we continued down the passageway, "Reeve and Tank are heading back after we meet this friend of theirs tonight, right? Back to the cave where they've been hiding out, so Reeve can get in touch with his people in town. I think one of us should go stay with him."

"Why?" said Luke.

"Just, you know, to help him out. Share information."

"Haven't we been doing that all day?" said Luke. "Anyway, you can't just disappear with them. You have to be here for Georgia and your mum. And I'm—" Luke stopped walking again. "Wait," he said, bringing me around to meet him. "Is this about me?"

"What do you mean?"

"Seriously Jordan, do you actually have a plan here, or are you just trying to get me away from Peter?"

"What's wrong with getting you away from Peter?"

I said, struggling to keep the volume of my voice under control. "Why not get you out of here while we've got the chance?"

"Right, because there's *no-one* up there who wants me dead," said Luke. "And, anyway, who says Peter's only interested in attacking *me?* Who says I'm the first person he comes after? All we know is what was on that video."

"Luke—"

"I'm not leaving you down here," he said. "That's not how this is going to happen. We're not going to solve this by running away from it."

I leant in again, touching my forehead to his. When had he started talking like this? When had he become the person who stared death in the face and kept walking?

"You can't die," I said.

Luke smiled ruefully. "I really don't want to." He bent forward and kissed me. "We'll work this out."

I nodded, still staring at him, my tongue brushing over my lip. Then I realized what I was doing and started down the corridor again. "Come on."

We stopped just around the corner from Peter's

door and I reluctantly dropped Luke's hand. He wasn't actually coming in with me. He never did any more; no point making things more volatile than they needed to be. But he always waited outside, out of sight, just in case. I left him there and started lifting the barricades away from the door. "Peter?"

He was at the window in a second. "Jordan! Hey – are you OK? You look like you've—"

"I'm fine," I said, setting the last barricade down against the wall, a dark edge slipping into my voice before I'd even made it inside.

Peter moved in to hug me as soon as the door was open. My skin crawled, but I tried not to show it. He let go and reached for my hand. I stuck it into my pocket, pretending I hadn't noticed.

We hadn't told him about the stabbing. We hadn't told him about any of it. Neither of us was interested in having that conversation with him. Besides, what if us talking about it was what put the idea in Peter's head in the first place?

Peter returned to his bed and patted the blanket beside him. "Come and sit."

"Thanks," I said, dragging the chair across and

setting it down opposite the bed, trying to ignore his not-so-subtle grunt of disappointment. "How are you feeling?"

"Better now," he smiled, recovering quickly. He dragged his computer across and spun it around, proudly displaying a screen full of programming gibberish. "I think I've almost figured out a way to bring down the surveillance network. Really this time."

"That's great," I said, although the truth was he'd been telling me the same thing for three weeks straight.

He put the laptop back down, leaning forward so that our knees were touching. "Is Tank still here?"

"Yeah," I said. "He and Reeve are taking us up to the surface tonight. He wants us to meet with a contact he's made in town."

"You and Luke," said Peter.

I rolled back my shoulders, edging my seat backwards under the pretence of stretching, fighting down the urge to just smack him across the head and walk out. Less than two minutes in here and already I felt like I needed a shower.

"Is Tank OK?" Peter asked. "You know, after—"

"You smashed him into a wall, Peter."

"It was an accident!"

"Was it?" I asked, before I could stop myself.

I braced for an outburst, but instead Peter let out a kind of strangled cough and put his head in his hands.

"I didn't mean for it to go that way," he said after a minute.

"Which way did you mean it to go?"

"I was angry. He should've – I don't know. I don't know what I wanted." He sat up, staring at his hands, slowly clenching and unclenching his fingers. When he spoke again, his voice was strained. "Do you think I don't get it, Jordan? Do you think I don't know what's happening to me?"

And somehow, the question pierced through everything else and I felt guilty for how I'd been writing him off. He was a million miles from the cocky, carefree kid I'd met three months ago, but he was still Peter. Somewhere under there, he was still the same person.

"Peter…"

"What?" he snapped. "You want to tell me to calm down? Try being locked up in this hole for a month and see how freaking calm you feel! Meanwhile, Soren's strutting around like he owns the place, my parents are trapped up there with Shackleton, and you guys won't even—"

"We're trying to help you, Peter! We're doing everything we can."

"You don't know what it's like!" he said, jumping up and pacing. "You have no idea what it feels like to not even be in control of your own—"

A shout of pain burst from my throat, cutting him off. I lurched to the ground, nausea rushing up inside me like there was something trying to claw its way out.

"Jordan!" said Peter from somewhere above me. "What's wrong?" But his voice was dim and warbled, like he was shouting underwater. I collapsed on my side, eyes squeezing shut, blocking out the blur of colour and noise as the whole world swirled around my head.

Another vision. The first in over a week. And either I'd forgotten how bad they were, or this was the most head-shattering one yet. I tried to keep breathing, riding out the shakes, waiting for it all to pass, terrified of what I was going to find when it did. Because even though I called these things "visions", they were quickly becoming more than that. In the beginning, all

I'd been doing was *seeing* things. Whatever my mind was doing, my body had stayed firmly in the present.

These days, it was a different story.

My body spasmed again, and Peter's shouting flickered out altogether, replaced by a deeper voice, still muffled but easier to make out.

"– second iteration, approaching peak stability."

I rolled over, hands reaching for my head. It was throbbing violently, like it might crumble to dust under my fingers.

"Event appears to be another Type B," a woman's voice chimed in, *"magnitude four, extent … two point two four metres."*

The pain in my head began slowly easing off, and I forced my eyes open. At first, I barely recognized it as the same room. The walls and ceiling were flat and smooth, actual walls instead of the mess of concrete and wreckage that formed them in the present. But Peter's door was still there, minus the chipping paint and smashed window.

I staggered to my feet and turned around, swaying as the world caught up. There was a whole other room behind me now, separated by a glass wall. On the other side of the glass, two people in white coats were staring out from behind a row of boxy computer monitors: a Japanese guy who was maybe in his twenties, and an older, round-faced woman with squarish glasses and dark hair pulled back into a tight bun. Neither of them had registered my sudden appearance in the room.

Because you're not here, I reminded myself. Not yet anyway.

"Diagnostic prepared," said the man, voice muffled by the glass. *"Ready to initiate on your mark, Dr Vattel."*

Dr Vattel.

Remi Vattel. Kara's mother. The woman who'd founded this place. Still down here, still alive. Which meant I'd come back at least twenty years.

"Soren," she frowned at the man next to her, *"call me 'doctor' one more time and I'll reconsider letting you marry my daughter."*

He smirked, breaking the clinical veneer. *"Sorry, Remi. Old habits."*

I glanced between the two of them, thinking I must have misheard. That wasn't Soren. Soren hadn't even been born until after the Vattel Complex was destroyed.

And then it clicked: this wasn't *our* Soren. It was his father. We knew Soren's dad had been killed in the explosion. Kara must have named their baby after him.

"*Well?*" said Vattel, staring over her glasses at the older Soren. "*What are you waiting for?*"

"*Right. Sorry.*" He glanced at his computer. "*Initiating scan.*"

Whatever they were "scanning", I couldn't see it.

A second later, I almost jumped out of my skin as Luke appeared, centimetres from my face. He reached for me, his expression desperate. Mouth open, shouting, but I couldn't hear a word of it.

And all at once, panic came rushing at me with full force. It was happening again.

I was slipping away.

Luke wasn't here. Not really. He was back in the present, watching me disappear, trying to drag me back to reality before—

Before what?

"Luke!" I called back, grabbing at him, my fingers passing straight through him.

"*Scan initiated,*" said Soren's dad, apparently oblivious to all of it. "*Adjusting focus. Three. Two. One.*"

The lights cut out on my side of the glass. Nothing left to see by but the glow of the computers.

I squinted, searching for Luke in the darkness. He stepped forward again, still mouthing silently from two decades away. I stretched out my hands to meet his, but I might as well have been clutching at his shadow.

A mechanical hum rose up. *"Temperature: normal,"* Soren's dad reported behind me. *"UV: normal. EM: Slightly elevated, but still within expected range…"*

Whatever was going on in here, I needed to get *out*.

I turned back to Luke, staring into his face. I tried to focus, to tune out the rest of the room, willing my body to co-operate, as though I could get back to the present by wishing it were true.

I reached for him again, swiping at the air in front of me. *Come on!*

"Anything?" Vattel asked from behind the glass.

"Not yet. All readings still report normal."

I tried again, and again, and—

And I tripped forward, losing my balance as Luke's hands clamped down around my wrist.

"–ordan!" he shouted, suddenly audible again.

"Yes! That's it. Just focus, OK? Concentrate."

I brought my other hand down, grabbing on to Luke's, and felt the nausea bubbling up again.

"Hold on," said Soren's dad. *"I'm getting something,"* and at first I thought he was looking at me.

Then I saw what he was really talking about. It was glowing around me, a cloud of gas or mist or something, fluorescent blue, like white paint under a black light. A shiver ran up my spine as I pictured another empty room like this one, a Shackleton Co-operative research facility – figures contorting on the ground as Tabitha ripped them to pieces.

"Luke!" I shouted, squeezing harder on his arms as the glow grew brighter, more solid. I couldn't see where it was coming from, but—

The churning in my insides reached full force, and my legs dropped out from under me. The room started collapsing again, everything blurring together, and for a second, I could see both places – both *times* – at once. Dark and light. Solid and destroyed. Vattel staring through the glass and Peter standing over me, screaming.

And then it all melted away. For a long moment,

the room disappeared completely, plunging me into blackness. Then it blinked back into existence again. Luke was there, another Luke, strapped to a steel chair. Then more darkness, invisible walls pressing in from every side. And through all of it, Luke was there, still holding on, the one solid thing in the whole world. I squeezed my eyes shut, biting down on my gag reflex, fingers digging into him until, finally, the universe stopped spinning and I crumpled to the ground.

Peter's shouts broke into my head again. "– are you *doing*? Let go of her! Give her to me!"

"No," I groaned, as Luke's arms lowered me to the ground. "Don't … it … I'm OK."

I gave it a minute, and then opened my eyes again. Luke was kneeling over me, looking ready to pass out. Peter was red-faced from shouting. He hadn't seen me go through this before. No-one had, except for Luke and my dad.

Peter crouched on my other side, and the two of them hoisted me to my feet.

"Thanks," said Luke, tugging me gently away from Peter as I found my feet again. "I've got her."

Peter's expression blackened. I struggled to get my

head back together, ready to intervene in whatever came next.

"Don't," Luke told him, surprisingly forceful. "Not now. Don't make this about you."

Peter stared at him for a moment longer, then swore and dropped my arm. He grabbed his laptop and slumped down on to his bed, not even looking up again as we closed the door on him.

Chapter 7

Saturday 1 August
12 days

"You know, I'd almost convinced myself it was a one-off," I said, voice low as Luke and I crept through the bush, a few paces behind Tank and Reeve. "The disappearing. At least, it's never been as bad as that first time, when I saw the Complex getting attacked."

"It has now," said Luke. "I thought you were gone, Jordan. You *were* gone for a couple of seconds there."

"Wherever *gone* is," I said.

Because that was the question, wasn't it? What would happen if I faded out altogether? Would I fade *in* to the other time? Or would I just vanish completely?

I tried to push it all aside. Right now, the best thing I could do was focus on not finding out.

It was just after midnight, and we were closing in on the makeshift graveyard at the north-west corner of town. The air was bitterly cold. How had these two survived so long out here without getting hypothermia or something?

Luke shot me a nervous glance, like I might disappear again at any moment. "You do realize there's no way I'm leaving you on your own after this, right?"

He hadn't seen any of it. It might have looked to me like Luke was with me in the vision, but as far as he was concerned, he'd just been standing there with Peter, watching my body fade away in front of him.

I reached over and squeezed his hand.

"Right," said Luke. "I'm going to take that as a yes."

It was amazing how quickly he'd become this critical part of my life. I'd known him for all of three months, but already it was a struggle to remember a time when he hadn't been there. It was as though the life I'd had before Phoenix wasn't even mine, just memories of something that had happened to some other person – netball games and family barbeques and being driven to school.

Somewhere along the line, I'd started seeing Luke's survival and my survival as pretty much the same thing. Like those two realities were tied together. And in a very real way, it was starting to look like maybe they were.

When I'd started fading out the first time around, Luke and my dad had both tried to grab hold of me, but only Luke had been able to do it. And this afternoon, Peter had apparently stood over me for almost a full minute, trying to make me come back, before Luke got him out of the way. Why was Luke the only one who'd been able to reach me? And what would happen if he wasn't around to do it next time?

Reeve and Tank came to a stop in front of us, just short of a little clearing in the bush. We were here. Reeve whispered something to Tank, who nodded, and took off around the edge of the clearing.

"Where's he going?" asked Luke, crouching low in the grass beside Reeve.

"Just making sure we're alone." A smile crossed Reeve's face, and something about it reminded me of Dad. "Good kid, that one. Good head on his shoulders."

It struck me that this was probably the first time

I'd ever heard someone say a positive word about what went on in Tank's head. Even more striking, it seemed like Reeve was kind of right. Something in Tank had changed. It was like he'd finally found an identity beyond being Mike's bodyguard.

"I think you've been good for him," I said. "Nice for him to have someone decent to follow for a change."

Reeve shrugged off the compliment. "We're all following someone."

He looked out across the clearing, fingers drumming on the butt of his rifle. I watched his gaze drift slowly from the path to the marble tombstone in front of us, marking the empty grave the Co-operative had dug for his funeral. Reminders of a time when Shackleton was still bothering to cover up the messes he made.

A few metres away, a mound of upturned soil marked another burial site. A real one. The place where Calvin had unceremoniously dumped Dr Montag's body after his murder, the night we broke into the medical centre.

If not for Reeve, we might've been down there with him.

"Thanks for that, by the way," I whispered. "Drawing those guards off. Letting us escape. You saved us."

"Yeah," Reeve shrugged again, "you saved me too." He reached into his jeans pocket and pulled out an old watch with half the strap missing, tilting it so its face caught the moonlight. They were late. "I've been thinking," he said. "If this Tobias of yours is anywhere, it'll be in the Shackleton Building, right? Up on the restricted level, where Shackleton can keep a close watch on it."

"Maybe," said Luke. "Probably. But going up there didn't work out so well for us last time."

"Last time wasn't smart." Reeve's focus flickered back to his tombstone. "I should have told you that myself. Should've taken the time to do it properly. But back then, I was too caught up in keeping my family out of harm's way. For all the good that did."

"What do you mean, *properly*?" I said. "We did everything we could."

"Not everything," said Reeve. "There's an armoury. Out in the bush, near the warehouse that holds all the town's food. I've never actually been posted out there myself, but—"

"There's another building on that road?" said Luke. "Why didn't Bill tell us about it?"

"Maybe he didn't know," I said.

"He went all the way out to the warehouse and then didn't bother to check what was further down the road?"

I shrugged. "We didn't."

"Yeah, but – we had other things on our minds at the time," said Luke.

"Tank and I went to check it out last week," Reeve said. "We've been looking at getting into Shackleton's communications room, and so first we need to pick up a few supplies. The armoury's guarded, but it's not impenetrable. Not like the Shackleton Building. I'm working with my guys in town to figure out how to get in and get what we need."

I bit my lip. "Weapons, you mean."

The idea of picking up a gun made me seriously uncomfortable. I tried to remind myself that Reeve wasn't a violent guy, that he wouldn't use force unless we really had to. But still, even talking about it made me feel sick.

"I don't like it either, Jordan," said Reeve. "But if we're going up there, we need to do everything we can to make sure it's not a repeat of last time."

"How are you even still *here* after last time?" asked Luke, and I shivered as my mind dredged up images of Reeve handcuffed to a table, getting slashed to pieces by an early iteration of Tabitha. "We saw what Shackleton did to you. You were…"

"Yeah," said Reeve. "I can't explain it, but—" He reached down and plucked a stalk from the sharp, spindly grass at our feet. "Here," he said, holding the stalk up in front of us. "Watch."

He yanked the stalk across his other hand, flinching as the sharp edges sliced into his skin. Then he held his palm up in front of us.

A line of blood oozed up where the grass had cut him, silvery blue in the darkness. But then, almost immediately, the wound began to scab over. The bleeding stopped, and the skin began to knit back together, healing right there in front of us.

Luke leant in closer. "Whoa."

"Yeah," I said. Since we'd arrived in Phoenix, everyone here (well, everyone except Luke and his mum) had developed a kind of accelerated healing ability. Something to do with the fallout that had saturated this area since the destruction of the Vattel Complex.

But this was way beyond that. If my body had got a boost, Reeve's had been strapped to a jetpack.

"I'm not the only one, though, am I?" said Reeve. "I mean, not *this* specifically, but all of us who were getting tested on in the medical centre—"

He broke off. There was a rustle of leaves from the far side of the clearing, and two men stepped out cautiously from between the graves. Security guards, both armed. One of them pointed at Reeve's tombstone. He turned towards us and I got a proper look at his face.

"Officer Miller," I whispered.

"You know him?" said Reeve.

"He's helped us out a couple of times."

"Yeah, he's a good bloke," said Reeve. "First one to jump onboard with all this."

The two officers stopped at the tombstone. Miller let go of his gun and scratched his left elbow.

"All clear," said Reeve, standing up. "Let's go."

He walked into the clearing, and Luke and I followed. There was a clatter of metal as the two guards raised their guns, saw that it was Reeve, and relaxed again.

Miller shot a curious look at Luke and me.

"Matt!" The other guard gaped at Reeve. He was an older guy, maybe my dad's age. "You're… You're actually here…"

Reeve smiled and reached out to shake his hand. "Hello, Ethan. Yeah, still kicking, whatever the chief might tell you." He turned back to Luke and me. "Guys, this is Officer Hamilton."

I recognized the surname. "You're Lauren's dad."

Lauren was a girl from school who'd helped Luke and me out when we were hiding from the Co-operative in town. Georgia used to go over to her place sometimes to play with her little brother, back in the days when kids lived in houses.

"That's right," Hamilton nodded, but for some reason he didn't quite meet my eye as he said it.

"Have you spoken to my dad?" I asked, advancing on him without really meaning to. "Is he OK? Can you pass a message on to—?"

Reeve's hand came down on my shoulder. "We might want to give Ethan a minute."

I stopped talking, stepping back again, but the uneasy look didn't shift from Hamilton's face.

"How are you guys holding up?" Miller asked, shrugging off a backpack and handing it to Reeve.

"Surviving." Reeve nodded at Luke and me, waving a hand at his new clothes. "Better for having run into these two. How's life in town?"

"About the same as the last time you asked," said Miller. "We're all just stuck in a holding pattern. Waiting. People get restless, start fights. We move in to break it up, settle things down before they get out of hand. Only a matter of time before it all blows up."

"Which is why we need to be ready to move when it does," said Reeve, pulling the backpack open, revealing a jumper and a few tins of food. "Thanks."

"The surveillance network," I said. "One of you needs to shut it down. Until that happens, we're—"

"Jordan," said Reeve, cutting me off. "Slow down."

"It's not that simple," said Miller. "Security personnel have no real access to the new network. We can monitor the feeds, but we're locked out of the network hub. Not even Barnett has clearance."

"Oh," I said.

"There's something else," said Miller, returning his attention to Reeve. "Weird rumours floating around town today. Something called Tobias."

A chill shot up my spine, piercing through even the cold of the graveyard. Reeve looked significantly at Luke and me. "We've heard that name too. Any ideas what it is? Or where?"

"Hard to say," said Miller, brow crinkling. "I mean, obviously there's no way to tell what's real and what's just speculation, but it definitely sounds like something the Co-operative doesn't want us to know about. The most convincing theory I've heard is that it's some kind of emergency shutdown mechanism for Tabitha."

I suppressed another sigh. That was no further than we'd got.

"Right. Well, keep an ear out. Let me know as soon as you hear anything more solid." Reeve zipped up the backpack. "Now," he said, focusing on Hamilton, who was starting to look like he regretted coming. "Let's get to business. I assume you know why you're here."

"Yes," said Hamilton, glancing nervously over his shoulder. "You want to drag me into this. You want me to join your revolution."

"Not yet," said Reeve. "Right now, I just want to know whose side you're on."

Hamilton's eyes flashed around the clearing. "Listen, Matt," he said, suddenly defensive, "you've got no right to drag me out here and start making demands."

"Who's making demands?" I said. "He just wants to know where you're planning on pointing that gun. That's not a reasonable question?"

"It's not that simple." Hamilton's voice was shaking now. He jabbed a finger towards Reeve. "And you know it's not!"

Luke shot me a warning look, and part of me knew that I should probably listen to him. But we'd been dealing with blind, useless townspeople since forever, and I wasn't about to let this one go without a fight.

"You want simple?" I said. "In less than two weeks, the Co-operative will wipe out every human being on the planet outside this town. They're going to murder seven billion people. You're either working to stop that from happening, or you're working to *make* it happen. So if you're still having trouble picking a side—"

"They have my daughter!" he shouted.

Luke flinched, glaring at him to keep quiet.

"They have my dad too. You think you're the only one who—?"

"No," said Miller. His voice was low, but it shut down my rant in an instant. "No Jordan, that's not the same." His eyes dropped to the ground, like he needed a minute to gather himself. Then he looked up at Reeve. "You haven't told them about the loyalty room?"

"The what?" Luke asked.

"The old staff cafeteria," said Hamilton. "In the Shackleton Building. Every security officer has a family member in there. As long as we're completely obedient to the Co-operative, they're well treated. Better than everyone else. Real beds, double food rations… But if we put *one foot* out of line, they get…"

"They get hurt," I finished, guilt surging up.

"Shackleton came to each of us – one at a time," said Hamilton, starting to break down now. "He – he described *exactly* what he would do to Lauren if I ever disobeyed an order."

My mind sparked with a thousand nightmarish

images. I'd been dealing with Shackleton long enough to know that he didn't waste time on empty threats. "I'm sorry," I said.

Hamilton didn't even look at me. He turned away, heading towards the path into town.

"Ethan…" said Miller half-heartedly.

He kept walking. Reeve dashed forward and caught him by the arm. "Ethan, just wait a minute."

"No." Hamilton whirled around, pulling free. "No. You can't ask me to choose between saving the world and saving my daughter. You can't."

"I don't like it any more than you do," said Reeve. "But Jordan's right. You're *already* choosing. We all are."

Hamilton just shook his head, refusing to hear it. He walked away again, and this time Reeve let him go.

Chapter 8

Saturday 1 August
12 days

"Sorry," I said, finally breaking the silence as Luke and I tracked back to the Vattel Complex alone. "I shouldn't have got fired up like that. He was twitchy enough already without me blowing up at him."

"Do you really think it would have made any difference?" said Luke, craning his neck to watch out for security. "I mean, yeah, maybe you could have been a bit more diplomatic or whatever, but it's not like you said anything that wasn't true."

"Mm," I said, still mad at myself, mad at Hamilton, mad at myself for being mad at Hamilton.

Really, it was Reeve I should have been apologizing to, but he and Tank had already gone back to the cave hide-out. Reeve's whole operation was set up to run from there, and he said it would be a while before he could safely shift things down to the Complex.

I sort of wished we were going with him. He might be sleeping in the cold and struggling to recruit anyone over to our side, but at least he was *doing* something. We were going to catch up in a couple of days to compare notes and see if we were any closer to getting into the armoury, but in the meantime, I was back to watching surveillance feeds.

I'd asked Miller to get a message to my dad and Peter's parents. Let them know we were OK. The last time Dad saw me, I was being carried away from him with a pickaxe wound in my gut.

"Here's what I don't get," said Luke. "How can there be all these rumours suddenly floating around town about Tobias, and still no-one knows what it is? Surely someone must have seen something."

"Not if it's up on the restricted level," I said, grateful for the change of subject. "That's the one place left in town that even security don't know about. Reeve's right: if we want to find Tobias, we need to find a way to ge— *EEUUGH!*"

I collapsed forward, slamming into the undergrowth like someone had shoved me over. My arms rushed to my stomach, and I swear I could *feel* it churning underneath my clothes.

"Crap," said Luke, crouching beside me, hands resting hesitantly on my side.

Not just my imagination, I thought. I started gagging, chest heaving, as though my body was trying to shove my guts out through my mouth. This was worse. They were definitely getting worse.

"Try to – try to keep your eyes open," said Luke, rolling me on to my side. "Try to focus, OK? See if you can—"

He swore, ducking closer to me as light flickered in the distance. Panic signals fired inside my head, but I couldn't work out what it all meant. Luke drifted in and out of focus above me, his face stretched with panic. I had just enough time to feel him clamp a hand over my mouth before he melted into the darkness and the whole scene folded in on itself.

The hand disappeared, and the light on the other side of my eyelids changed colour.

A cockatoo squawked above my head.

I sat up gingerly in the scraggly undergrowth.

I was alone.

The sky was shot with pink and gold. Sunset. I was still surrounded by bushland. No clues at all about how far I'd shifted this time. It might have been hours or years.

Voices rose up from somewhere off to the south. Not loud, but obviously not trying all that hard to be secretive either. Whoever was speaking obviously didn't think they were in any danger out here.

I was still dizzy. Disoriented.

The voices got closer. My head began to clear, and I realized who was talking a second before he stomped in front of me. It was Mike, smiling and clean and dressed in a school uniform that looked almost new. He studied the crumpled bit of paper in his still five-fingered hands.

"Over here!" he called back into the bushes.

Tank and Cathryn walked into view behind him. Tank was lugging a giant cardboard box. It was stamped and labelled just like the ones Luke and I had taken from the truck.

"This was a bad idea," said Cathryn, picking

97

something out of her stocking, looking extremely unimpressed to be getting this close to nature. A thick coil of rope was weighing down one of her shoulders. *"What if someone catches us out here?"*

"Like who?" Tank taunted. *"Security? Come on. What are they gonna do?"*

"Hurry up and get over here," said Mike. *"We need to find a tree stump."*

"You find a tree stump. You're the one not carrying anything."

"I'm carrying the map," said Mike.

Despite the obvious weirdness of following a note from their overseers out into the bush, there was something impossibly *light* about their conversation. Like this was all just some exciting adventure. This was months ago, back before everything got swallowed up in darkness and the constant threat of death.

The thought dragged me back to reality and my mind rang with the sudden realization of what I'd seen back there in the present. The light was a torch. Someone had heard us. And now Luke was stuck out there, trying to bring me back.

So where was he? What was taking him so long?

Or worse, what if I'd finally slipped out of his reach entirely?

"Found it!" said Mike, darting closer to me. I pressed down into the bushes. If I really *was* here, I didn't want to take chances.

Mike shoved his hand into the tree stump he'd spotted and pulled out an envelope sealed with black wax. A message from the overseers.

"Here," he said, handing the other paper he'd been holding to Cathryn. *"Burn this one."*

Cathryn took a lighter from her skirt pocket and held it to the old note, while Mike tore open the new one. I pushed up from the ground again, trying to get a look at it, but then the bushland was blocked from view as a face flashed into existence, right in front of me. Luke.

"How come she gets to burn everything?" grumbled Tank.

"Because if I let you do it, you'd start a bloody bushfire," said Mike. *"Besides, you've got a box to carry."*

I sat up, reaching for Luke, but my hands sank straight into him like he didn't exist.

"What do the overseers need so many freaking candles

for, anyway?" Tank muttered, pulling my attention away.

"How should I know?" said Mike. *"Not your job to ask questions, man. Just do what you're told."* He looked up from the note in his hand and pointed towards the lake. *"All right. This way."*

The cave, I realized. That was what the candles and the rope were for. We were way back at the beginning. Kara and Soren were luring these guys out to set up their creepy little cult headquarters.

Luke launched himself back into my field of vision. *Jordan!* he snapped silently. *Pay attention!*

"Yeah," I muttered, turning away from Mike and the others again. I held out my arms, trying to focus.

Luke reached for me again. Nothing.

"What about Peter?" Cathryn asked behind me.

"They didn't ask for Peter," said Mike. *"They chose us."*

I tried to tune them out, but part of me kept getting drawn back into the conversation, wanting to know why I was here in the first place.

"No, I mean—" Cathryn began, the lightness vanishing from her voice. *"Why do they keep asking us to find stuff out about Peter? They're acting like he's*

dangerous or something. What if— What if they're going to do something bad to him?"

"You saying you don't trust them?" said Mike.

Luke grabbed at my shoulders like he was trying to shake me. Snap me out of it. His hands dropped through and he almost overbalanced.

"No!" said Cathryn, horrified, like she was sure they could hear her. *"No, I do! I do trust them! But—"*

"You swore an oath, Cat! We all did. We swore that we would die *for them if we had to!"*

Luke jolted, startled, and whirled to look over his shoulder. He turned back, face white. Whoever was out there, they were coming closer.

"Get moving," Mike spat.

"Mate, come on," said Tank. *"Don't be such a—"*

"DO IT!"

Mike set out in the direction of the cave, and the others followed.

I locked eyes with Luke, willing my hands to make contact, furious at myself for putting him in danger. If my stupid curiosity had just got us—

My hands smacked down hard into Luke's arms. I held on tight, pulling him towards me.

"That's it. That's it," he hissed. "Hurry!"

"Hey..." said Tank behind me. *"What the crap is that?"*

I turned around. He was staring right at me.

And then the bile rose up in my throat again and everything collapsed.

And just like last time, the two worlds blurred together. Day and night. Warm and cold. Cathryn and Mike there and gone at the same time. And Tank looking straight through me, almost like I was actually there. I spun my head around, fighting the sick feeling in my gut, trying to take in everything at once. The moment stretched out. I hung there, suspended at both ends. Like time was standing still. Or like it didn't even exist any more.

Then Luke's voice rang in my ear, "Jordan, get back here!" and it all sped up again, the world flaring around me, just random snapshots, like someone was flicking through a slideshow.

I was sitting under a blazing sun, surrounded by knee-high saplings.

I was engulfed in complete darkness.

I was watching the day break over a barren wasteland.

I closed my eyes against the pounding nausea, clinging to Luke, sure it was all that was keeping me alive. And then finally, I was back in the present, mouth clamped shut to keep myself quiet, head throbbing like I'd smashed it into a wall.

"Shh…" Luke breathed, cradling me like a little kid. "Shh…They're almost gone."

I opened my eyes and the world swung slowly into focus. Two bright torch beams cut through the trees. I held my breath. They were pointing away from us, back towards town, but all it would take was one sound…

Slowly, the lights dimmed into the distance. By the time they were gone, I'd got my head back together enough to stand without collapsing or throwing up. Luke held on to me anyway, fingers lacing themselves around mine. I could feel him shaking.

Twice in two days.

Why? Why *now*, with everything else that was going on?

"That was – I thought we were dead," breathed Luke. "Seriously, if they had taken like two more steps…"

"What stopped them?" I asked, moving closer and

resting my arm around him.

"I don't know. I was too busy hanging on to you." He glanced over, like he wasn't sure how much more he wanted to say. "It was worse this time, wasn't it?"

"Yeah," I said. "Wait. Why? Did you see something?"

"No. I don't know. It just scares me, Jordan. It freaks me out that one day you might just – that I might not be able to bring you back."

I shivered, looking up at the stars, wondering for a moment if all of it – everything I was seeing – really was just random. Just chaos. An unguided by-product of an unguided universe that was completely indifferent to everything we were going through down here.

But no, there had to be more to it than that. There had to be more than I was seeing.

All of this might not make sense now, but that didn't mean it wouldn't ever.

A minute or two later, we were stepping through the low, overgrown ruin that marked the entrance to the Vattel Complex. There was a dull rattle as someone downstairs opened the trapdoor, and I glanced around one last time to make sure there was no-one waiting to follow us in.

A thought struck me as we started down the mouldy stairs. "What if those guards had shot you?"

"They didn't," said Luke.

"Yeah, but what if they did? What if you'd, like, jumped up and waved your arms around and got yourself killed back there?"

"That would've been a pretty bad tactical decision."

"You'd be dead," I said.

"Yeah," said Luke, sounding slightly exasperated. "That's why I didn't do it."

"You would have been *shot* dead," I said, lowering my voice as we neared the bottom of the stairs. "Shot. Not stabbed."

"That's not exactly an improvement."

"I know, but you get what I'm saying, right? You could have changed it. You could have changed what we saw on that video. None of it would have happened."

"That's not what Kara says."

I breathed a frustrated sigh. This was not a new conversation. And as far as Kara was concerned, there was only one way this was all going to play out. The way she'd explained it, there was no *last time* and *this time*. It was all one time. All the same. What we'd seen on that video wasn't just *going* to happen, it had *already* happened. It was just as unchangeable as anything else in the past.

"Kara's not a scientist," I said. "She's a doctor."

"Right," said Luke, squinting at the sudden brightness as we walked into the corridor. "Yeah. I hope you're right."

Mum and Mr Hunter were both waiting up for us in the surveillance room, nursing mugs of tea. The teabags sat in a little dish on the table, ready to be dried out and reused.

Mr Hunter came over to meet us. He frowned at the expression on Luke's face. "Everything OK?"

"Yeah," said Luke quickly. "Almost ran into security on the way back, but we're OK."

Mum hoisted herself out of her chair, grunting with the effort. "I can't believe I keep letting you do this."

"I'm fine," I said. "What about you guys? Is everyone else—?"

I jumped back, startled, as I realized for the first time that Amy was in here too. She was sitting in the corner on the edge of the table, staring into space like she was hypnotised.

I walked up to her. "Amy…?"

"Whoa. Hi," she said. "Sorry. I guess I kind of spaced out for a bit there, huh?" She blinked hard and got to her feet. "I think I'm going to go to bed."

I stared after her as she left the room.

"How long was she sitting there?" Luke asked.

"A while," his dad said. "We did ask if she was…" He looked up. "Did you hear that?"

Everyone stopped. For a moment, all I could hear was whirring computers and the buzz of a fluorescent tube flickering in the next room.

Smash!

A noise like a battering ram, violent but far off. It was coming from somewhere in the research module.

"Crap," said Luke, standing over one of the monitors. I joined him just in time to see a cloud of dust billow up into the camera lens.

"Is that…?" asked Mum, behind me.

"Yeah," I said. "Bill's room."

Chapter 9

**Saturday 1 August
12 days**

"Hey!" Peter shouted, as Luke and I sprinted past his door. "HEY! What's going on out there?"

We ignored him. Another explosion of sound echoed up the corridor. Creaking, twisting metal.

"Are you sure we should be running *towards* him?" Luke panted.

"I don't think Bill's going to hurt us," I said. "He needs our help, remember?"

"He put me in the hospital!"

"OK, yeah, but – we'll be careful."

I could see something silhouetted in the dim light, blocking our path up ahead. I slowed as we reached it.

The metal bookcase that had sealed the entrance to

Bill's room was lying on its side, bent in half like it was made of cardboard. It was wedged into the debris at a particularly narrow section of the corridor, forming a makeshift barrier to keep us out.

"Help me move it," I said, gripping the bookcase with both hands. Luke leant in next to me. I dug in with my heels. The bookcase shifted slightly, scraping against the walls, but only seemed to get itself more tightly lodged into the surrounding bits of debris.

"You really want to be doing that?" said Mr Hunter, coming up the corridor behind us.

"No," said Luke.

"Yes," I said.

"OK, fine. Yes."

Mr Hunter shouldered his way in between Luke and me. "OK. Three. Two. One. *Push.*"

The bookcase buckled, angling forward, grinding against the concrete on either side. We pushed again. All at once it came loose, crashing to the ground.

I clambered over and ducked into Bill's room. The dust was clearing by now. Bill's bed had been thrown across the room, and was now lying on its side against the wall. The contents of Kara's medical kit were scattered all over the place. I scanned through the mess, snatching up a sedative pen and the penlight Kara had used to check Bill's eyes. We kept moving, deeper into the research module.

Another, smaller tunnel came up on our left and I almost stopped running again. I'd been down there only once before, into a room stained with Luke's twenty-year-old blood.

"What's wrong?" Mr Hunter asked.

"Nothing," said Luke. "Come on."

More noise up ahead, like someone beating at the walls with a hammer. I flicked on the torch as we left the last of the functioning ceiling lights behind. We barely ever came down this deep. The tunnel pressed in all around us now, the remnants of the old labs almost impossible to pick out in the ocean of concrete. The hammering sound was louder now. Slow, irregular smashing.

"So what's the plan here?" asked Luke.

"I just want to talk to him," I said.

"Yeah, but—"

"He knew about Tabitha!" I said. "He knew about stuff that *no-one* was meant to know! Don't you think we should find out if that includes Tobias?"

The light from behind us had all but faded away, leaving us to navigate by the light of Kara's little torch. I flashed it around at the tunnel walls. Luke and I had spent a whole week mapping this place out, but it was such a labyrinth that I still got lost every time I came down here.

"Hang on a sec," said Luke, pointing past me. "Turn your torch off."

I clicked the button on the penlight, plunging us into total darkness. *Almost* total darkness. A dim light slid across the wall up ahead, in and out of view, like it was coming from around a corner.

"There!" said Luke.

I edged towards the light, leaving the penlight switched off. The tunnel squeezed even tighter for a few metres, then widened out again, opening on to a room that seemed to have escaped the explosion and the concreting almost completely.

It looked like Peter's room had looked back in my vision with Soren's dad and Remi Vattel. Two separate areas, divided by a wall of glass that had long since shattered to the floor.

Bill was up the other end, standing with his back to us, waist-deep in smashed computers and upended tables and chairs, swinging a pickaxe out wide over his shoulder. He had one of Kara and Soren's excavating helmets strapped to his head, which explained the light we'd seen coming in.

Bill slammed the pickaxe down again, sending chips of concrete shooting into the darkness. He let out a wild, animal laugh, like nothing could give him more joy than tearing into that wall.

"Hey Bill," I said, walking slowly towards him. "It's good to see you awake again."

He whirled around, face masked in shadow, spot-lighting us in the beam from his helmet. "You're early."

"Oh," I said. "I'm sorry. We didn't realize—"

"No, no, no, that's *enough!*" said Bill, raising a finger like a parent scolding their kid. "Leave. You are the wrong one. I have *told* you this. You are not right, and you are all *far too early* for my – my purposes." He dropped the pickaxe and put his hands to his head.

"Maybe we should come back later," said Mr Hunter out of the corner of his mouth.

"You told us you needed our help," I said gently,

edging forward again, flicking my torch back on to see him properly. "Remember? Out at the airport. You said you needed Luke and me to—"

"NO!" Bill bellowed, and I had to throw myself out of the way as a computer monitor suddenly leapt from the rubble and flew at me. The monitor smashed to pieces against the back wall, narrowly missing Luke and his dad.

I straightened up again. "Please, Bill. Talk to me. If you explain what you're doing, maybe we can help."

"No, I already—" Bill muttered, hunching over like he was trying to get his head around something. "That's not how it works! I have seen this! You can't— *Argh!*"

He broke off in a rage, fists in the air, stomping the floor. The ground between us started moving.

Something was rising up off the floor. Glass. The shattered dividing wall, thousands of jagged, glimmering shards, lifting into the air to form a deadly barrier between us and Bill.

"Jordan!" said Luke urgently, running up to grab my arm. "Let's *go.*"

"Leave!" Bill shouted, his face fractured and

glinting behind the wall of glass. "Leave me! I will come when you are needed!"

He snatched up the pickaxe. Luke yanked at my arm again, dragging me towards the corridor.

"The time is coming!" Bill raged on. "It is coming! I will come for you!"

Mr Hunter grabbed my other hand. They hauled me into the shadows, a second before Bill fired the shards at the wall, drowning his own shouting in a furious explosion of splintering glass.

Chapter 10

"I want to go back and talk to him again," I said quietly, ducking under a low-hanging branch.

"Jordan…" I could hear Luke switching into voice-of-reason mode. "Do you really think you're going to get anything out of him? I mean, he's made it pretty clear he doesn't want to talk to us."

It was early morning, two days after Bill's breakout. We were heading out past the south end of town to catch up with Reeve. It was a bit of a hike, but we'd made use of the journey to set up another fake campsite in the bush – half-buried rubbish and remnants of a makeshift shelter, just to keep the Co-operative guessing. And beyond that, I think Luke and I were both grateful for an excuse to get outside.

Luke's parents hadn't spoken to each other since last night, when Mr Hunter had tried to intervene in an argument between Ms Hunter and Kara about not hanging up laundry in the kitchen. Luke's mum had been furious at him for "taking that impossible woman's side", and angrier still when he'd refused to keep arguing with her about it. This, apparently, was the same "pig-headed, passive-aggressive crap" that had led her to divorce him in the first place.

Meanwhile, Cathryn had lost it with Georgia again – first for playing on her bed, and then for catching her making a grab at Ms Hunter's kitchen keys – and Mike had taken to sneaking around with his old overseer notebook, trying to eavesdrop on my conversations with Luke. I had a feeling Soren had put him up to it.

Bill was still roaming around in the depths of the Complex, smashing at walls, volatile as ever. It terrified me to think what might happen if he strayed into the living area. But all that didn't excuse us from trying to get answers out of him when there were only ten days left until the end of the world.

Kara was looking for a way to contain him. The

sedative pens might have been an option if we'd had enough cartridges left to put him under and keep him there, but we were running low and had decided it was best to save them in case of an emergency.

Soren, on the other hand, wanted to deal with Bill the same way he wanted to deal with every other inconvenience in his life: by putting a bullet in him. Between him, Bill, Peter and Mike, it was a miracle no-one had got seriously hurt yet.

"I just want to know what Bill's *doing* down there!" I said. "I mean, Kara said there's nothing left to dig up but exploded labs and concrete, so what does he—?"

And then a thought dropped into my head. An explanation, not just for Bill's newfound pickaxe obsession, but for Bill himself.

"What?" said Luke.

"What if he's one of them?" I said.

"One of who?"

"Vattel's people!" I said. "One of her researchers from twenty years ago! What if that's why he's so obsessed with finding something down there? Kara was just their doctor. She wasn't involved in their research. So, what if there was something going on that she didn't know about? Something that could help us. What if—?" I hesitated, stomach jolting. "*I need to go back.*"

Luke's brow furrowed. "Back where?"

"No, that's what Bill said at the airport when we first met him. *I need to go back.* We thought he was talking about going home – going back to wherever he came from on the outside – but what if that *wasn't* what he was saying? What if he was talking about going back to the *Complex?*"

"Then why didn't he just *go* back to the Complex?" said Luke. "Why drag us into it?"

"I don't know! But that's exactly why we need to *talk*—" I cut the sentence short as we came up on a wide dirt path through the bush. The road to the former airport. "Hold on a second."

I crept low through the undergrowth in the direction of town, ignoring Luke's hisses of protest. I stopped at the edge of the bushland, just out of view of the security cameras, and reached into my jeans pocket, pulling out the video camera Luke had given to Georgia. I flipped it open and hit record, panning slowly across the town. Rows of identical houses, all abandoned. And beyond them, the town centre.

My vision blurred with tears but I kept my hand steady, determined to capture as much as I could. I zoomed in, passing over the office complex, the hospital, the Shackleton Building, everything still, dead, eerily quiet, apart from a few security guards out keeping an eye on the emptiness. Even the fenced-off exercise area was deserted this early in the morning.

We could see all this on the security monitors whenever we wanted, but not like this. This was different. Sitting here in the bushes, actually *seeing* it all, knowing Dad was in there, knowing just how close and how far away he was…

I wiped my eyes on the back of my sleeve. We had to get in there.

"What are you *doing?*" Luke whispered, crouching.

I pocketed the camera again, getting hold of myself. "Done. Come on, we should keep moving."

"Jordan … what was that about?" asked Luke, as we backtracked to a safe distance.

"I don't know," I said, rubbing my eyes. "I'm not – I just figure, why wait around until I've got this camera thing completely figured out before I start using it?

I have to believe it's meant to be more than just a toy for Georgia to play with."

"Why?" said Luke. "Why can't it just be a random thing you saw in a vision?"

"Because I saw it *in a vision,* Luke! My brain got *dragged through time* and saw *this* camera. You want to tell me that doesn't mean anything?"

For a second, Luke looked ready to drop it. But then he said, "What do you want it to mean? Kara already gave us an explanation. The fallout. The same thing that's causing Amy's speed and Georgia's mind thing and Peter's – whatever. We *know* why you're having these visions. Why do you need to add—?"

"No, we *don't,*" I said. "We don't know why I'm having visions. We know *how* I'm having them. That's not the same thing."

"What do you think this is? Some, like, higher power controlling your mind? Making you see things?"

"I don't know!" I snapped, caught off-guard by how negative he was being. "But how far do you think we would've got without them? Where did we figure out how to get into Shackleton's tunnels? How to find Kara and Soren? How to open that thing they had Bill trapped in? That was all just random too, was it?"

I realized I'd started speeding up, pulling away from Luke, angry without knowing exactly why, except that I *needed* him to believe me about this, even if I wasn't entirely clear on what I believed myself.

Luke ran to catch up, sidestepping in front of me. "Jordan, look, don't – I'm not saying there isn't something to all this. I'm just saying be careful. You're not the first person in this place to start listening to powers they couldn't see."

"You think this is—?" I clenched my fingers. "So, because Mike was stupid enough to believe in Kara and Soren, that means no-one should believe in anything?"

"I didn't say that. But we've had a pretty solid *vision* of me getting stabbed to death sometime in the next two weeks. So if you're wondering why I'm not more willing to just jump onboard with this…"

Luke trailed off and I felt my anger bleed away. That was what this was about. Of course it was.

"That's different," I said. "That wasn't one of my visions."

"Doesn't feel much different," said Luke.

"It's not going to happen, Luke. We'll change it.

121

We'll find a way."

I could see he wasn't convinced, but he nodded anyway, and we pushed on again. I held on to his hand, focusing on that connection, that physical reminder that we were both still here, keeping each other alive. Even now, with both of my feet firmly in the present, he felt like the only solid thing in the whole world.

We skirted around the south-east corner of town and deeper into the bush, eventually meeting up with one of the bike tracks. We followed it for a kilometre or so, until finally a familiar rock formation loomed in front of us. A giant boulder with a couple of smaller boulders sitting on top of it. We'd met Reeve here once before, the day we first told him about Tabitha.

Luke and I circuited the rock and found him waiting at the same outcropping we'd cowered under, all those weeks ago.

"Hey, kids," said Reeve. "How's this for déjà vu?"

I looked out through the bush. The sun was still rising, light streaking in between the trees. "Least it's not raining this—"

The words died in my throat as Reeve moved out of the shadows and I took in his clothes for the first time. He was wearing the new jumper Miller had brought him from town. I realized I'd seen it before. A hundred times before. Over and over again, on the grainy old video and in the pictures that replayed in a constant loop in my mind. Reeve was wearing the same jumper that Luke had worn in Kara's tape. The jumper Luke was going to be murdered in.

One look at Luke told me he'd seen it too.

Reeve's eyes shifted between the two of us. "Something wrong?"

"No," said Luke.

"All right. Sure," said Reeve, clearly not buying it. Then he smiled. "Your dad says hi."

My head jerked up and I felt the tears pricking my eyes again. "Is he OK? What's—?"

"He's fine. Miller spoke to him. He sends his love to you and your mum and your sister. He – he says he knows he can count on you to keep them safe."

I crashed into Reeve, hugging him, like for a minute Dad was right there in front of me. "Right," he said, patting me on the back, and I realized he was on the verge of tears too. "I'll make sure Miller passes that on to him."

I pulled away, smiling weakly, wiping my eyes dry again. "Thanks. What about your family? Have you heard anything?"

"Yeah," Reeve sniffed, determinedly pulling himself together. "Miller keeps me posted. They're keeping their heads down. Doing as well as anyone. And Katie knows I'm alive now, so that's... That's something."

Luke gave us a minute to gather ourselves, and then said, "So, what's the news? How's the revolution going?"

"Slowly," Reeve admitted. "The boys are all scared. Everyone's waiting for someone else to move first."

"But you've already made the first move," I said. "I mean, you have *some* of the guards onboard, right?"

"We've made a start," said Reeve. "But it's only a start. There are seventy-eight security staff in Phoenix, not including those who are out of action."

"And how many are on our side?" Luke asked.

"Hard to say." Reeve laced his fingers together behind his head. "I reckon there's only about a third of them that are actually *loyal* to the Co-operative. But, like I said before, most of the rest are like Hamilton. Too scared of crossing Shackleton to commit to anything."

"All right," I said, "so where does that leave us? How many could we actually count on in a fight?"

Reeve chewed the inside of his cheek. "Four."

"Four?"

"Like I said, it's going slowly. Miller, Lazarro, Ford and Kirke are all solid. There are others who could go either way when the moment comes, but it's not much to mount a mission on. The guards get six hours a day to sleep, but otherwise they're on duty. Take out the guys posted to other parts of town, and you're still left with something like forty guards awake and on duty in the Shackleton Building at any given time."

"Yeah," I said grimly. We'd come up with a similar number from the surveillance feeds. "So we'll just have to sneak in again, right? Just a couple of us. Get up there and find Tobias. I mean, we've only got ten days left. That's our first priority."

"No," said Reeve, suddenly grave. "It can't be."

"Reeve—"

"Think about it, Jordan. What if you succeed?"

I shook my head. "What are you *talking* about?"

"Let's say it works," Reeve pushed on. "Let's say, somehow, you get in and out of there in one piece.

125

You get Tobias to the release station. You stop Tabitha. What happens next? What do you think Shackleton's going to do with those two thousand prisoners he suddenly doesn't need any more?"

Reeve leant against the rock, letting the answer to that question sink in. Letting my mind fill with images of security officers mowing down the crowd with their rifles, transforming the town hall from a concentration camp to a mass grave.

Luke let out a heavy breath, his expression just as bleak as ours. "What are we supposed to do, then?"

"We need to get to the cafeteria," I said. "That *loyalty room* or whatever you guys call it. If we take away the danger to the guards' families, we take away their loyalty to Shackleton."

"Exactly what we're thinking," said Reeve, digging a hand into his pocket. "Which brings me to the next piece of good news I have for you kids. Miller's done some digging. Managed to get his hands on this." He pulled out a scrap of paper with five numbers scrawled on it.

"What's that?" asked Luke.

"This," Reeve grinned, "is our way into the

armoury. What do you say we go get what we need to end this nightmare?"

Chapter 11

**Monday 3 August
10 days**

I rolled over in the bed, eyes shut, trying to find a position where the mattress springs didn't dig into me so much. It was late now, probably around midnight. I'd been drifting in and out for a couple of hours now, too preoccupied to rest properly.

Finally, we were getting somewhere. After weeks of just treading water, we finally had a solid direction to head in, something that could make a real difference in the fight against Shackleton. Reeve had a couple more meetings up on the surface, and then he and Tank were coming down here tomorrow afternoon to figure out a plan. An *actual* plan, with a beginning, middle and end, which was kind of new territory for us.

I pulled a scratchy blanket over my shoulder, listening to the gentle rhythm of Luke's breathing from the bed next to mine. He finally seemed to have fallen asleep.

Mike, meanwhile, still hadn't come in from the surveillance room. It wasn't like him to sit in there pining for his family. He barely even spoke about them, as though the only way he could cope was to shut them out of his mind altogether. Mostly he sat in the bedroom, drawing in his sketchbook, but even that was a frustration now with his injured hand. The floor under his bed was littered with scrunched-up paper.

I tried not to think about it. But after several minutes of turning it over in my head, I realized I was never going to get to sleep until I'd seen what he was really doing out there.

I sat up, grunting as one of the mattress springs jarred the newly-acquired bruise on my shoulder. I'd picked it up earlier tonight when I'd gone to see Bill and take him some food. Like Luke had predicted, he wasn't interested in talking.

I'd asked him about Tobias. He'd shot me a disdainful look and said that "wasn't his concern".

I'd tried to push the issue, but all I'd got was more indecipherable shouting and another computer monitor thrown at me. Phoenix's healing powers would take care of the bruise soon enough, but right now it was just one more little hassle.

And for what? The one person down here who might give us a chance of finding Tobias, and he was too busy smashing at walls to help us.

I froze in the bedroom doorway, hesitant to let Luke out of my sight. *Let him sleep,* said the rational part of my brain. *You'll be ten metres away.*

I started towards the surveillance room, but then something made me change course and I found myself heading for the other bedroom instead. I eased the door open and peered inside. Georgia was murmuring in her sleep, curled up next to Mum. I thought of Dad, sleeping at gunpoint on a chair in the town hall. Counting on me to keep them safe.

I knew he'd only said it to be encouraging. He wasn't trying to burden me with anything. But he didn't need to. I'd already been carrying that around with me since day one.

"You too?" said a voice in the darkness.

I whirled around, heart pounding, then breathed again as I realized who'd spoken. Amy was sitting up in her bunk, staring into space again.

"Sorry," I whispered. "Did I wake you?"

She waved the question away. "No. I was awake."

Her voice was more controlled than I'd heard it in weeks, almost none of the speeding and slowing that had haunted it since the fallout took hold.

"Are you doing OK?" I asked. "You seem like you've been a bit out of it lately."

Amy smiled. She'd turned to look at me, but it was like she was staring straight through my head and out the other side. I shivered, bringing a hand up to my face to remind myself that I was still here.

"It's funny." She crossed her legs under the blanket, dark hair tumbling over her shoulders. "This thing – whatever's happening to me – you know, I was always so obsessive at school. About everything. My classes, my gymnastics, my music. Just obsessed with *achieving*. And there was never enough time for it. I was like this constant battle, trying to be better, smarter, *faster*."

"Faster."

"I know. Be careful what you wish for, right? But

that's the thing. It's like the fallout gave me exactly what I wanted, but now none of those things even matter any more. And not just because the school's abandoned and the teachers have been captured by terrorists. This speed thing – you all think of it as me being fast. But to me, it's not like that. It's like the whole universe has slowed down. Like my *life* has finally slowed down enough for me to stop and pay attention to the important stuff."

"And what's the important stuff?" I asked.

"I don't know," said Amy, smiling again. "Still working on that one." She tilted her head, sending ripples through her hair. "Anyway, don't you want to go check on her?"

"Check on who?"

"Cathryn. She left ten minutes ago. Usually she'll talk to me, but – anyway, I thought that was why you were here."

My eyes shot to her empty bed. "Wonderful."

Amy started to apologize, but I was already out in the corridor.

Mike and Cathryn, both out of bed. That couldn't be good news. But they'd barely even spoken to each other for over a week, so why the sudden change?

I ducked into the surveillance room. There was Mike, over in a corner, deep in a whispered conversation with Soren. But no Cathryn.

"What do you want?" said Soren, spotting me.

"Where's Cathryn?"

"How should we know?" said Mike.

"But – crap," I said, realizing where she must have gone. I darted back out, racing down the corridor towards Peter's room. Part of me wondered whether I should stay back to figure out what Mike and Soren were up to but, no, Cathryn and Peter were the more immediate problem right now, and unfortunately I couldn't be in two places at once. Not on purpose, anyway.

It wasn't long before I heard voices booming up the passageway. "How many times do you need me to say it, Cat? I can't."

"Yes you *can*," said Cathryn. "You can get up right now and walk out of this room. We'll go together."

"No," said Peter.

I slowed down, just around the corner from Peter's doorway.

"Why are you doing this? Why are you letting them treat you like an animal?" Cathryn's voice was thick with tears. "Come on, Pete. Please. Come with me."

"*No.* Not like this. I'm not leaving her."

My fist clenched against the wall.

"Oh, *honestly*," spat Cathryn, "you think Jordan cares about you? You think she's keeping you locked up in here because she *wants* you or something?"

"As if you would have any idea what—"

"Have you *seen* her and Luke together?"

A surge of heat swelled in my stomach. I strode around the corner, breaking in before this went completely to pieces. "Peter? What's going on?"

They were sitting together on the bed. Cathryn was a wreck. As soon as Peter saw me, he leapt away from her, holding out his hands like he was trying to fend her off. "Get out."

Cathryn spluttered and stood up. "I'm sorry. I'm sorry, OK? I'm trying to help—"

"Get out of here!"

"Look at him!" she screamed, turning on me. "Look what you're doing to him!"

"Cathryn..." I caught her arm as she pushed past, lowering my voice to a whisper. "Not now. Please. I'll talk to you—"

"Don't bother," she said, shoving past me.

Peter watched her go, waiting until her footsteps faded out. "She wanted me to run away," he said. "She wanted me to break out, but I didn't. I stayed."

He sat back down, and I was so tempted to just walk out and shut the door on him. So sick of these blatant attempts to score points with me. But that was always the choice, wasn't it? Stick around and validate it or walk away and risk infuriating him even more.

"Thanks," I said, letting go of the door.

Peter stretched out a hand as I came over. "I won't leave you, Jordan. I'll find a way to bring down the cameras again. I will. And then we'll go out there and get our parents back."

"Yeah," I said, ignoring the hand. "You keep trying." More and more, it seemed like a pointless exercise, but at least it gave him something to do. "Anyway. I should get back to bed."

"Wait." Peter stood up. He took a steadying breath, like he had something important to say, then rested his hands heavily on my arms. "I'm sorry. For all of it. All this – whatever's happening to me. I know I keep stuffing up. I get it. But I'm *trying*, Jordan. You know that, right? You have to let me keep trying. Because if you give up on me…" He swallowed hard, eyes boring into me. "I *need* you, Jordan. I can't do it on my own."

He snaked his hands around my waist. I returned the hug, just for a second, then leant back to release him. Peter leant with me, moving us around. I took a backwards step, felt the cold steel of the bed frame behind my knees, and a second later I was down on the mattress with Peter on top of me.

I twisted under him. "Peter—!"

His mouth came down against mine.

I grabbed him by the shirt, trying to push him away, but he held on, lips working furiously, one hand rubbing up and down my arm and the other moving to my face. His body pressed against me, a writhing, paralysing weight.

Peter's eyes stayed closed, either not noticing or not wanting to notice me fighting to shove him off. I parted my lips to yell at him again, and he took the opportunity to force his tongue into my mouth.

I hesitated just a second and then bit down hard.

Peter screamed into my mouth. He scrambled off me, spitting blood on to the concrete. "*What was that for?*"

"Don't," I said, getting up, shaking with anger, backing out of the room as he approached me again. "Don't touch me."

"Wait! Jordan, no, please—"

I slammed the door on him, leaning against it while I dragged the first barricade over with my foot. I shoved it into the brackets, grabbed the second one, and stood up to find Peter's face filling the gap in the door.

"I'm sorry!" he said. "I thought we were—"

"Go to bed, Peter."

I smashed the barricade down across the door and walked away.

Chapter 12

"All right," said Reeve, sticking the cap on the whiteboard marker in his hand. "That's about it. What do you think?"

We were standing around a cracked marble table down in some old back room of the research module, listening to Reeve outline our way into the armoury. All of us except Mum and Georgia, who were up the other end of the Complex, probably reading some of the "picture books" the two of them had been making in PowerPoint on one of the laptops.

I could tell Mum was torn about it – she wanted to be in on the planning as much as anyone – but the last thing Georgia needed to hear was more talk about guards and guns.

Reeve had been drawing on the table as he went, sketching out a diagram of the armoury. I looked it over again, taking it all in.

Two storeys. Weapons on the ground floor, vehicles on top, with a ramp running up the outside to let them in and out. Four guards on duty at any given time; two inside and two guarding the perimeter.

We were going to break in, grab what we needed, then load it into a few skids (the fire-fighting units Calvin's men used out in the bush), and make a break for it down the second-floor ramp.

"It's a good plan," I said, looking up again. "Good as we're going to get it, anyway."

There were nods from around the table.

"OK, great," Reeve said. "So. Numbers. We've got Kara, Jack and myself as our designated drivers, plus Amy as runner. Luke, Jordan, I'm assuming you guys are in? That gives us six."

"I'm coming," said Soren, speaking up for the first time since we'd started. "And so is Michael."

Mike's head jerked in surprise, but he didn't argue.

"Yeah," said Tank, "me too, boss."

Reeve held up a hand. "No. Too many. Sorry guys, but we can't afford to get slowed down by a crowd."

"Screw that!" said Mike. "If Soren wants to go, he's—"

"Oi!" Tank barked, glaring at him. "You shut up and do what he says."

Mike raised his crippled hand to give Tank the finger, and Tank's anger evaporated. Mike stared at his missing digits, realizing what he'd done. He jerked the hand away, looking sick.

"He's coming," I said, breaking the uncomfortable silence that followed. "Soren's with us."

Luke looked at me like I'd gone insane.

"Trust me," I breathed. I didn't *want* Soren to come with us, but something told me leaving him and Mike down here together was an even worse idea. Better to split them up. "Soren's coming. But Mike stays."

"Fine," said Soren, stifling the argument halfway out of Mike's mouth.

"What about me, boss?" Tank asked Reeve.

"Stay here," I said, before Reeve could answer. I walked around to his side of the table. "Keep an eye on my mum and my sister. And keep an eye on *them*,"

I said, pointing at Mike and Cathryn. "Make sure no-one goes in to see Peter. And if anyone comes to the entrance, if anyone figures out we're here, you *run,* down into the panic room, and you *hide my family* until we get back."

"Boss?" Tank asked.

Reeve nodded. "Do it."

"OK," said Tank. "I can do that."

I went back to my place at the table, rubbing my eyes with the bases of my palms. Sick of this. It should have been *simple.* Two sides: us and the Co-operative. Was that really so impossible for everyone to get?

"Right," said Reeve. "I reckon that should do it. We'll head out tomorrow arvo. Two o'clock. It'll be a good few hours on foot. Ideally, we'll get there around sunset: dark enough to give us some cover but not so dark we go smashing into trees on the way out."

"Hang on," I said. "What should we be looking for? I mean, what are you actually hoping to find in there?"

"What do you think?" Soren sneered.

"No. This isn't—" I faltered, already regretting the decision to let him come. "We're not starting a militia here. You really think we're going to get Shackleton's men to switch sides by shooting at them?"

"They don't need to switch sides if you've shot them already," said Mike.

"Mike!" said Cathryn, appalled.

"Look," said Reeve, putting both hands down on the table. "We've got a partial idea of what's in there, but nothing even close to a full inventory. Some of these decisions have to wait until we're in there. But, yeah, I'll be looking to pick up rifles, ammunition—"

"And then what?" I said, voice rising to cut him off. "We shoot our way into the Shackleton Building? Murder anyone who gets between us and Tobias?"

Reeve looked me right in the eye. "Is that really what you think of me, Jordan? I don't want this any more than you do. And I'd love to say there'll be a convenient, non-lethal way to deal with the guards we need to deal with, but I just don't know. We may not be able to get out of this without spilling some blood."

"Exactly," said Soren, punching the table. "We need to make them understand that we are serious. We are at war. Collateral damage is an acceptable risk."

Mike nodded in agreement, as though Soren had just delivered some rousing speech. Kara made a kind of disgruntled noise.

"Right," I spat, rounding on Soren. "Yeah, as usual, *other people's* deaths are an acceptable risk to you!"

"What's your solution?" Mike stepped in front of Soren, like he was getting ready to stop a bullet. "Hug it out?"

"*Enough,*" said Luke's dad, pulling the three of us apart. "He's just told you he doesn't know what we're going to find until we get there. Let's survive that step first, OK?"

"Agreed," said Kara. "May I remind you that, even armed with all the weapons we could carry, we would still be hopelessly outnumbered against the Co-operative in a direct assault on the Shackleton Building. This argument remains a pointless exercise until we can deactivate the surveillance network again."

"Fine," I said. "But don't think this is—"

I crashed down into the table.

"Jordan!" Luke rushed over, pushing everyone else out of the way.

I screamed as the vertigo kicked in. The room whirled around me, colours bleeding together. I dropped to my knees, losing my grip on the dusty table, stomach hurtling around inside me, matching the pace of the disintegrating room. I fell back, hearing the shouts, feeling the hands grabbing at my arms and legs, cradling my head.

And then all of it disappeared. I was gone again.

The floor flattened out under me. I lay there gasping, tears streaming from my eyes, until a nearby spluttering sound brought me around.

I wasn't the only one crying in here.

I sat up. The room was gleaming, pristine. The cracks and chips in the marble table had vanished, and it was now surrounded by half a dozen leather chairs. The door was wide open, revealing a brightly lit corridor.

There was another little sniffle, and I realized the sound was coming from underneath the table. I crawled over, reaching to pull one of the chairs aside, but my hand went straight through it. I bent closer to the ground, peering under. It was a girl, maybe five or six years old, face in her hands, long brown hair spilling past her shoulders and down across her lap.

I jumped as another face appeared in my peripheral vision. Luke, here for me already. I turned to look at him, trying to fix my mind on getting back, but my attention kept flickering back to the girl under the table. Even without seeing her face, there was something familiar about her.

A shout echoed in the distance, harsh and guttural. The girl's head snapped up, revealing dark eyes shot with red, and again I could have sworn that I'd seen her before. She cringed and buried her face again. Someone out there was badly hurt.

Luke was still reaching for me. Reaching through me. I reached back, catching fistfuls of air – and then crashed straight through Luke's body as a furious explosion shook the room from somewhere up the corridor.

I sprawled across the ground, grazing my hands. The shaking continued, more and more violent, sending chairs toppling over and dust raining down from the ceiling, and a deafening roar rose up in the room, like a horrible dark creature sweeping up the corridor towards us. The little girl screamed, cowering in a ball. It took me a second to realize that I was screaming too.

I fought my way to my knees, grabbing desperately

at Luke's arms and still not making contact. The roar intensified to an impossible, mind-crushing sound – and then the whole room was swept up in a wave of white-hot light. It spewed through the door, blinding, shattering, swallowing everything.

He was gone. *Everything* was gone but that roaring, all-consuming light.

"LUKE!" I screamed, clawing blindly at the air. "Luke! Get me out of here! *Please!*"

Two hands came down around my wrists. I let out a terrified shudder, falling into him, fingernails digging into his skin.

The others flashed into view around me. Reeve, Mike, Soren, Amy, Mr Hunter, silhouetted against the light. Then all of it dissolved again, swirling away like someone had pulled out the plug.

Everything shifted, and I found myself drowning in darkness. It rushed through me, penetrating every part of my body. Luke pulled me towards him, arms wrapping around my back. It all changed again, and I landed back in the meeting room. Remi Vattel was alone at the desk, surrounded by paperwork. She jumped up, knocking her chair over.

And then I was back. Back in the present, still shaking, gagging, face pressed into Luke's chest. Panicked voices broke out around me, adding to the throbbing in my head.

"Get back!" said Luke, face white. "Guys, come on, give her some space!"

Luke's dad stooped over me, and the two of them heaved me to my feet, shuffling me out of the room, tears still streaming down my face. I glanced blurrily at Kara on the way past. She frowned like she was trying to piece something together.

"What was it?" Luke asked when we were out of earshot of everyone else. "What were you screaming at?"

"I was there," I said, still shaking. "I was right in the middle of it. I think I just saw this whole place come down."

Chapter 13

Wednesday 5 August
8 days

"You sure you're OK with this?" I asked Amy, sneaking down the dark corridor ahead of her.

"It's fine. I – oops, sorry," she said, accidentally speeding up and bumping into me again. "It's fine. Good practice for tonight."

I stopped at the first glimpse of light up ahead. "All right. He's up there. Just around the corner."

I turned sideways, letting her past, listening to the *shink – shink – shink* of Bill's pickaxe driving into the wall. I readjusted the rope over my shoulder.

"OK," said Amy, psyching herself up. "OK." She raised her fists in front of her, and I could just make out the dark shapes of the sedative pens clenched in each one.

A rush of footsteps and she was gone. I waited, hoping. Bill let out a howl of rage, and suddenly Amy was right on top of me again, almost knocking me to the ground.

"Sorry, sorry," she panted, the words speeding out of her mouth. "Oh my goodness. That was nuts."

"NO, NO, *NO!*" Bill shouted, charging around like an angry bear if the sporadic flashing of his helmet light was anything to go by. There was a series of loud smashing noises, like he was determined to tear the whole room apart before he went under. "I DON'T HAVE TIME FOR THIS! This is not— This is *unacceptable* – I need … I have to…"

Bill's throat gave out and the torch on his helmet drifted to a standstill.

"Nice work," I whispered, flicking on my own torch and heading down the corridor for a look.

Bill was on his stomach, face pressed into the concrete. He'd made a lot of progress with his excavating since I'd last been in here. There was now a hole in the back wall big enough for a person to climb through, leading into what looked like a whole other room.

I walked past Bill, tiptoeing around him despite the fact that he'd just been pumped with a double shot of sleeping drugs. The empty space on the other side of the wall turned out to be part of another old corridor, blocked up with concrete and junk in both directions. The far side was all gouged and cracked, where Bill had made a start at clearing a path.

What could possibly be down here that was so important to him? If Tobias wasn't his concern, then what was? And why didn't he just *tell* us about it?

I turned back, shrugging the coil of rope off my shoulder. I prodded Bill with my foot to make sure he was really gone, then got down by his side, dragging his arm out from under him.

"Do you, um, need a hand?" asked Amy behind me.

"No, I've got it." I crouched over him, one foot on either side of his body, roping his wrists together behind his back, and then moving down to start on his legs. I looked up. "You get why I have to do this, right? I mean, I know he hasn't come near us since he woke up, but you know what he was like back in town. He's not stable. I can't have him roaming around the place while Mum and Georgia are—"

"Whoa. What the—?"

I swung the torch around. It was Mike.

"I told you not to come down here," I said.

"I heard shouting," said Mike. "Anyway, screw you. Since when did I start taking orders from—?"

I grabbed him by the front of the shirt, dragging him up to me until his face was an inch from mine. "Listen Mike, don't think I haven't considered knocking you out too. But honestly, we can't afford to waste the sedatives on someone whose arse I could kick with my eyes closed. So here's the deal: you go back to Tank right now, and you don't leave his side until we get back."

"And why would I—?"

"Because," I said, twisting his shirt around my fist, "if anything happens while we're gone – if anything happens to my *family* – I'm going give you to Peter. Let him decide what to do with you. You understand me?"

Mike swore at me bitterly, jerking out of my grip.

I bent back down to finish dealing with Bill. "Good."

* * *

The rain came out of nowhere about two hours into our hike to the armoury, pounding through the trees and turning the ground to mud. Reeve said it was a good thing, that the noise of the downpour would disguise our approach. But then, as Luke had pointed out, it would do a pretty good job of disguising anyone who was approaching *us* too.

We trudged on. By the fourth hour, I could barely feel my feet and yet the rain showed no sign of easing up. We'd moved into some particularly sparse bush. A few scattered trees and not much else. I didn't like it. But the sun was setting now, so hopefully the darkness would help hide our escape on the way out.

Reeve was in front, checking our trajectory with a compass. He stopped as we reached the road again, meeting it for the third time that afternoon as it wound itself around and around the town.

"Don't forget to look both ways," he said, scanning for any sign of movement.

We darted over the road.

"Right," said Reeve. "I think that was our last cross. Shouldn't be too far now."

I looked over at Luke, who'd been talking quietly

to his dad for the last few minutes. Mr Hunter was carrying another one of our three rifles. Not because he wanted it, but because it meant Soren couldn't have one. Luke patted his dad on the back and came over to me, rain sticking the shirt down against his front, outlining a body that was really starting to show the strain of being underfed for so long. A body that was going to have a knife plunged into it any day now, if history played out the way it was supposed to.

I shoved the image away as he reached me. "What's up?"

"Sounds like Soren's not too happy with you," said Luke, holding my hand and leaning in to be heard over the rain.

"And?" I said. "When is Soren *ever* happy with me?"

"Mike told him you threatened him."

I rolled my eyes. "Only to make sure he didn't do anything stupid while we were gone. And where does Soren get off, lecturing me on being kind to others?"

I glanced over my shoulder at Soren. He was skulking along behind the rest of us, eyeing the rifle in his mum's hands. It wasn't loaded yet – we were down to Reeve's last two clips – but if things went to plan, it would be soon enough. Kara looked back and waved at Soren to hurry up.

I hadn't asked her yet about the little girl in my vision. I was still trying to work out a way to approach the subject without raising too many questions about how I even knew the girl existed.

"So what are you going to do when he wakes up?" asked Luke. "Bill, I mean."

"He'll still be out when we get back," I said, hoping I was right. "I guess we just wait and see what happens after that. We can always put him under again if we need to."

"Not for long," said Luke. "How many sedative cartridges do we have left?"

"What else was I supposed to do, Luke? Just leave him down there with Mum and Georgia?"

"No, that's not—" He stared at the mud, rain dripping off the end of his nose. "I'm not saying you did the wrong thing. We just need to think about it, that's all."

Reeve threw out a hand, signalling us to stop. A narrow dirt road cut across in front of us. He raised his rifle and then signalled us all to cross.

After about five minutes, the bushland dropped away and an enormous grey warehouse appeared, the same one that Luke, Peter and I had broken into almost three months ago. I slowed down, pulling out Georgia's camera to do a quick pan across the clearing. The warehouse was surrounded by a towering razor-wire fence with padlocked gates at the front to let the delivery trucks in and out. A guard slumped lazily against the wall, barely even bothering to watch the entrance.

"C'mon," said Luke, pulling me away.

"We could get back in there," I said. "I mean, if it comes to it."

"Yeah," said Luke. "Although Mum reckons our supplies should be OK for a week or so. And by then…"

By then, one way or the other, it probably wouldn't matter.

On our last trip to the warehouse, we'd escaped through a hole in the fence and run straight back into the bush, too focused on evading security to wonder if there was anything else out here. But it turned out Reeve was right; the dirt road kept going, and about five hundred metres further up, we came to a second clearing.

The armoury was twice as big as the warehouse. Its walls were plated with a gleaming silver metal that reminded me of the tunnels under the town. Narrow, black-tinted windows dotted the building at regular intervals.

The one positive was the lack of cameras. Reeve said that was because back before the concentration camp, this place was meant to be hidden even from most of security.

The dirt road curved around to the front of the building, dead-ending at the ramp. We crouched in the undergrowth, keeping well back from the edge of the clearing. I grabbed Georgia's camera again. The rain and the trees obstructed my line of sight a bit, but I still had a pretty good view of the front of the building, and down one side. A tall, broad-shouldered security officer stood guard at a huge set of double doors. He looked much more alert than the guy at the warehouse. I guess you took things more seriously when you were guarding explosives instead of groceries.

I glanced sideways at Amy and Reeve, who were

peering out from a fallen tree a little way off. Reeve whispered something to Amy. He pointed down the side of the armoury. Amy nodded. I leant out from my hiding place, trying to see what they were looking at. A second guard had come around the corner. Officer Cook. We'd run into him before.

There was an explosion of wet leaves, and Amy was away. I caught a glimpse of her flitting through the trees, and then she was out of sight.

"All right," said Reeve to the rest of us. "Get ready."

I turned my attention back to Officer Cook just in time to see Amy sprint up behind him, swinging the sedative pen above her head like a dagger. She plunged it into his neck.

Cook whirled around with his rifle and a shot exploded through the bush. Amy screamed, sprinting back into the bush, apparently unhurt. Cook moved to follow her, but the sedative was already starting to kick in. He staggered to the edge of the clearing and fired again.

There was a shout from the other end of the building as the front guard came splashing around. Officer Cook turned to yell something at him, then collapsed into the mud. The other guard slowed, nervous now. He stared out at the bush, weapon raised.

Cook tried to push himself up into a sitting position, but his arms were giving out. He barked at the other guard to help him. The guard backed towards Cook, still not taking his eyes off the edge of the clearing. He took one hand off his weapon to help Cook to his feet.

Amy flew back out into the clearing. The other guard dropped Cook, aiming his rifle again. Too late. Amy blurred behind them, jabbing the guard in the back, and disappeared into the trees again. The guard staggered back, tripping over Officer Cook.

More crashing bushes and splashing feet and Amy was right back on top of us. "Oh my goodness. Oh my goodness. Come on! Hurry!"

She kept moving, out to the front of the building, and the rest of us jumped up and got ready to follow.

There was a keypad next to the entrance. Amy hammered in Reeve's code. The double doors edged slowly apart, trundling away into the walls. Amy leapt back in case anyone decided to come at her from inside.

"*Go!*" said Reeve, vaulting over the fallen tree in front of him. We sprinted into the clearing.

Amy shifted from foot to foot. We must have seemed torturously slow to her. "Hurry! Hur–!"

Another blast of gunfire ripped through the clearing, and she fell to the ground, screaming.

Chapter 14

I spun in a circle, heart hammering. Where were they shooting from?

Soren froze. "Back! Go back!"

"No! Get her inside!" Reeve pointed his rifle up above our heads and any argument from Soren was silenced by another roar of weapons fire.

Then I saw it. An open window on the top level.

"Jordan!" shouted Kara, wrenching my attention away. "Over here! Now!" She was stooped over Amy, stretching out her leg. Kara dug her fingers into an already-tattered patch of Amy's jeans and pulled, ripping them open at the thigh. Amy cried out again, a strained, accelerated sound, way past controlling the speed of her voice. Her right leg was a mess, torn open and glistening with blood. The rain spattered against the wound, trailing pale red streaks across her skin.

Kara tore the jeans down to the ankle and pulled the shredded fabric aside. "Take that off," said Kara, nodding at my jumper. "Give it to me."

I pulled it over my head as Reeve let off another spray of bullets. Amy groaned, clutching her leg.

"Calm down," said Kara, squeezing the worst of the water out of the jumper and knotting it around Amy's leg. "You're going to be fine. Hold still and let me stop the bleeding." She pulled the knot tight and Amy gasped.

I glanced over my shoulder at Luke's dad, who was standing guard at the door, rifle in hand. Luke was with him, staring at Amy with wide eyes. It looked like Soren had already run inside.

"Can you stand?" I asked Amy as I hefted her up.

"I – I don't know," she said. "I think—" She broke off into a shrill scream and slumped down again.

"Here," said Luke's dad, scooping her over his shoulder in a fireman's carry. He ran through the door just as Reeve came racing up behind us.

"Quick as you can, guys," Reeve said, forcing himself to stay calm.

We followed the others inside, and I realized the firing from upstairs had stopped. "Did you…?"

"Hurt him?" said Reeve. "No. Just a warning. Not the best way to start a conversation, but he didn't give me a whole lot of choice."

"Idiot," said Soren, appearing in the doorway with a rifle he'd found inside. "You are here to *end* a conversation, not—"

"Quiet," said Kara tersely, and Soren shut up.

The ground floor of the armoury was one huge, open room divided up by row after row of racks and shelves and storage units. A department store for dictators. Reeve moved to the front of the group and led us down the nearest aisle. "Stay low, everyone."

We passed by racks of rifles like ours, followed by shelves piled with hundreds of boxes of what I assumed was ammunition. Reeve stopped. "Somebody grab some of these."

Luke started piling boxes into the empty bag on his dad's back, careful not to bump Amy, while Kara and Soren stopped to load their weapons. I dug my nails into my bare arms, wanting to go over there and rip the rifle right out of Soren's hands.

"Good," said Reeve, as Luke tugged the zipper closed. "All right, this way."

We moved off again. Kara and Soren stayed back, still stuffing around with their weapons. I hissed at them to hurry up.

Reeve led us down the next aisle, past big stacks of boxes with labels I couldn't make any sense of. Reeve seemed to know what he was looking at though, because he shook his head and said, "No. None of this."

I looked around at the ceiling. According to Reeve, there were two more guards. So what were they—?

Reeve spun around, signalling us all to stop. Kara and Soren scurried to catch up. Reeve put a finger to his lips, and they stopped moving. Amy's ragged, rapid-fire breathing continued for a second longer before she bit down on her fist, holding her breath.

Silence. Almost. All except for the faint footsteps padding on the concrete floor, maybe a couple of aisles over.

"That you, Webb?" Reeve called out.

No answer. The footsteps stopped.

"Yeah, I thought so," said Reeve grimly. He raised his voice. "We're not looking for a fight, mate. How about you just sit tight and let us get what we came for?"

Still nothing. Reeve nodded down the aisle and we kept walking. Soren fell back again, muttering something about Reeve giving away our position. He pointed his weapon behind us, ready to open fire on anything that moved.

Down the next aisle, still no guards in sight. Reeve brought us to a stop again alongside a cabinet filled with bricks of grey-white plasticine-looking stuff that I recognized from a hundred different action movies. C-4. Plastic explosives.

Shackleton really had planned for every contingency.

Reeve smashed the cabinet open with the butt of his rifle. "Don't worry," he said, catching the look on my face. "Not going to use it on people. Stick some in my bag, will you?"

Luke eyed Reeve nervously as I piled the bricks into his backpack. "Is that safe?"

"Should be," said Reeve, picking up some other wires and stuff and passing them back to me. "This stuff doesn't detonate on physical impact. You'd need—"

A volley of gunfire cut the conversation short. I looked back to see Soren clutching his rifle with jittery fingers and Officer Webb ducking for cover at the end of the aisle.

"Stay back!" Soren yelled. "Next time, I will not miss!"

"You really want to do this, Webb?" called Reeve, shooing us all away to the other end.

"You shouldn't have come here!" said Webb. "You know we have to defend this place."

"She's only sixteen, Webb. The girl you shot—"

"That wasn't me! It was Reynolds!"

"And what about you, mate? Coming up behind us with a—"

"They have my *kid!*"

Soren opened fire again, knocking something loose at Webb's end of the aisle and sending a pile of boxes crashing to the floor.

"Soren!" I snapped.

He glared back at me. "No more talking!"

"Yeah," said Reeve. "He's made up his mind. Come on."

We raced to the end of the aisle. All except Soren, who stayed planted to the spot, aiming another spray of bullets down at Officer Webb.

"Soren!" I yelled again. "Get up here!"

"Jordan," said Reeve from around the corner.

I darted around the end. Reeve was up at the back wall, hefting what looked like a gas canister down into Luke's arms. "I think we've found what we're looking for."

Luke grunted under the weight. Kara had slung her rifle over her back and was lugging a second canister. Reeve brought down a third and handed it to me. "Here."

"What's this?" I asked.

Bits of concrete shot into the air as bullets tore up the ground only a metre or two away from us. We dived for cover, crouching low behind the shelves. I closed my eyes, forcing myself to stop shaking and breathe.

Reeve pointed his rifle towards the ceiling, searching for the source of the gunfire. He shifted around, sights landing on a figure crouched at the top of the emergency stairwell in a far corner. "There you are."

Reeve fired up at him. The other guard – Officer Reynolds, I assumed – stopped shooting and hid.

Luke's dad crouched beside me, still lugging Amy across his shoulders. Her eyes were shut tight, tears streaming down her face. "Where is he?" asked Soren, appearing next to us. "Where is the other guard?"

Reeve ignored him. "Time to get out. Let's head up top. Lift's just a bit further along. Everyone stay low and follow my lead. Ready? *Now.*"

We sprinted along the back wall of the armoury. Somewhere in the middle of our thundering footsteps, I was sure I could hear Officer Webb off to our left, running to catch up.

We reached the lift and I hammered the button until the doors slid open. We piled inside and I turned back to see Officer Webb sprinting up the aisle towards us.

Soren fired at him through the closing doors, drowning the whole world in the sound of it, the force of the weapon knocking him backwards into me. His backpack crunched into my chest and I made a mental note to take it from him as soon as we got back.

Something exploded between us and Webb, detonated by Soren's haphazard gunfire. Flames swelled into the air. Then the doors slid shut, sealing it all away.

"You moron!" I said, as the lift trundled upwards. "You could have—!"

"Up against the sides," Reeve ordered, crouching low and aiming his weapon at the doors. "We've still got Reynolds to worry about."

We all did as we were told, except Soren, who got down next to Reeve, rifle raised. The lift slowed to a stop, and the doors edged open again. Reeve and Soren leapt out, scanning the room. But if Reynolds was there, he wasn't giving himself away just yet.

I crept after them on to another open floor, dimly lit, all laid out with neat rows of security vans, skid units, big chunky things that looked like missile launchers or something, and—

"Whoa – Jordan!" said Luke. "Over there!"

"Yeah," I breathed. "Yeah. I see them."

There were three of them, side by side in the very centre of the room.

Glimmering black helicopters.

Chapter 15

**Thursday 30 May
14 days**

A sudden, reckless hope flared inside me, threatening to cloud out my brain altogether.

"You didn't feel it was worth telling us there were *helicopters* in this facility?" said Kara, spotting a toolkit up against the wall and shoving it between the lift doors with her foot to keep them from closing again.

"Might have mentioned them if I'd known," Reeve whispered, eyes brightening. He started across the floor, sticking close to a row of parked trucks.

I fell into line behind him, one hand slipping from the gas canister in my arms to the little rectangular bulge in my pocket. Georgia's camera.

This was it.

This was what it was for, why I'd been gathering footage all this time. *We were getting out.*

"Look up there!" I said, mind buzzing with nervous energy. The middle third of the ceiling was different. Long, interlocking plates instead of the seamless steel on either side. "That looks like it opens up."

"Sure," said Reeve, stepping out from the last truck in the line. "But we're not talking about driving a car here. Unless one of you has a secret pilot's licence you haven't told me about—"

He reeled back as a guard opened fire from off to our left. Glass shattered above his head, and the whole truck shifted as a bullet blew out one of the tyres. Amy gasped, and Mr Hunter ducked lower, pulling her clear of the windows.

"I can fly them," said Kara. "If those helicopters are open and fuelled, I can fly one of them out."

Luke twisted around, like he thought he'd misheard. "Really?"

"How do you think we came and went before the Co-operative arrived?" she asked.

"You're talking *out* out?" said Reeve. "*Civilization* out?"

I could hardly take it all in. It was too big. I was dizzy, my whole body and brain charged with a kind of wild electricity.

But then another stream of bullets pelted the far side of the truck, dragging me back to earth. Mum and Georgia were waiting back at the Complex. This was no time to get stupid.

Reeve pointed to a big metal box near the choppers. "We're going to make a run for that storage unit. I'll do what I can to keep our mate over there busy. The rest of you, don't stop until you're under cover again. Ready? Three, two, one—"

He leapt out, firing in the direction of the guard. I bolted past, hefting the gas canister up against my chest. I looked left. The guard was out of sight again.

Luke and Kara sprinted along on either side of me. Ten metres to the storage unit. Five.

The guard fired again, his rifle flashing in the corner of my eye. Someone shouted behind me. I dived for cover, the canister crushing against my arm as Luke and Kara dropped to the ground next to me.

"Everyone OK?" panted Luke's dad, lowering Amy to the ground.

"Y-yeah," I said, jumpy with adrenalin. "I think we're—Wait, where's Soren?"

I glanced back to see Reeve tearing towards us, rifle firing with one hand, dragging Soren along with the other. He pulled him down behind the storage unit. "Haven't got time for heroics, mate. If I want backup, I'll ask for it."

"It won't be a pleasant takeoff," said Kara grimly. "That wind might not have seemed like much from the ground, but—"

"We can't go," I said, holding on to one little part of me that was still capable of being pragmatic. "Not all of us. We need to keep fighting here too."

I peered out between the choppers to the skid units, way over on the other side of the building. Only sporadic bits of cover between here and there, and even when we reached the skids, we'd still need to figure out how to open that door at the top of the ramp.

"Right," said Reeve, peeking out around the side of the storage unit again, "we've got work to do. But I don't think Kara should be heading out on her own, either. Someone else needs to go with her. Someone with firsthand—"

"Me," said Soren.

"No," I said. "How about Luke?"

Luke gave me a weary look. "Jordan, don't even— You know I can't."

"Amy then," said Mr Hunter. "Get her to a hospital before—"

"No…" Amy murmured. "Not without my mum and dad."

"Not Amy," said Reeve. "Look, I hate to be cold about this, but she'll heal fine and we're going to need her. We can't afford—"

Another round of gunfire spattered the storage unit behind us. Reeve jumped up and returned fire. The concrete shook with the sound of it.

The guard fired again. Reeve cried out, lurching. He landed on top of me and I felt something warm against my arm.

"No!" Luke shouted.

Reeve rolled off me, landing on his back. Blood dribbled from his side. Kara rushed over to him, but Reeve weakly shoved her away. He winced and pulled the jumper up to reveal a ragged gash at his hip.

"Just – a graze," he grunted, struggling to sit up.

"Reeve, don't – don't move," I said breathlessly, eyes darting in search of the guards. "You shouldn't be—"

I broke off. The blood flow had stopped. As I watched, the wound dried and scabbed over. In a few seconds, he was on his feet like nothing had happened.

"Reynolds is coming around the side," he reported, as I gaped at him. "If we're doing this, we need to do it."

"Dad," said Luke, pulling his eyes away from Reeve. "I think it should be you."

"No," said Mr Hunter. "*No*, Luke. I'm not leaving you out here on your own again."

"You won't be. I'm not on my own. And I don't *want* you to go, you know I don't, but—" He broke off, swearing, as someone opened fire right behind us.

Soren. He was backing away from the storage unit, shooting erratically in Officer Reynolds' direction. Reynolds fired back, but stopped instantly as Soren rolled behind one of the missile launcher things.

"Going to get himself killed," Reeve muttered. Then, to the rest of us: "That security van over there. Ready? Go."

We ran, weaving between the helicopters. Reeve hung back to cover us. Gunfire exploded all around me, but I had no idea where it was coming from. It was all just noise. I didn't stop running until I was around the other side of the van.

Amy moaned again as Luke's dad slammed into the passenger door beside me.

Luke flew after them, breathing hard. "It's – open!"

I saw where he was pointing, risked a look around the van and felt my heart skip a beat. Kara had just tried the door on one of the helicopters. And she was climbing inside.

I couldn't believe they'd left it unlocked like that. But I guess if you keep your secret helicopter inside a secret armoury protected by guards armed with semi-automatic weapons, you probably figure you've got security covered.

Kara jumped out of the chopper again. She did a frantic circuit, yanking a bunch of red plug things out from the engines and exhausts and throwing them aside.

Reeve leant out to lay down some covering fire. He swore under his breath at the sound of bullets tearing through glass. "What in the world is Soren trying to—?"

A giant, echoing groan boomed down from the roof of the armoury. The ceiling was moving, splitting apart. Rain streamed through the gap like a waterfall.

I peered around again. Soren was way over the other side of the armoury, half-hidden in shadow. His hand hovered over a black control panel. He pressed another button and a metallic clattering sound joined the groaning of the roof. At the far end of the room, the door at the top of the ramp had just started rolling open.

"I take it back, kid," Reeve grinned, sticking out a hand to let Soren know where we were. "We'll make time for all the heroics you want."

Chapter 16

Wednesday 5 August
8 days

Soren weaved through the vehicles, firing an occasional burst from his weapon. Then Reynolds must have caught sight of him, because he stopped running and hit the ground behind some machinery.

The rain hammered down louder and louder as the roof split further apart, drenching the concrete behind us, then the top of the van, and then pouring down on our heads. The sky outside was growing dark.

I heard a shout from one of the security guards. And then another noise, something I hadn't heard since the day I got here: the long, high drone of a helicopter powering up.

Over my head, on the far side of the van, I saw the

rotor spring to life, pushing the blades in a slow circle.

I tried to steady myself, but my attention was sucked up completely by the whir of the engine and the spinning of the blades.

Reynolds switched targets, opening fire on the chopper. Reeve shot back, pinning Reynolds down behind wherever he was hiding.

"Dad, please!" Luke shouted over the noise. "It can't just be Kara. Go. People will listen to you."

"Come with me," said Mr Hunter. "They can listen to both of us."

"I can't!"

Luke's dad stepped away from the van, Amy still hanging in his arms. "Why? Why can't you?"

"I have work to do!" he said, voice unsteady. "*Here.* I can't just—"

Thunder cracked the sky overhead, swallowing up the sound of his voice.

"Luke…" I said.

"I'm the only one who can bring you back!" he shouted, and even in the pounding rain I could see that he was crying. He turned back to his dad. "I *have* to stay. I have to."

I shivered, wet fingers slipping on my gas canister. If he stayed here and got himself killed because of me...

Mr Hunter looked sick. He lifted his eyes to the ceiling, rain sliding down on his face. The noise from the chopper was shifting, the high-pitched whining overtaken by the *whump-whump-whump* of the blades. The downdraft swirled around us, like a blizzard to our saturated skin. "All right," he said, sitting Amy down against the van, then shrugging off his backpack and handing it to Luke. "All right. But I'm coming back, OK?" He clutched Luke with both hands. "I'm bringing help. We are *all* getting out of here."

Luke didn't answer. He put his gas canister on the ground and squeezed his father into the same kind of desperate, crushing hug he'd given him when he first arrived here.

I pulled Georgia's camera out one last time, panning the armoury just as Reynolds fired at Soren again. "Here," I said, handing the camera to Mr Hunter. "Take this. Show them what's happening here."

He shoved it into his pocket and turned back to his son. "Hey. Tell your mum..."

But Luke was already bending down to get Amy, staggering under the weight of her and the weight of everything else.

Mr Hunter clapped a hand to my shoulder. "You get him home, Jordan. Keep each other safe."

"All right," said Reeve, from the front of the van. "Count of three, you run to the chopper. I'll keep Reynolds off. One. Two—"

Mr Hunter ran. Reeve leaned out around the corner and fired again. Luke hovered on the spot for a few seconds, then put Amy down again and dashed forward to see what was going on. Reeve stuck a hand out to block him. "Don't. He's OK. He made it."

Luke slumped back against the van, then jolted upright again at another flash of gunfire. Soren was sprinting towards us from out beyond the choppers.

"Time to go," said Reeve, ejecting the ammunition clip from his rifle and smacking in a new one. He hoisted Amy up off the ground and handed her back to Luke. "Gonna do all the rest in one shot. Load those skids and get down that ramp." He picked up Luke's gas canister and tucked it under his arm. "GO!"

Gunfire exploded behind us the second we were

out from the van. Reeve fired back, but only for a second. He let go of the trigger, shouting something behind me, but my ears were still ringing from the noise of the rifle. We kept running, deafened and shivering, buffeted by the wind from the chopper, and a few metres later we were out of the rain again, back under the cover of the roof. Almost there.

I glanced over my shoulder and saw the chopper lifting up into the air. For one tiny moment, I felt my heart lift with it. And then I realized Reeve wasn't with us any more.

He was running back to the chopper. Back to Soren, who was standing there in the rain, completely exposed. Soren turned in a circle, hands to the sky, screaming up at his mother. "No! No! Take me with you!"

"Soren, *get over here!*" Reeve roared, crouching behind the van. "You want to get yourself killed?"

Luke and I kept moving, closing the last ten metres to the skid units. I dumped my gas canister in the back cage of the nearest one, shifting the fire-fighting gear aside to make room, then gave Luke a hand lowering Amy in with it.

Reynolds fired his rifle and I almost dropped her. But he wasn't aiming at anyone on the ground. He was targeting the helicopter.

Someone in the helicopter fired back.

The shooting silenced Soren for only a couple of seconds before he started shouting at his mum again. Wild, desperate nonsense on an almost Crazy Bill level. He was melting down. Losing it completely.

His whole life, Soren had never been separated from his mother for more than a couple of hours. She'd been his only family, his only friend, his only *anything*. And now she was leaving him.

Reeve dropped Luke's gas canister and bolted out from the van. He grabbed Soren from behind, spun him around and smacked him across the face, yelling at him to shut up and get it together. The chopper kept rising, swaying erratically in the wind.

Reeve threw his free hand out past Soren, firing his rifle again.

And then more gunfire, much closer this time, shredding the concrete at my feet. Officer Webb was taking aim at us from the top of the stairwell. His hands were shaking on his gun, attention flitting from us to the chopper. My stomach lurched at the thought of what Shackleton would do to these guys when he learned they'd let a helicopter escape.

I ducked between our skid unit and the one next to it, crawling past the massive tyres to the driver's seat. The skids only had one seat up front, but there were platforms around the cage where other people could ride standing up.

I peered under the line of skid units and saw Webb's legs dashing across the floor. I couldn't work out whether he was coming after us or the helicopter, and I don't think he knew either.

"Quick!" I climbed into the driver's seat. "Hop on!"

"You don't know how to drive!" hissed Luke, but he was already clambering into the cage with Amy.

The key was in the ignition, and the set-up looked pretty similar to Mum and Dad's car back home. Steering wheel. Accelerator. Brake. I could do this.

"*Go!*" Reeve shouted behind me. "*Go, go, go!*"

He'd finally got Soren away from the helicopter and was dragging him, still screaming, to catch up with us.

I turned the key. The skid unit roared to life and started rolling forward. I stomped my foot down on one of the pedals, which turned out to be the brake, and the skid ground to a stop.

Webb fired again and Luke cried out behind me.

"Luke!" I yelled.

"No, I'm fine! I'm fine! Just go! Hurry!"

I hit the other pedal. The skid jerked forward. We hurtled straight for the back wall, and I spun the wheel just in time to avoid a collision. Too far. The skid hurtled around, heading almost directly back the way we'd come. Luke cried out and I heard the cage rattle behind me as he fought to keep Amy steady.

I caught a glimpse of Soren shoving Reeve away as he tried to pull him aboard another skid; the chopper pitching forward, almost catching on the roof; Webb lining up his next shot; Reynolds running towards us. I turned the wheel again, gentler this time, and we veered away at a right angle.

Webb fired. I ducked, swerved, almost fell out of my seat and, miraculously, found myself staring straight down the ramp. We lurched forward, speeding through the door and into the rain. And even over the storm and the shooting and the noise of the engine, I could still hear the glorious thumping of the chopper as it floated into the air above the armoury.

We shot down the ramp. I squeezed the steering wheel with both hands, terrified I was going to drift sideways and send us rolling over the edge. But we made it. Off the ramp and onto the dirt road. I glanced back and saw two more skids shooting out of the building behind me. Soren had somehow pulled himself together enough to drive on his own.

An exultant laugh escaped my throat. We were all out. Kara and Mr Hunter were clear of the building, clear of the trees, rising into the charcoal sky.

Finally – *finally* – the world was going to know about us. We were going to be OK.

Bright light flashed in the corner of my eye from somewhere in the bush. A rumble echoed out from the source of the light, starting low but quickly getting louder, and a dark shape streaked above our heads.

I had just enough time to register that it was heading straight for the helicopter before the sky was torn apart by a blinding explosion.

Chapter 17

Wednesday 5 August
8 days

I slammed on the brakes and the skid spun to a stop in the mud. Luke was screaming. Raw, gut-wrenching cries. I looked back, expecting to find flaming wreckage raining down behind us, but the explosion had passed and everything was shadowy grey again.

"Keep going!" yelled Reeve.

A fourth skid unit shot out from the top of the ramp. They were coming after us. Soren zoomed past me, screaming and screaming but still streaking forward, like he'd forgotten he was in control of his skid. I hit the accelerator again.

"NO!" Luke gasped behind me. "Go back! You have to go back!"

"For *what?*" I said desperately, heart plummeting from my chest. "There's nothing we can—" I swerved again, narrowly avoiding a tree as we sped up the muddy track, back to the main road, right behind Reeve. "Wait. Do you hear that?"

I strained my ears, trying to tune out the rain and the skids, making sure it wasn't my imagination. But no, I could still hear it. Fainter now, but definitely there. The helicopter was still flying.

Back in the cage, Luke let out a kind of coughing sob. He'd heard it too.

But I had no time for feeling relieved right now. I glanced down at my hands and realized there were mirrors on either side of the steering wheel, reflecting what was behind me. Officer Webb was right on my tail, leaning forward in his seat, close enough for me to see the look of terrified determination on his face. Reynolds stood on one of the platforms at the back.

I floored the accelerator, knuckles white against the steering wheel, more or less OK as long as the path was there. But sooner or later, I was going to have to pull off into the bush, and then things were really going to get interesting.

Another dark blur rocketed past above our heads, lighting up the sky as it exploded.

"He'll be OK!" I said, not needing to see Luke's face to guess at his expression. "If they dodged one of them—"

I coughed, catching a mouthful of dirty water as Reeve's skid hit a dip in the path in front of us. I splashed through after him, wiping my eyes clear with the back of my hand.

I glanced at the mirrors again. Security were still coming. They'd gained another couple of metres on us. Officer Reynolds was leaning out the cage, hanging on with one hand, aiming his rifle with the other.

"Turn!" Luke shouted. "Get off the road!"

It was all too fast. The trees blurred past us on both sides. There was no way I could turn off without smashing the skid into a ball. Not until the bush thinned out.

"I can't!" I said. "Do something!"

"What am I supposed to—?"

Reynolds fired his rifle. I swerved again. There was a *crunch* and a snapping of branches as I drifted too close to the side of the road. The skid shuddered horribly, spinning its wheels, and then jolted forward again.

Another burst of brilliant light flashed overhead. I couldn't hear the chopper any more, but that didn't mean much with everything else that was going on.

I felt the skid tip slightly as Luke started moving around in the back. "OK – OK – just go straight for a second."

"That's what I've been trying to do!"

I checked the mirrors again and saw Reynolds lining up another shot.

Luke grunted, lifting something. Whatever it was clattered against the back of the cage. There was a dull, wet thud and a jangling of metal behind us and suddenly Webb and Reynolds were skidding into the bushes at the side of the road. We pulled away and I caught the reflection of a giant toolbox lying in the mud.

"Nice one," I said, teeth chattering in the cold. The rain pelted down against my arms, turning my fingers numb. Amy moaned, and I wished we had a blanket or something to put over her.

I squinted through the spray from Reeve's tyres. The landscape had just shifted abruptly, trees falling away from the side of the road. We'd reached the other clearing. The warehouse.

A rifle erupted on the other side of the razor-wire fence and I almost dived out of the driver's seat. Reeve fired back, aiming the rifle up above head height, trying to scare the guards off without actually hurting them.

"What's he doing?" Luke panicked, clambering up behind me.

"It's OK," I said, "he's not—"

"No, what's *Soren* doing?"

Soren had made it to the far end of the warehouse. Despite his meltdown, he was somehow managing to keep his skid in one piece. He peeled off the road, sending his skid hurtling down the narrow gap between the fence and the edge of the clearing. Reeve's skid plunged in after him.

"Slow down!" said Luke.

"What?"

"When you turn, you're meant to slow—"

I spun the wheel hard to the left, foot shifting to the brake pedal. We slid across the wet grass, spraying mud, and crunched sideways into a tree. Amy gasped in pain.

"Sorry, sorry, sorry!" I said, hitting the accelerator again. We surged straight over the gap, colliding with the fence on the other side.

Luke shouted behind me. "JORD—!"

Gunfire roared in my ears, tearing into the cage behind me. My left mirror exploded and disappeared. I pumped the accelerator. The skid shuddered, still scraping against the fence. The guard fired again. I twisted the wheel to the right and the skid finally broke free.

"You guys OK?" I called back, gunning it after Reeve, who'd slowed down at the warehouse to wait for us.

"Yeah," said Luke. "I think so."

I could still hear the guard splashing through the mud on the other side of the fence. He shouted at us to stop and give ourselves up. Yeah, right.

Reeve picked up the pace again as we approached. Into the bush. I followed after him, scanning frantically for a safe path through the trees. Soren was way up ahead by now, almost out of sight.

I felt like I was getting the hang of the steering now, as long as there were no more sharp corners, anyway. The skids were definitely at home out here.

Their oversized wheels tore through the undergrowth like it was nothing. I was just starting to think that I could get this thing home without any more disasters when I heard the growl of another engine.

Webb and Reynolds. Still coming.

I looked into the bush, searching for the source of the noise, taking my eyes off the path for just a second too long.

A boulder loomed out of nowhere. I heaved at the steering wheel, pulling us away to the right, but it wasn't enough. The skid's left wheel ran up over the rock, tipping us sideways. There was an awful sliding and crashing from the cage as everything – and everyone – rolled to one side.

The shifting weight was enough to bring the skid over completely. We hit the ground and I was flung out of my seat, ribs smashing against something sharp in the mud. Amy screamed in pain.

Another skid roared up in front of us. Reeve jumped out of the driver's seat and came over to pull me up. I steadied myself against the closest tree. Luke was already back on his feet. He bent down, trying to help Amy who was crying on the ground, but he couldn't lift her. It looked like he'd sprained an ankle or something.

"Get in," said Reeve, pointing Luke towards the upright skid. "I've got her."

Luke left Reeve to it. I saw a gas canister lying in the mud and hobbled over to grab it, battered arms protesting as I hefted it into the air. I dumped the canister in the back of Reeve's skid and jumped in after it. Reeve lowered Amy on top of me, and then helped Luke over the side of the cage.

The guards' skid raced closer, coming at us from the side, near enough for me to see Reynolds lining us up with his rifle.

Reeve jumped into the drivers" seat as Reynolds fired.

"GO!" said Luke. "What are you waiting—?"

Reeve whipped his weapon around and shot back. The guards' skid shuddered, throwing Reynolds to the ground as the front tyres blasted apart.

Officer Webb hit the brakes, bringing the skid to a stop only a few metres away from us. He threw his hands into the air, the rain pasting his blond hair to the sides of his face. "I'm sorry! I'm sorry! Please don't—"

He shrieked and leapt from the skid as Reeve shot out the other two tyres.

"I'm not going to hurt you, mate," said Reeve, lowering the rifle. "We're the ones trying to *stop* the bloodshed. Might be a good idea for you to remember that."

He pushed the accelerator, driving us away into the night.

Chapter 18

"It must have been some kind of automated defence system," said Reeve, shifting his grip on Amy and scanning around us one last time as the entrance to the Vattel Complex rolled open at our feet. "To take out anything that might fly over and spot us. I'm so sorry, mate. I had no idea."

"Yeah," Luke croaked, limping down the steps. "Not your fault."

We'd left the skid out in the bush at a safe distance, and made the last leg here on foot. The rain was still coming down. Not that we could get any wetter or colder at this point.

I gazed down into the tunnel, eyes barely focusing.

I needed to rest. *Not yet,* I told myself. Not until I'd made sure everyone else was safe.

"We *know* they dodged the first one," I told Luke, coming down behind him. "They have to have dodged the rest."

Luke made a kind of noncommittal noise.

"She's right," Reeve grunted, struggling a bit on the stairs under Amy's weight. "That was one of *his* choppers. You don't think Shackleton's got a way of dealing with his own defence system?"

I couldn't tell if he honestly believed what he was saying or if he was just trying to make Luke feel better, but I was grateful for the effort either way.

Mum and Ms Hunter rushed to meet us at the bottom of the stairs. Mum gaped at Amy, at the bloodied mess of my jumper hanging from her leg. "Are you OK? Where are the others?"

"Where's Soren?" I asked, following Reeve as he headed for the laboratory. "He needs to patch Amy up."

Luke's mum pursed her lips. "He's not with you?"

"We got separated on the way out," said Reeve. "He was ahead of us, though. He should've beaten us back."

We pushed through the surveillance room, past Mike and Tank, who jumped up and followed us into the lab.

"What about your dad?" Ms Hunter demanded, trailing behind us. "And Kara? Are they with him?"

Luke turned around to face her, threatening to fall apart again. "They're gone."

"Gone. Luke – what are you saying?" She held him with both hands, just like his dad had done before he left.

"There were helicopters at the armoury," I explained, helping Reeve lower Amy on to one of the beds. "They took one of them—"

"They got out?" said Tank, lighting up.

Mum's mouth fell open. She closed it again at the look on my face. There was a long silence.

"We're not sure," said Reeve, looking Amy over. "They triggered some kind of automated weapons system on the way out. They survived the first shot. We didn't see what happened after that." Amy winced as Reeve loosened the jumper around her leg. He looked back at Mum and Ms Hunter. "Don't suppose either of you have any medical experience?"

Ms Hunter shook her head. She dragged Luke towards her, hugging him, looking like she might start crying herself.

"No," said Mum. Her hands rested absently on her stomach, and I realized the full weight of the words. That baby was coming any day now, and we'd just lost our only doctor.

"Not much more than a scratch, anyway," said Reeve, peeling back the fabric from the mangled flesh of Amy's thigh. "I'll just have to sort you out myself."

Mum came over and put an arm around me. "My brave girl," she said softly.

I reached up, clasping her hand in mine. "What about you guys? Any drama while we were gone?"

"No, everyone's been behaving themselves."

"Georgia already asleep?"

"About an hour ago," said Mum. "Cathryn turned in not long after."

Luke pulled silently away from his mum and left the room, wincing at his injured ankle.

"Back in a sec," I said, releasing Mum's hand. I went to the boys" room and found Luke dragging his towel down from the end of his bed. He turned to look at me as I came in, but didn't say anything.

"They made it out," I said, putting my arms around him and resting my head on his shoulder.

"You don't know that."

"No. I believe it, though."

Luke didn't answer. He just held on to me, the warmth of his body slowly radiating through all the layers of wet clothes between us. I thought back to the nights we'd spent hiding out from the Co-operative in that abandoned house, just the two of us, taking turns watching each other sleep.

A lot had changed in that week.

Luke lifted his head. "Even if he did get away, chances are I'll be gone by the time he gets back."

"Don't." I leant back, hands slipping to his hips. "Don't even—"

But then a voice cut into the room from out in the hall.

"*No,*" Cathryn was hissing, apparently not asleep after all. "They're back! You need to get out of here."

"Get your bloody hands off me!" yelled a second voice, sending panic jolting through my stomach.

Peter. Out of his room.

I heard the sharp *smack* of a hand against skin and Cathryn stumbled into the doorway, clutching the side of her face. Peter appeared and shoved her out of his way. He froze in the doorway, staring at Luke and me. At Luke's hands *on* me.

And then he was charging at us like a crazed animal. He grabbed Luke's head with both hands, fingers digging into his eyes and mouth, tearing him away from me.

"Peter!" I snatched at the back of his jumper, attempting to hold him back as Luke rolled to the ground, grabbing his ankle and moaning in pain.

Peter twisted around, tearing free.

"HEY!" boomed Reeve from the doorway, Tank right behind him. Reeve's voice had such force behind it that Peter actually stopped and looked up. He eyed the rifle hanging from the strap over Reeve's shoulder.

"You should go back to your room now, Pete," said Tank.

Peter stared down at Luke, dark fury in his eyes. "You *stay away* from her."

"All right, mate," said Reeve, stepping forward, "that'll do." He put a hand on Peter's arm, and I flinched, half expecting Peter to throw him across the room or something.

But whatever else the fallout was doing to Peter, I guess he still had enough reason in him to feel threatened by the presence of a gun in the room. He roared, backing away, hands shaking like he didn't know what to do with them. But he didn't attack again. Reeve and Tank steered him through the door.

I bent down to help Luke to his feet.

"Sorry," said Cathryn, back in the doorway. A tear streaked down the red mark on her face where Peter had hit her. "I didn't – he was so *calm* before. I thought if I just let him out for a little bit—"

"Get out," I snapped.

She sniffed and disappeared, leaving Luke and me alone on the floor.

Chapter 19

**Thursday 6 August
7 days**

"It's about us, isn't it?" said Luke dully, hobbling sideways to get through a particularly narrow section of the passageway out to Bill's excavation site. "That's why Peter's going to do it. He comes after me because he wants me away from you."

I felt my fist tighten on the torch in my hand. "That's such—" I growled in frustration. "How does that even make *sense*? Even to *Peter*?"

"I think we left sense behind a long time ago," Luke said. "I mean, even *before* all this fallout stuff started, he was pretty obsessed with keeping you to himself."

"When have I *ever* given him any reason to think that I was—?"

"You haven't. You didn't need to." He kept his voice steady enough but I could hear how shaken up he was.

We were down to our last week. Down to *his* last week. And, whether Luke's dad had made it out or not, losing him again hadn't exactly improved Luke's outlook on life.

I took a breath. "There has to be more to it. Surely. You did not come all the way out here and go through all this crap just to get killed over some stupid thing about a girl!"

"Trust me, I'm totally open to suggestions on how to stop that from happening." He sighed. "Hopefully Cathryn's learnt her lesson about letting him out of his room, at least."

Tank had spent all last night apologizing for letting Cathryn out of his sight. But the funny thing was that the apologies weren't directed at Luke or me. They were directed at Reeve. As if Tank's biggest regret in all of this was letting *him* down.

The two of them had gone back to the surface this morning. Reeve wanted to see if he could use our newfound weapons supply to leverage some more support from security before we started planning our attack on the Shackleton Building.

Not that there *could* be an attack on the Shackleton Building as long as that surveillance network was still online. Whatever we might have achieved by going to the armoury last night, it was worthless without a way to bring down the cameras.

I lowered my torch as we got closer to the end of the passageway, listening for any sign of movement. According to our previous experience with the sedatives, Bill *should* still be unconscious on the ground, but there was every chance the usual rules didn't apply.

Everything was silent. I moved forward again, feeling for the auto-injector pen in my pocket loaded up with Kara's last sedative cartridge. Just in case.

I would've breathed slightly easier if it was Amy wielding the pen instead of me. But given she'd already taken a bullet for us in the last twenty-four hours, it seemed like a stretch to ask her back down here.

Like Kara had said back at the armoury, Amy's injuries were nothing too serious. Reeve had put his Co-operative security first-aid training to work, stitching and bandaging her up, and we were hoping the fallout would take care of the rest. Already, she was limping around on her own. Still, she'd gone straight back to bed after breakfast this morning and hadn't gotten up again since.

Soren, meanwhile, had made it back to the Complex about half an hour after us, still a bawling mess and covered in mud from head to toe. Apparently, he'd taken a wrong turn and run off into a ditch. Not surprising, given the mental state he was in.

Mike had gone crazy with relief when Soren reappeared at the entrance, like he couldn't imagine anything worse than not having a violent psycho to run his life. He'd been delivering food and drink to Soren's room all day, and had got into another fight with Ms Hunter after she'd refused to give him Kara's share of the rations as well.

I stopped again at the end of the passageway and shone my torch cautiously around the corner. Bill was right where I'd left him, tied up on the floor with his arms and legs behind his back.

"OK," said Luke, limping behind me, "what now?"

"I want to find out what he's doing down here."

"Didn't you look already, when you knocked him out?"

"Yeah. I want to talk to him," I said. "While he's still tied up. It's been twenty-four hours. The sedative should be wearing off by now."

I felt Luke's hand tense on my shoulder. "You really think him being tied up is going to make any difference?"

"Guess we'll see," I said, walking out and crouching in front of Bill's face.

"He broke out of a prison cell," said Luke, exasperated. "You don't remember that?"

"This is different. He needs us."

"Didn't stop him throwing a computer at your head."

I shone the torch into Bill's face. He grunted, shrinking away from the light.

"Hey," I said gently. "You awake, Bill?"

Bill's eyes snapped open. He rocked from side to side, trying to push himself off the ground, and I saw the anger flare up behind his eyes as he realized he was bound.

"THERE IS NO TIME!" he shouted. "NO TIME FOR THIS! I must – I must be released!"

"I'll untie you," I said, getting up. "I'll let you go,

but I want you to tell me—"

"No, no, no, *NO!*" An invisible force pounded my stomach and I staggered backwards into Luke. "I don't need you! Not yet. You are an obstruction."

"We should go," said Luke.

"What are you trying to do?" I straightened, not ready to back off without an answer. "What are you looking for down here?"

"*Nngh!*" Bill groaned, his face screwed up in concentration. He rolled over on to his side, and I saw the ties begin to loosen all by themselves. "I need to – *Nngh!* Timing is critical for the undertaking to be… to be…"

"What undertaking?" I asked. "Bill, please, does this have something to do with the Co-operative?"

"I don't care about it!" Bill spat. "Not until – not until – no. All things in sequence. Your concern is premature."

"Not until *what?* What are you looking for?" The invisible hands shoved me again, harder this time. Luke's injured ankle rolled under him and he collapsed.

Bill dropped on to his stomach, face contorting again. All at once, the ropes came undone, slithering apart like they were alive. Bill stumbled to his feet, woozy from the sedatives. He gave his hand an angry shake and the last coil of rope fell to the floor. "These two will take me back," he said, switching his helmet light back on. "That is the mandate. But first – first, I need the space. This is critical. Cyclical." He was pacing now, hands clutching his head. "I require the location. It must end the same. Inevitable. Inevitable. It cannot be altered."

"Bill…" I said slowly, wary of interrupting him. "Anything that was down here – it all got destroyed twenty years ago."

Bill's head snapped up, like he'd only just realized we were still here. "NO!"

He lumbered up to the other end of the room, grabbed his pickaxe, and crawled through the hole he'd made in the back wall. I heard the *shink* of splintering concrete as Bill returned to his excavation.

Friday 7 August
6 days

"Freakin" stupid dumb-arse *morons*," spat Tank. "All of them!" He kicked his chair, sending it skittering across the surveillance room floor. "Don't they get it? Don't they have people *outside* that they care about?"

Reeve sighed. His last round of meetings had not gone well. "Yeah mate, I know it's frustrating," he said, resting a hand on Tank's back, "but you've got to see it from their point of view. Our trip to the armoury hasn't exactly improved Shackleton's mood." He smiled at the rest of us. "And we did pick up *one* piece of useful information while we were away. Word on the street is that we were right about where Shackleton's keeping Tobias. Miller's heard several officers talking about an emergency shutdown mechanism hidden somewhere in the Shackleton Building."

"The restricted level," I said. "Has to be."

Luke frowned. "But security don't know about the restricted level, do they? So where's this information coming from?"

"Hard to say," said Reeve. "But we're hearing lots of voices all saying the same thing, and it seems to tally pretty well with what we've figured out on our own."

"And have these voices said anything about *what* Tobias is?" Luke asked.

"No," Reeve admitted. "Nothing specific, anyway."

He turned to the bench behind him and grabbed the padlock on a big steel box with a red Co-operative logo on the side. A toolbox, like the one Luke had dropped into the path of the security officers. Reeve had gone back to the other skid and retrieved this one for us to use as a weapons locker.

I looked around the surveillance room, which was suddenly feeling extremely empty. Soren and Mike were holed up in Soren's room again. They'd been weirdly quiet all day, especially Mike, who'd skipped breakfast and spent most of the morning sitting alone on his bed. Luke said he'd heard him throwing up in the bathroom last night. I didn't want to think about it. The last thing we needed was some flu or whatever sweeping through this place.

Mum and Georgia were across the hall too, setting up another video camera for Georgia to replace the one I'd given to Luke's dad. Georgia hadn't been too happy with me when she'd found out it was missing.

That left six of us. Reeve, Tank, Cathryn, Amy, Luke and me.

I spaced out for a second as Reeve undid the padlock on the toolbox, distracted by a glimpse of Dad and Mr Weir lining up for lunch on one of the monitors. I knew both of them would jump at the opportunity to help us out, but what chance did they have against a pack of armed security guards?

"Here's what we've got," said Reeve, grabbing my attention back. I got up to join the others, who had already gathered around him (all except Amy, who was staring into space again, bandaged leg propped up in front of her). "There's the ammunition from Jack's bag, plus those few extra clips Jordan confiscated from Soren when he got back. Still only two rifles, though, since the others went up in the chopper."

Reeve moved his hand across to the neat stacks of grey-white bricks at the other end of the box. "Then there's the C-4. We've got enough to do a decent amount of damage, but there's a bit of fiddling around with detonators involved. If we're going to use it, we'll need to get the timing right."

"What about that stuff?" Tank asked, pointing at the gas canister standing up behind the toolbox.

Reeve picked it up, spinning it around to reveal the words *Inhalational Anaesthetic* followed by a bunch of letters and numbers. "Sleeping gas," he said, "or something like it. One of Dr Galton's concoctions."

"Brilliant," Luke muttered. Galton was Shackleton's second-in-command. She was also the person we had to thank for Tabitha.

"How do you know it's one of hers?" I asked.

Reeve turned the canister over again. The words *Sparkbrook Technologies* were stencilled on to the other side, next to a logo with eight black arrows spinning out from a central point.

"Sparkbrook Tech was the company Dr Galton founded before she came to Phoenix," Reeve explained. "I wouldn't be surprised if the whole thing was a front for what they were planning to set up here. Back in the early days, before you kids got here, there were rumours going around that a few of the construction workers who'd helped build this place were called away to take part in some testing. We'd hear stories about— Well, I guess they were more than stories, weren't they?"

I shuddered, mind burning with slow-motion images of a young couple being torn inside out. Sleeping gas wasn't the only thing the Co-operative had been testing.

"Anyway," said Reeve, replacing the canister behind the toolbox, "if we want to get into Shackleton's "loyalty room" and take away security's reason to—"

"Um … guys?" a voice broke in, making me jump. It was Amy, suddenly right behind me. "Should they be doing that?"

I followed her gaze to the row of monitors along the wall and saw movement in the feed of the tunnel entrance.

Soren and Mike had just clambered up on to the surface. Something about Mike's body language made me think he was going to be sick again. Soren twitched around like a cornered bird, checking that the coast was clear. He tugged on Mike's arm, pointing at something, and then the two of them were swallowed up by the bush.

Chapter 20

Friday 7 August
6 days

"Jordan!" Luke panted behind me as I leapt up the steps to the tunnel entrance. "Wait, are you sure this is—?"

He gave up, saving his energy for running. His ankle still wasn't a hundred percent, but he pushed on anyway, determined to keep up.

Reeve had started to follow us too, but I'd told him to stay put. If Soren was about to do something stupid – which was almost a certainty at this point – I wanted to deal with him myself. And if he was going to bring trouble on the Complex, I wanted someone down there who I trusted to take charge.

As soon as my head was above ground level, I scanned the bush and saw Soren and Mike skulking towards the east side of town. I hurried after them, quick as I could without giving myself away.

The rain had stopped since the last time we were up here, but the sky was still a pretty menacing shade of grey. Soren spun around as he ran, weird little pirouettes, as though he was trying to see in every direction at once, far less sure of himself now without Kara. He'd thrown a white lab coat on over his clothes, the one he used to wear when he was playing overseer. Stupid to wear something that bright out here, but I doubted he'd even done it consciously.

After a few minutes, they pulled away to the right, heading south in the direction of the airport road.

I broke into a full run, abandoning the thought of sneaking up on them. Almost instantly, I felt a stitch in my side. I kept running, ignoring the pain, but then my stomach started churning and I realized what was really going on. I let out a groan that was equal parts fear and frustration. *Seriously? Right now?*

Luke called out behind me. My vision blurred, collapsing the bushland, reducing it to liquid. My foot caught on something and I dived into the swirling undergrowth. I rolled on to my side, writhing on the ground, fighting with everything I had not to cry out, sure I was going to just disintegrate completely this time and melt away into the dirt.

But somehow, my body managed to hold itself together. The convulsions finally began to ease and slowly, slowly, the world spun back into place. I lay there, remembering how to breathe again, then opened my eyes and sat up.

The landscape had shifted completely. I was still surrounded by trees, but not the towering, ancient-looking things that filled this place in our time. I was sitting in a vast field of saplings, as though someone had swooped in here overnight and planted a whole forest. Phoenix was nowhere to be seen.

Kara had told us about this. It wasn't just people who'd been affected by the fallout. Before the destruction of the Vattel Complex, this whole area had been nothing but wasteland. The seemingly centuries-old bushland that surrounded Phoenix had all sprung up from nothing in the last two decades.

Which meant that, judging by the shoulder-high growth all around me, I'd probably landed not too long after the Complex went down.

"Why did you bring me here?" asked a girl's voice over my shoulder. *"You know I hate this place."*

I searched for her, standing up to see over the saplings, and found a large, dome-shaped tent only a few metres behind me. An older man and a teenage girl were sitting out the front on folding chairs.

"No, you don't," the man said patiently, pressing his fingertips together, and I felt a chill stab through me as I realized who I was looking at.

It was Shackleton. Maybe ten years younger than he was now, brown hair instead of grey, and dressed in a tan safari shirt instead of his usual jacket and tie, but there was no mistaking the calm, icy malevolence glinting in his eyes.

The girl stared up at the sky, brushing a strand of hair away from her face, and I recognized her as well. She was the girl from the Vattel Complex in my last vision. The one who'd been crying under the table when it all blew up. Older now; maybe my age.

What was she doing with Shackleton? Kara and Soren had never mentioned either of them, so why—?

Then Luke was there in front of me, derailing my train of thought. He was mouthing at me, hands hovering at my arms.

"Seriously, Noah—" the girl began, but Shackleton cut her off.

"Father," he said, the patient tone vanishing from his voice. *"You are to call me 'father.'"*

I leant past Luke to look at them. Luke mouthed a word I'd never heard him use before.

"You're not my real dad," the girl said sulkily.

"I adopted you, did I not?" said Shackleton. *"I took you into my home. That makes me your real father. The past is dead, girl. You would do well to remember that."*

Luke sidestepped in front of me, reaching for me again, and the frustration on his face dragged me back to reality. Soren and Mike were getting away. And I was probably disappearing almost completely by now.

I reached for Luke's hands, fingers passing through his only once before he locked on and took hold of me.

Behind him, Shackleton leant forward and put a hand on the girl's knee. *"And as I have told you before, you do not hate this place. This place has made you who you are."*

"What are you talking about?" The girl jerked her

leg away, suddenly defensive.

"You are a very special girl, Victoria."

Victoria. I stretched up to look over Luke's shoulder, taking in the girl again. Dark brown hair, piercing eyes, slim build, sharp jaw line…

It was Dr Galton.

Luke tightened his grip on my arm, pulling me closer to him. *Come on! Get back here!*

"Wait!" I said. "Just let me—"

But it was too late. The nausea flared up again, and the world of the present crashed into this one. And just like before, I was in both places at once, the sky simultaneously grey and clear, the bushland ancient and new. I could still see Shackleton and Galton, but they were flickering in and out with everything else. I held on, pushing down my gag reflex, trying to catch as much of their conversation as I could before they were gone.

The teenage Dr Galton was looking up at Shackleton like he'd caught her doing something shameful. *"I'm not. Why would you say that? I'm not – I'm just like everyone else."*

"Your body is resilient beyond any normal human

standard," said Shackleton gleefully. *"I can use that."*

Now I felt two kinds of sick. But instead of being appalled by Shackleton's blatant desire to "use" her, Galton looked almost relieved. Like she'd been expecting him to say something else.

"The world is a mess, Victoria," Shackleton continued. *"Humanity has lost its way. It is our job to rectify that. If this place can be used to change others the way it has changed you—"*

Galton's eyes narrowed. *"This is about your Tabitha project."*

I was shaking harder now, leaning into Luke for support. I dropped one of his hands to wrap an arm around my convulsing stomach.

"What are you doing, Noah?" Galton pressed. *"What's this all about?"*

"Patience," said Shackleton. *"That is all a good many years away. For now, I just want to conduct a few—"*

My legs fell away and the campsite disintegrated, along with the rest of the universe. It all spun together, like mixing paint, and I squeezed my eyes shut, clutching Luke's arm, sure I was going to throw up all over him.

Light sparked on the other side of my eyelids and

for a few seconds, I felt rain pouring down across my back. Then everything went dark and I was dry again. The light shifted a few more times, and then everything straightened out again and I felt Luke lowering me to the ground.

"Are you OK?" he asked, completely spooked. "What was going on over there? It was like you didn't want to leave or something."

"Sorry," I said, letting him pull me to my feet. "Did you see where Soren went?"

Luke pointed in the direction they'd been heading when I flashed out. I jogged off again, but slower than before, still recovering from the after-effects of my vision.

"You sure you don't want to stop for a minute?" asked Luke, racing to catch up.

"Why? I'm fine."

"Because," Luke caught my wrist, pulling me back, "Jordan, you were – I don't even – even after I grabbed you this time, it was like you were still stuck back there. Or, I don't know, like you were stuck halfway or something. I could see you, and I could feel you, but – I don't know. You definitely weren't fully here. And then you – you started glowing. Well, not – like, it wasn't bright or anything. But *something* was happening to you. I – I thought I was going to lose you."

"I'm sorry," I said again, trying to ignore the little ripple of anxiety running through me at the idea that I had "glowing" to add to my list of bizarre symptoms. "I was holding on, trying to hear as much as I could. That might have been what did it."

"Holding on?" said Luke. "You can control it?"

"No, not like – I don't know. A little bit." I released Luke's hand and we picked up the pace again.

"What did you see, anyway?" he asked.

"I think I just found out how Shackleton first discovered this place. It was—"

But then I spotted something white through the trees up ahead of us. Soren. I broke into a sprint again. He jerked his head around, seeing me coming, but didn't try to run away. I caught up and found him standing at the edge of the airport road, hands twitching excitedly at his sides.

"You are too late," he said.

"For what?" I demanded. "Where's Mike?"

Soren smiled. "He's coming."

I shoved Soren into a tree. "What are you doing?"

"I am doing what is necessary," said Soren coldly.

A low rumbling noise rose up. Something was coming down the road. I backed into the bush, taking cover behind another tree.

It was a skid unit, zig-zagging all over the road, like the guy behind the wheel had about as much driving experience as I did. Like he was just another fifteen-year-old kid.

"Crap," Luke breathed.

The skid shot past, finally straightening out, and I saw Mike hunched over the wheel, eyes fixed on the path ahead, black hair fluttering out behind him. He'd taken a pair of scissors to the sleeves of his shirt, exposing the black spiral of his overseer tattoo for the whole world to see.

"Where's he going?" I hissed at Soren.

He said nothing.

I started sprinting after the skid.

"Jordan, no!" Luke shouted. "You can't—"

There was a crash of bushes and I heard his footsteps come pounding up the path behind me.

Mike hit the end of the dirt path and kept driving,

out on to the bike track that would take him straight into the town centre. Every second, he pulled further away from us.

I should've stopped at the end of the path. I should've just turned back to the safety of the bush and left Mike to it. But I hammered forward, hesitating for only a moment at the edge of town before sprinting out in full view of the surveillance cameras. Luke shouted another half-hearted protest, but kept following. Back into town for the first time in weeks.

The skid rocketed between two blocks of identical houses, all lifeless and empty, overgrown grass in the front yards.

"MIKE!" I yelled, pounding after him but still losing ground. At the end of the block, the bike track opened up on to the town centre. Mike slowed down just a little bit, glancing off to his right. Further up ahead, the prisoners in the fenced-off exercise area out the front of the Shackleton Building looked up. A few of them ducked for cover. Others shouted out words of encouragement.

I stopped at the end of the block, just short of the town centre, survival instincts finally kicking in.

Security were already pouring out of the Shackleton Building and the security centre, spreading across the street to head us off. Mike veered away to the right.

One of the guards opened fire. I dropped to the ground. The skid kept moving, full throttle again, and the guard dived out of the way.

Mike was heading straight for the security centre.

More gunfire. The skid rattled and shook but somehow kept going, swerving erratically and then resuming its collision course, juddering up the security centre steps and smashing through the front doors.

For a long moment, everything seemed to stop.

The guards held their fire.

The prisoners fell silent, gaping out from behind the fence.

"No…" I breathed, leaping to my feet, realizing what he was about to—

The whole world shook and I was thrown to the ground as the security centre blew apart in a ball of fire.

Chapter 21

"Jordan!"

The voice was muted, distant, like he was yelling underwater.

Fire fell from the sky all around me. Glass shattered as the windows of surrounding buildings gave way. There were shouts, screams, thundering footsteps, all of it muffled by the ringing in my ears and the splitting pain in the back of my head.

Luke swam into view above me and thrust out a blurry hand to drag me up. I swayed, finding my feet, eyes watering at the haze of dust and smoke.

The security centre was a shell, flames towering above what little was left of the roof, spewing inky smoke into the air. The heat was unbearable.

There was a shout from behind the fence and one of the guards fired his rifle into the air. Apparently, a couple of the prisoners had made an escape attempt.

More guards moved in to subdue the crowd, trying to herd them back inside. I craned my neck, looking for my dad, but couldn't see him.

Another wave of security officers came out from the Shackleton Building. A few of them were wearing backpack things with hoses twisting out from the sides, but the rest of the fire-fighting stuff was stored in the security centre. It had all gone up in the explosion. One of the guards turned in our direction, squinting through the smoke.

Luke tugged at my arm. "We need to go."

I staggered again, pressing a hand to my head, and felt the blood seeping through the mess of matted hair.

A security van screeched to a stop in the middle of the street and half a dozen officers piled into the back. The van roared away again, gunning it for the south end of town. Out to the armoury for more gear.

There was an enormous cracking noise and the

guards with the hoses ran for cover as a section of the security centre wall that had somehow survived the initial explosion came toppling down above their heads. For a second, I thought I saw the charred remains of Mike's skid unit lying upside down in the middle of the flames, but then a fresh cloud of dust billowed up, swallowing it all again.

"Jordan," said Luke, putting an arm around my shoulder, steering me away.

"Yeah. OK."

We raced back out to the cover of the bush.

We made it back to the Complex and found Soren heading into the ground just ahead of us. I sprinted down after him, dizziness fading now, the shock of what I'd just witnessed giving way to a cold, dark fury.

Mike was gone.

Dead.

Hysterical screaming echoed up the stairwell. Cathryn. "Stop! Let me *go! Let me GO!*"

"He's— *Oof!*" Tank grunted like he'd been bashed in the stomach. "He's gone, Cat!"

Cathryn kept screaming.

"Jordan!" cried Mum, throwing her arms around me as soon as I reached the bottom of the stairs. We were both knocked sideways as Ms Hunter brushed past to meet Luke.

"I'm fine, I'm fine," I said, disentangling myself and going after Soren. I caught him going into the surveillance room and slammed him against the doorframe with my forearm across his throat. "YOU KILLED HIM!"

Through the crack in the door, I saw Cathryn, half-collapsed and sobbing in Tank's arms. Reeve stood behind them, stony-faced. He'd had friends in that building.

"No," Soren coughed. "I did not kill him. He chose it. Michael gave his life to give us a chance at—"

"His life!" I shouted. "His! Not yours! You sent *him* out there to die because *you*—"

"*Look!*" Soren shoved me off and pushed the door open, storming across to the surveillance computers. "Look at what he died for and tell me it was not worth the sacrifice!"

I stared at the circle of computers. The feeds were gone, replaced by flickering static on every screen.

When the security centre was destroyed, so was the surveillance network.

"You think that changes what you did?" I said. "You think you can justify a murder by—?"

Cathryn let loose another agonized scream and tore herself out of Tank's grip. She charged at Soren, grabbing at his hair. "You killed him!"

Soren shrieked, pulling back, but she dug her nails in, swinging her other hand around and smashing her fist into his nose. He kicked her away and she fell to the ground, sobbing. "You killed him… You killed him…"

Soren brought a hand up his nose, trying to stop the flow of blood. He moved in to kick her again.

"Oi!" barked Reeve, "that's enough." And suddenly he had a rifle trained on Soren's chest. "Touch her again, and we are going to have a serious problem."

"She attacked me!" said Soren, throwing his hands in the air.

Reeve twitched his rifle to the side of the room. "Up against the wall."

"You going to shoot him, boss?" asked Tank.

Reeve didn't answer. He gestured at the wall again

and Soren leant up against it. "Hands behind your head," said Reeve.

"I just handed you the keys to the Shackleton Building!" Soren spat, but he did what Reeve told him.

Reeve's rifle came down between Soren's shoulder blades.

Soren's knees began to buckle. "He was supposed to get out! He was supposed to park the vehicle and—"

"Shut up."

"Reeve…" I said, moving to intervene. I wanted justice for this as much as anyone, but shooting Soren wasn't the solution. More bloodshed wouldn't fix anything.

Reeve turned to Luke, who was standing in the doorway behind me. "Where can we put him?"

"In his room," said Luke. "We'll barricade the door."

Reeve grabbed Soren by the back of his collar and hauled him towards the door. "Get moving."

Luke led them along the corridor. I left Tank with Cathryn and followed, feeling cold all over.

Mike was not a good guy. He was obsessive, ruthless, borderline psychotic. Sometimes not even borderline. We had never been anything but enemies. But he was gone now. And somehow, none of that other stuff made this feel like any less of a waste. Not to mention the guards on duty in the security centre that Mike had taken down with him.

Reeve shoved Soren into his room and held him in the corner long enough for us to drag out a couple of beds to barricade the door with. Soren gave up protesting pretty quickly and sat on his bed, sulking. Luke's mum stood in the corridor, watching, but didn't say anything.

When he was safely sealed away, we returned to the surveillance room and found Cathryn lying on the floor, head resting on Tank's lap.

For a long moment, no-one spoke. No sound except the hum of the computers and Cathryn's muffled, spluttering sobs.

Tank looked up, teary-eyed but stoic. "What now, boss?"

Reeve pulled a chair over and slumped down with his arms on his knees. "This changes things. What those two did was—" He breathed out, gathering himself. "It was inexcusable. But we've just been handed an incredible opportunity." Reeve stood up again. He looked back at the sea of static. "I'm going to need a couple of days to meet with my people. Assuming they're still out there."

"Reeve, we're running out of days," I said.

"Which is exactly why we need to take the time to get this right." Reeve pulled a few clips from the weapons locker and padlocked it shut again. "The price on our heads just went up again. Shackleton's going to be more determined than ever to find us and snuff us out. But Mike just took the Co-operative's eyes out. I don't need to tell you kids how huge that is." Reeve ejected the empty clip from his rifle and slapped in one of the new ones. "Give me two days. Whatever we do next, we need to make it count."

Chapter 22

**Saturday 8 August
5 days**

A nauseating jolt shot through my body and I shuddered awake. It was dark. Everyone else still asleep.

Slowly, I registered the sound of my own breathing, hard and uneasy, like I'd just woken up from a nightmare. I reached up to rub my eyes. My face was slick with sweat. But whatever I'd been dreaming about, I couldn't remember it.

The lights in the bedroom were all off, but I could still make out the shape of Luke's body sprawled on the bed above me.

Wait. Above—?

I was on the floor. I sat up, groggy, feeling like I was missing something important. I hadn't fallen out of bed since I was Georgia's age.

Voices drifted in from over the hall and I got up to investigate, head spinning. I yawned, barely awake, ignoring the weird rumbling in the pit of my stomach. I stumbled through the open door to the surveillance room and gasped at the figure looking up from the circle of computer monitors.

"Kara!"

She didn't answer. She was too busy staring across the room.

Cathryn had just come in from the laboratory. The security feeds were all back online, and she was gazing at them, open-mouthed. *"This is how you watched us…"* she said, taking a hesitant step towards Kara. *"It was just cameras."*

And finally, it clicked. This wasn't happening. Not now. It was a vision. I must have slipped into it in my sleep.

The night we'd brought Cathryn and Mike down here for the first time, we'd dragged Mike straight into the laboratory so Kara could operate on his bullet-shredded hand. He'd passed out on the way downstairs without laying eyes on Kara or Soren. Even after the surgery was done, Cathryn had refused to leave his side, so we'd let her sleep in there on the other bed. Kara and Mr Hunter had taken turns keeping an eye on them so Luke and I could rest.

But now here I was again.

I felt a stab of panic as I finally woke up enough to realize the full danger I was in. Luke was still asleep. There was no-one to come for me.

I glanced out into the hall, thinking about going back to the bedroom, but what was the point? I could scream all I wanted but he still wouldn't hear me. I was too far gone. Too deep into the vision.

"Mike!" Cathryn called back through the door. *"Get in here!"*

A shiver ran up my spine as Mike's terrified voice rang out from the next room. *"No. Not – not until she tells me I can."*

I watched Kara's face shift from resignation to something deeper. And I realized that *this* was the moment. This was when she'd finally started to take it in, to feel some of the weight of the damage she'd done to these guys. *"You may come in, Michael."*

I tried to tune them out and focus in on my own

body – maybe somehow I could get back by myself – but my concentration shattered as Mike stepped out from the laboratory.

He edged slowly, hesitantly, into the room, holding his bandaged hand up against his chest, eyes to the ground like he still thought Kara might strike him down with thunder if he looked at her. His other hand was clenched into a fist, but it wasn't anger. It looked like he was trying to keep himself from shaking.

For a minute, I forgot about trying to get back to the present. I forgot about everything. He was right there. Still standing. No idea that he only had about two weeks left to live.

"Mike!" I shouted, knowing it was pointless but calling out anyway. *"Mike!"*

He stepped straight through me, edging towards Kara. *"That letter,"* he said, still refusing to lift his head. *"That – that was really from you?"*

"Yes," said Kara.

I let out a startled yelp as Luke suddenly appeared between Mike and me, bleary-eyed and frantic.

"Luke!" I said, grabbing at him. "How—?"

"It was a test," said Mike behind him, nodding like

he understood. *"The letter. After what happened out at the lake – after we f-failed you – you had to test us to make sure we were still –"*

"No, Michael." Kara's voice was steady, but I could see tears glinting in her eyes. *"It was not a test. It was the truth. We are not who we claimed to be."*

Luke's hands crashed down against my sides. "– up and get back here!" he shouted.

I sneaked a quick glance over his shoulder. Mike hadn't moved. His fist was still clenched. His head hung there, face hidden in his ragged hair, and all at once it hit me that I had seriously underestimated just how deep Mike's obsession with the overseers had gone.

A tear ran down Kara's cheek. *"Please, Michael. Look at me. There's nothing to be afraid of. It's over."*

But it wasn't over. Not as far as Mike was concerned. He just stood there, shaking his head.

"Jordan!" said Luke, shaking me. "C'mon, *please*—"

"Let me speak to him," said Soren behind me, slinking in from the corridor. He took Mike gently by the arm. Mike flinched, but didn't pull away. *"Let me explain the situation. I believe he will listen to me."*

"NO!" I shouted, struggling under Luke's grip. "No, you filthy piece of crap! Get away from—!"

A tidal wave of nausea slammed into me, knocking the words from my throat. The two timelines blended together again, and Mum and Georgia flickered into view, standing in the same place Kara was sitting in the past. One of them must have heard something and run in to get Luke. They hung there for a moment, horrified, and then the room was dashed to pieces, everything falling apart and me falling apart with it. My insides clenched, like my body was trying to turn itself inside out.

The pieces rushed back together and suddenly there was sunlight streaming down on top of me. I looked up and found myself standing at the bottom of an enormous square hole in the ground. Construction workers milled around me, drilling holes and laying concrete and scooping up the soil with heavy machinery. Building the Vattel Complex.

My knees buckled and I dropped to the ground, bringing Luke down with me. The scene shifted again and I found myself back in the surveillance room. But it wasn't a surveillance room now. Soren's dad and another man I didn't recognize were locked in a heated game of table tennis while more people in Vattel Complex jackets stood around, cheering them on.

They all disappeared in a swirl of colour and then the lights switched off around me. Darkness took over, surging through my body like it had done before, rushing into every part of me but somehow never filling me up. I shuddered, convulsed, nails digging into Luke's skin.

And then it was over. The darkness drained away and the surveillance room slowly took shape around me. The convulsing stopped. My muscles relaxed again. Luke was kneeling over me, chest heaving. He pulled me up into a crushing hug, breath hissing in my ear. I looked over his shoulder and saw Georgia crying behind him.

"Is she OK?" Mum asked desperately. "Jordan, are you—?"

"Yeah," I said, releasing Luke and getting to my feet. "I'm fine. That's not the first time that's happened."

Mum threw her arms around me, squinting as Luke switched the lights on. "Your "fainting spell" out in the meeting room. Emily told me – but it was this, wasn't it? Jordan, what—?"

"Gross!" said Georgia, cutting her off. She'd come over to hug me to, but then stopped herself. "Why are you all dirty?"

"Huh?" I backed off from Mum and looked down at myself.

"See?" said Georgia. "Where did that come from?"

Yeah... I thought, stretching my arms out for a better look. *Good question.*

Every centimetre of my body was caked in a layer of crusty black mud.

Sunday 9 August
4 days

"He believed it," I said, hunched over the surveillance room table with my head in my hands. "All the way to the end, even after everything he'd seen. He still believed in the overseers. He was totally devoted to Soren."

"I guess we're all like that about something," said Amy from her seat in the corner. Her bandage was off, leg almost completely healed.

"Yeah," I sighed. "Well, Mike picked the *wrong* something." I sat up, feeling like pulling my hair out. "But – why did I get the vision *now?* If I was going to see all that, why not show me two days ago when it might have made a difference?"

"Maybe it did make a difference," said Mum, who was slumped back in a chair, watching Georgia drawing with some old crayons we'd found. "Maybe you saw that to help you understand why he did what he did. To help all of us understand."

"Yeah," I said, head dropping down into my hands again. "Maybe."

But there were things I would have liked to understand even more than Mike's death wish. Like what Tobias was, and where the Co-operative was keeping it. And how in the world Luke was going to wind up dead twenty years in the past.

I'd finally explained to Mum about the visions. After last night, I didn't really have a choice. She'd been surprisingly calm about it all, under the circumstances. I guess when you've already got one daughter who can read minds, finding out that the other one sometimes dislodges herself in time is just the icing on the cake.

The door swung open and Luke backed into the room, carrying a tray crammed with bowls of rice.

We were running low again. According to Luke's mum, we had food enough for a few more days. Maybe a bit longer, now that—

I suppressed a shudder, disgusted at myself for the thought that losing some of our number at least meant more food for the rest of us.

In any case, with four days left until Tabitha was released, it wasn't food we were short on. It was time.

Luke went over to Mum, who sat forward and took down a couple of bowls.

"Careful, sweetheart," she said, as Georgia abandoned her drawing and reached up to grab one of them, "that's going to be hot."

I stretched across the table and picked up one of Georgia's crayons. For all we knew, they might once have belonged to Dr Galton.

"Shackleton must have changed Galton's name after the adoption," I said. "Kara and Soren would've worked out who she was ages ago, otherwise."

"Is that normal?" Luke asked, moving around to pass a bowl to Amy. "I mean, you said she was six or

243

something, right? Bit late to be changing someone's name. And if he was going to change it, why not make her a Shackleton?"

I tossed the crayon back into the box. "Something tells me it wasn't the only thing about the adoption that wasn't normal."

I caught myself staring absently at the laptop in front of me, like I was expecting to see my dad wandering around in the static somewhere. We'd left the computers switched on, just in case anything changed, but it looked like Shackleton's surveillance network really was gone for good.

Two days had passed since Reeve went out to get in touch with his people. He'd taken Tank and Cathryn with him, which I think was good for everyone. In fact, with Soren and Peter still locked up in separate rooms and Bill at the other end of the complex, digging, the past couple of days had been surprisingly peaceful, apart from the incident last night.

"But, hang on," said Luke, as his mum walked in with a jug of murky water and some glasses, "what about Galton's crazy mind powers? If the Co-operative's known about her all along, then why were they so surprised when they found out about Bill? Why were they so unprepared when other people started changing? Surely they should've seen it coming."

"Could Galton's abilities be more recent than that?" asked Mum. "What if they didn't appear until she came back here as an adult?"

"Maybe," I said. "Or she might have – I'm not sure. When I saw them talking, it almost seemed like Galton was hiding something from Shackleton. Like maybe *she* knew what she was capable of, but didn't want to tell him."

"There's something else that doesn't make sense," said Ms Hunter. "If Dr Galton lived in this place as child – if she knows where it is – then why hasn't she led them to us already?"

"Galton couldn't have been any older than Georgia when she left here the first time," I said. "I don't know how much she'd even remember."

"Plus, the Co-operative doesn't think this place exists any more," said Luke, sitting down. "They think it was all abandoned and flooded with concrete twenty years ago. That's why they're all up there, searching the bush."

In the last two days, it seemed like Shackleton

had diverted a bunch more resources to scouring the bushland, trying to track us down. We'd seen more than a few guards near the entrance to the Complex. None of them had stopped or shown any sign of suspicion, but I still held my breath every time they crossed the path of Kara and Soren's security camera.

And in the meantime, what was I doing? Babysitting prisoners. Lying in bed, worrying that Peter was going to break out and kill Luke while I slept. Sitting around eating rice while Reeve was out there getting things done.

It wasn't that I didn't trust Reeve. I did. But the waiting was driving me insane. It just didn't feel right. This was *my* fight. I wanted to be *doing* something.

"Tomorrow," said Luke, like he was reading my mind. He leaned in, rubbing my arm. "He's back tomorrow night. We'll come up with a plan. I'm sure you'll get the chance to do all the running and screaming you want."

I shivered at his touch. *Four more days.*

The invasion of the Complex. Mum's baby. Luke's murder. Whatever Bill was digging for. And the end of the world. It was all coming. All of it at once.

Luke was right. I should be saving my strength. Enjoying the peace while it lasted.

If I was looking for a chance to risk my life for the cause, there was going to be no shortage of opportunities in the days to come.

Chapter 23

Monday 10 August
3 days

"We're going to have to bring Soren with us," said Reeve.

"*No*," I said instantly, almost shouting it. "Reeve, he's completely unstable!"

We were back in the conference room. We'd spent the last hour thrashing out our plan to get into the Shackleton Building, which was actually shaping up to be three plans that had to be pulled off all at the same time.

Plan number one involved two of Reeve's guys, Miller and Ford, creating a distraction to keep security busy, and then heading up to the old staff cafeteria – Shackleton's loyalty room – with our sleeping gas. They were going to incapacitate the guards on duty and free the security staff's families – and they were going to film the whole thing.

Meanwhile, the rest of us would be sneaking in the back way: through the secret tunnel underneath the school. While Reeve's guys held the cafeteria, Reeve, Tank and Amy would run their footage down to the audio-visual control centre on the third floor, hijack the P.A. system and the big screen, and let every security officer in the building know we'd just taken away their reason to co-operate with Shackleton.

That left Luke and me with one job: head up to the top floor of the Shackleton Building, find Tobias and get it out to the release station.

It was our last shot, our *only* shot, at taking Shackleton down. It was risky, complicated, and the whole thing was completely reliant on our ability to work together.

No way in the world was I about to let a maniac like Soren come in and derail it all.

"Look," said Reeve, "I know it's not ideal, but—"

"No," I said again. "It's insane. *He's* insane! What could you possibly—?"

"We need someone to get past the security on the

A/V computers and feed through that camera footage," said Reeve. "And they're going to need to do it in a hurry. So unless there's someone else here who knows how to do all that…"

"Peter could do it," said Cathryn.

"Right," I said, "because things went so brilliantly the last time you let him out."

"What do you expect? You want him to be grateful or something? You keep him locked up like a circus animal for a whole freaking month and then he finally gets let out and the first thing he sees is this guy –" Cathryn jabbed a finger at Luke "– with his hands all over the girl he—"

Tank banged his fist down on the table. "Both of you, shut up! We're not talking about Pete. We're talking about Soren."

"Right," said Luke. "No way are we bringing Peter into this. I'm not ecstatic about the Soren option either, but if those are the choices we've got…"

"Jordan, all of this hinges on getting the word out to the guards about their families," said Reeve. "Soren will be with me the whole time. He'll be unarmed. I'll make sure it doesn't get out of hand."

"He goes straight back to his room," I said, admitting defeat. "I don't care if he finds Tobias and saves the world single-handed. As soon as it's over, he goes back to his room and he stays there until it's over. We're not going to forget what he's done."

"Sure, absolutely," said Reeve.

"Wait a minute," said Mum from the other end of the table. She was lower than the rest of us, sitting on a chair that Tank had brought in for her. "What about everyone else in town? I realize we're doing everything we can to convince security to switch sides, but some of the guards will still be loyal to the Co-operative, won't they? Even without the threat to their families."

"True," said Reeve.

"Well, they're not just going to surrender. If we go ahead with this, won't we risk putting everyone else in town in the middle of a fire-fight?"

"I don't think so," Reeve said. "Both sides have a vested interest in keeping the prisoners alive. They'll keep them out of it as much as possible."

The room fell silent. And despite everything, despite Soren, despite the countless other ways this could fall apart, I felt the excitement rising inside me.

This might just work.

"All right," I said. "How soon can we leave?"

"Well, first Miller and Ford need to set up our little distraction out at the mall. That's no small job, and they'll be doing it right under Shackleton's nose. Still, Miller reckons they can get it done within forty-eight hours. We'll move out as soon as they're ready."

"Forty-eight hours?" said Luke. "That's the night before Tabitha is meant to be released! You don't think that's cutting it a bit close?"

"Yeah, mate. I do," said Reeve. "I realize we're down to the wire here but, look, this either works or it doesn't. We're not going to get another chance. This is it, folks. One way or another, this ends here."

Tuesday 11 August
2 days

"How is she?" I asked, hanging the last pair of wet jeans over our makeshift clothesline just as Luke came in. Not that our clothes actually got *clean* any more, but it didn't hurt to wring out the worst of the grime once in a while.

Luke crashed on the couch behind me. "She's freaking out a bit. I mean, this isn't exactly within Mum's comfort zone. She'll be fine, though. She's gone into project-manager mode. She's got a job to do and she'll get it done if it kills her." He smirked. "Still can't believe she put her hand up in the first place, though."

"Yeah," I said, coming over, "no offence to your mum, but I'm hoping this will all be over by then and Mum's baby can be delivered by an actual doctor."

Luke pulled me in for a hug as I sat down next to him. "Pretty sure that's what Mum's hoping for too."

At some point in their lives, Reeve, Mum and Ms Hunter had all taken a trip to the delivery room, and between the three of them, they'd come up with a plan for how Luke's mum was going to deliver the baby if Mum went into labour while we were gone.

Part of the plan involved getting Cathryn to babysit Georgia. I wasn't totally comfortable with *that* arrangement either, but at least it would keep Cathryn away from Peter.

"Two days…" said Luke, shaking his head. "How did that happen?"

I curled my legs up on the couch, snuggling in

closer. "Do you even remember life before this?"

"It's so weird," he said, playing with one of my hands. "Like, four months ago, we were just— Everything was *normal*. I thought Mum and Dad getting divorced was the most traumatic thing that would ever happen to me. And now…"

We sat there for a while, the familiar torn-apart feeling swelling in my stomach. Yet again, my mind returned to Kara's surveillance tape, replaying Luke's twenty-year-old murder in a grainy, black-and-white loop.

It's not going to happen, I told myself. *You're going to stop it. You'll find a way. Even if you have to keep Peter tied up and sealed away until all of this is over…*

But even as my mind started running through ways of keeping Peter and Luke apart, I couldn't escape the feeling that it wasn't going to be that simple. Luke's murder wasn't just a thing in the future. It had already happened. I was fighting to save someone who had *already* died.

Forget about it. Forget what happened before. He's not dead. Not now. Deal with what's in front of you.

And there was Luke, right in front of me. He shifted on the couch, shot a furtive glance out the door, then leant forward, his lips closing softly on mine. His hand brushed my face, fingers slipping into the mess of my hair, and I closed my eyes, arms lacing around his, a tear running down my cheek and over his fingers, and for a moment, all the clutter and chaos in my mind seemed to fade a little.

When we finally broke apart, Luke's face was serious. "Jordan… You know I love you, right?"

I sat bolt upright. "Why? I mean, yes. Yeah, I do. But why are you saying that? Why now, I mean?"

"Because," said Luke, holding my hand, "Jordan, we've got *two days*. I'm running out of time to—"

"No you're *not*," I said. "You're not. Don't talk about it like that."

"Like what?"

"Like it's already over! Like you're just going to die and there's nothing we can do about it."

Luke stared at our interlaced hands. "And what if there *is* nothing we can do about it?"

"I could go down there right now and shoot him through the hole in his door," I said. "That would change everything."

"Could you?" said Luke. "How do you know he

wouldn't throw you across the room with his brain again? Plus, we both know you *wouldn't* do something like that."

"No, I know, but—"

"And what if we *can* change it? If I *don't* go back? Then what? The only reason we even know to look for Tobias is because I went back and told Kara about it. If I don't go back – I mean, if the future changes, won't that mean the past changes too? Won't that mean we never get the warning about Tobias in the first place?"

"I don't know!" I said. "I don't know how it works. None of us do. But I'm not going to let you roll over and die just because some surveillance tape says you have to."

"Listen," said Luke, "I am *more* than happy to avoid the dying part. But I can't just act like that tape doesn't exist. And anyway, you're the one who keeps saying there's a reason for all of this." He took my hand again, his grip almost painful. "What if you're right? If I really am here for some kind of bigger purpose or whatever… then what if this is it? What if this is what I have to do?"

Chapter 24

**Tuesday 11 August
2 days**

I couldn't sleep.

I sat alone in the surveillance room, everything dark except for the grainy glow of static from the monitors. Everyone else had gone to bed hours ago.

I should have been excited. After all this time, we were finally confronting the Co-operative head-on. But all of that was crowded by the screaming dread that churned through my insides every time I thought about—

I stood up, finally coming to a decision. I couldn't do this any more. I wasn't just going to sit around, waiting for Peter to snap. I had to confront him. Make him understand what was going on here.

He's still a person, I told myself, turning to the bank of old computers along the wall to see what Peter was doing before I went charging in. *He's still in there somewhere. There has to be a way to get through to him.*

He was awake, standing in the middle of his room, staring out through the gap in his door.

A face stared back from the other side. Bill.

I raced back to the bedroom, grabbed the sedative pen I'd been holding on to since Kara left, and then ran all the way to Peter's room.

Bill was gone.

"Peter...?" I said hesitantly, approaching the door. The barricades were in place. He should still be—

"Jordan!" Peter's face appeared in the window and my heart skipped a beat. "Hey, listen, I am *so* sorry about before. You know, when we were—" He dragged his hands through his hair. "I shouldn't have – I don't want to do anything you're not comfortable with. I just thought—"

"Peter," I said, biting down on a rush of revulsion. "Why was Bill here? What was he saying to you?"

Peter cocked his head, like he couldn't understand why I was changing the subject. "He was— It didn't really make sense. Like, first it was about a room or something. Something he was looking for—"

"The room he's digging to out there."

"Digging?" said Peter, looking slightly confused. "Yeah, OK. Yeah. He didn't tell me anything about it, though. He was just really set on making sure I knew where it was. And then the rest was like he was trying to warn me about something. "Get back faster." That's what he kept saying. "Get back faster." But then he totally veered off again, like he was arguing with himself. Just, 'inevitable, inevitable,' over and over again."

Inevitable. He'd said it to us as well. That was the last word I wanted to hear right now.

He's insane, I reminded myself. *He's worse than Peter. Don't read into it.*

"Anything else?" I asked.

Peter frowned. "No, that's it. He bolted when he heard you coming."

I stuck Kara's sedative pen into my pocket, hoping Peter hadn't had a chance to spot it.

"Peter—" I paused, steadying myself, realizing I was shaking. "There's something I need to talk to you about. If I come in, will you promise me—?"

"Yeah," he said eagerly. "Of course. We don't have to do anything you don't want to do."

I pulled the barricades away from the door and eased it open. Peter reached out to grab me, then thought better of it and sat down on the bed, looking up expectantly. I brought his chair over and sat on it.

"What did you want to talk about?" he asked, leaning forward to touch my leg.

"You care about me, don't you, Peter?" I said, gently taking his hand and lifting it away again. "You wouldn't do anything you thought was going to hurt me."

Peter's mouth fell open. "No, of course I— How can you even ask that?"

I took another deep breath, forcing my voice to stay even. "A few weeks ago, the day after we broke into the medical centre, Kara and Soren came to Luke and me with an old surveillance video from the day this place was destroyed. We don't know how, but you – you were in that video. You and Luke."

"What do you mean?" said Peter, putting his hand on me again. "They, like, edited us in or something?"

"No. You were *there,* Peter. This thing opened up. Some kind of – I don't know – like a portal, I guess. Luke appeared out of it. And then you came through after him, and you—" I stopped, seeing it all over again. I could feel the tears coming, but I held them off long enough to finish. "You *killed* him, Peter."

Peter didn't respond. If anything I'd said had reached his brain, it didn't register on his face.

"Did you hear me?" I shouted. "I said you killed him! You stabbed Luke through the chest and you left him back there to bleed to death!"

I buried my face in my hands, breath coming in gasps, suddenly overwhelmed with the weight of it all. In a few seconds, I was sobbing openly.

And still, Peter kept silent.

"Please," I said, looking up again, hardly getting the words out. "*Please,* Peter. Don't do it. Don't hurt him. If you really care about me— If you really—"

"Why him?" he asked, voice low.

"What?"

"Why Luke and not me?"

I brushed the tears out of my eyes. "Peter…"

"It's not like you didn't know how I felt," he said

coldly. "Admit it. I had you first. And then Luke came and—"

"That's not how it works!" I said, standing up. "You don't get to call shotgun and then act like you own me!"

"Like it was all me!" Peter jumped up too, eyes flaring. "You think I didn't see how cut you got when you saw Cathryn kissing me, back at school? You think I missed all of your—?"

"All of my *what?* Peter, in case you've forgotten, Cathryn was trying to kidnap you!"

Peter balled up his fists, growling in frustration. The chair I'd been sitting on bounced up and smashed into the wall behind me. *"He's not even supposed to be here!"*

"Stop!" I said, backing off. "Please, just listen to me. Hurting Luke is not going to fix anything!"

"He took you," said Peter, advancing on me. "We were *fine* without him, but he—!"

"No, he didn't!" I shouted. "None of this is his fault! If you want to blame someone, blame me. But if you do anything to him, you can forget about me ever even speaking to you again. Understand me? I will *never*—"

"You will!" Peter grabbed hold of my arms, fingers digging into me. "I won't let you leave me!"

He started shoving me towards the bed. I jerked one arm free and ripped the sedative pen out of my pocket. Peter thrust his hand out to grab me again but I knocked it aside, lunging forward and jamming the sedative into his leg.

Peter reeled away, howling, and I got shakily back to my feet, tears still flooding down my face.

"YOU CAN'T DO THIS!" he screamed, coming after me again, unsteadier now as the sedative kicked in. "You can't just walk away like nothing ever—"

I sidestepped him and he fell down against the bed. He barked out a string of obscenities and wheeled around again, diving at me, grabbing my leg. I kicked him off and he collapsed on the ground, cursing some more. He rolled, trying to get up again, but his body wouldn't co-operate.

I stood there, watching Peter until his body gave out completely, reeling at the realization that I'd just made everything much, much worse.

The door creaked behind me and I whirled around. Bill was standing just outside, staring down at

Peter's unconscious form. His eyes drifted up to meet mine.

"You're too late," he said, with a hideous smile. "Both of you. It has already happened. All of it. It will happen again. All of this – all of this is inevitable."

Chapter 25

Mum groaned, gripping the sides of the mattress, eyes squeezing shut. The sound echoed off the laboratory walls. It was happening. Right now. Right as we were leaving.

My mind kept circling around my vision from a few weeks ago of security storming into the Complex, but what was I supposed to do about it? There was no way Mum was giving birth down in the panic room.

Georgia was in my arms, clinging to me, staring at Mum with a look of terror on her face. I hugged her back, not much calmer than she was.

Mum looked over from the bed as the contraction passed, obviously struggling to keep us in focus. "It's

265

OK, sweetheart. Mummy's fine." She took a couple of heavy breaths, and her eyes fluttered shut.

I felt a jolt of panic. "Mum?"

"That's normal," said Reeve, coming in from the surveillance room, rifle hanging from his shoulder. "The drowsiness. My wife did the same thing when she was in labour with Lachlan."

"She's three months pregnant with a full-term baby!" I said. "Like we have any idea what 'normal' is!"

Georgia whimpered, fingers clawing my back.

"Sorry," I whispered. "I didn't mean to yell. Mum's fine. She's fine."

"You're scared too," said Georgia accusingly.

"Yeah," I said. "Yeah, I am. We're all a bit scared. But everything's going to be OK."

Luke and his mum bustled into the room, lugging the old bathtub we used for laundry, splashing hot water on to the floor. They set it down beside the bed.

"OK," said Luke's mum frantically, smoothing down her hair. "OK, I think that's everything."

Luke put an arm around her. "Breathe, Mum. You're doing—"

But then her head snapped up. "Towels!" She ran

out of the room, almost bowling Cathryn over as she and Tank arrived from the hall.

Tank had the other rifle slung over his shoulder. It made me kind of uncomfortable, but I trusted him not to do anything Reeve didn't order him to do. Better Tank than Soren.

Cathryn came over and held out her hands to take Georgia from me.

"All right, Georgia," I said, trying to ease her off me, "Cathryn's going to look after you while I go up to—"

Mum jerked in the bed, wide awake again as the next contraction hit. She let out another groan and Georgia seized hold of me again. "No, you're not going!"

"Georgia—"

"Hey," said Luke, coming up behind me and brushing a hand over Georgia's hair. "It's all right. I'll look after Jordan for you. I'll make sure she's OK. Hey, have you got any paper left for your crayons?"

Georgia looked up. "It's on my bed."

"Well, how about you and Cathryn go and draw a picture for the new baby?" he said. "You can show it to

Jordan and me when we get back."

Georgia thought about it for a minute, then nodded and relaxed her grip on me. I gave her one last hug and passed her over to Cathryn.

"Thanks," I said, turning back to Luke.

He shrugged and went to say goodbye to his mum as she raced back in with a stack of almost-clean towels.

"Where's Amy?" asked Reeve.

Cathryn glanced over her shoulder. "Bathroom."

"Is she peeing or throwing up?" asked Tank.

"You're disgusting," said Cathryn, pulling a face. But then she put her free arm around him and stretched up to kiss his cheek. "Be safe, OK?"

"Yeah," he said, patting her on the back.

Cathryn took Georgia out of the room, and I went across to Mum's bed. She had her head on the pillow now, catching her breath between contractions. I bent down and kissed her cheek. "See you soon."

Mum wrapped her arms around me. "Love you, Jordan. *Please* look after each other out there."

"We will," I said. "I love you too."

I grabbed Ms Hunter as she bustled past again. "Remember, first sign of movement outside—"

"Panic room," she finished, glancing uneasily at Mum. "But, Jordan, how exactly—?"

"Just make it happen," I said. "Please." I crossed to the bed again, just as Amy appeared in the doorway.

"Sorry," she said, wiping her mouth. "Ready."

Reeve did a quick head count. We just had to pick Soren up on the way through and we'd be ready to go. Reeve's fingers snaked around the grips of his rifle.

"Right," he said. "Let's go save the world."

Chapter 26

Wednesday 12 August
1 day

"I am not going back," Soren muttered as we climbed in over the back fence of the school. "After tonight, you are all going to owe me your lives. You are not making me a prisoner again."

"Shut up," said Tank, shoving him. Soren went sprawling to the grass on the other side of the fence. His hands shot to his lower back, like he'd landed on something hard, but I couldn't see what it was in the darkness.

It was almost 10.30 p.m. Only a few minutes until Miller and Ford pulled the pin on their diversion in town.

This was it. The end. By this time tomorrow, it

270

would all be over – either for the Co-operative or for everyone else. And here we were, fighting each other in the school playground.

"Get up," I said, nudging Soren roughly with my foot. He stood up and rounded on Tank and me, looking like he'd really love to start something with him, but then Reeve stepped in between them and Soren backed off.

We crept out towards the front office, sticking close to the shadows of the buildings. The security lighting was still on all over the school, shooting spotlights through the cold drizzle drifting down from the sky.

It was so bizarre. Like visiting an old house you used to live in as a kid.

The last time we'd been here, the whole place was packed with students. Normal teenagers grinding through normal school days, blindly going about their lives like the biggest hassle in this town was a curfew or a blood test. We'd spent weeks wishing everyone would wake up and realize what was really going on.

This wasn't exactly what we'd had in mind.

Reeve slipped out from the end of the English block and swept his rifle around through shadows. He waved at us to follow and we darted across the quad to the admin building. Amy flitted in circles around us, burning off nervous energy.

"Well, this is familiar," I whispered, peering through the glass door into the front office. It felt like almost an exact replay of our last trip up to the Shackleton Building, right down to the weather.

There was a second set of glass doors on the far side of the room. I could see all the way out to the main street. The mall was directly opposite us, completely intact – at least for the moment.

Luke came up next to me and squeezed my hand. It was cold and slick with the rain. I breathed out, fogging the glass in front of me.

Any second now…

My thoughts went back to Mum. Her contractions had started just after lunch today and for a while, I'd been holding out hope it would all be over before we had to leave, but apparently these things take longer in real life than they do in the movies.

At least Peter wasn't going to be a problem. I'd gone back this morning while he was still unconscious and tied him facedown to his bed. Then I'd got Luke to help me lug a big chunk of concrete in front of his door. Even if Cathryn was stupid enough to come looking for him again, there was no way she'd be able to—

BOOM!

The sliding doors of the mall blasted apart, sending bits of glass and metal raining down over the street. Distant shouts rang out from the Shackleton Building.

Time to go.

"Out of the way, kids," said Reeve, bringing his rifle up over his shoulder. He drove the butt of the weapon into the door, smashing through the panel at the bottom and stepping through. I ducked in after him and dashed to the front doors, eyes landing on the big glass dome of the food court.

That first detonation was just a warning. A chance for anyone in the exercise area to run for cover before—

"Jordan, get back!" Reeve shouted.

BOOM!

The noise was incredible, even bigger than the security centre. An enormous ball of flame erupted inside the dome, lighting up the whole street. The glass shattered, exploding outward in all directions, and then it was swallowed up in roiling black smoke.

Everything shook. I staggered back, momentarily blinded. Loud *thunks* split the air as debris hammered down on the office roof.

Amy raced up, screaming. *"Jordan!"*

Reeve dragged us to the ground as a big hunk of something smashed in through the front door. Half a food court table. It bounced off the back wall, flames licking up the sides, curling the plastic veneer. Any second now, that fire was going to spread to the carpet.

"Go!" shrieked Soren. "Run!"

"No, wait, they haven't—"

BOOM!

Light flashed in my peripheral vision as a third and final explosion shook the hallway off to our left, much smaller but deafeningly close. Smoke billowed in the hall and a heavy *thud* signalled that the door to the head teacher's office had just been successfully removed from its hinges.

Outside, the rumble of skid engines rose up over the shouting and snapping of flames.

"C'mon!" I said, staggering up the hallway, feet crunching on broken glass. Through the smoke and plaster dust I saw more wreckage burning at the far end of the hall, flames splaying out across the ceiling.

I stopped outside Pryor's office, glancing back to make sure we were all still here, and almost tripped over the heavy steel door at my feet.

"Hurry!" said Reeve, clambering after me. "In a few minutes, this whole place is going to be burning too."

We piled into the room. Reeve heaved the door aside. As soon as it was out of the way, Luke crouched and started rolling Pryor's ornate antique rug back from the floor, while I darted behind her desk to the giant tapestry that hung on the back wall. I pushed the tapestry aside and flicked the two switches on the power outlet underneath. A hiss of compressed air cut through the room as a metre-squared section of Pryor's floor slipped away into the ground.

"This was here the whole time?" said Amy, staring at the shining silver stairs leading down into the ground.

"Thieves," said Soren under his breath.

"OK," I said, pushing past him and leading the way into the tunnels, "this is where it really gets interesting."

Chapter 27

The trapdoor hissed shut above our heads, sealing us off from the chaos outside.

The six of us were squished into a tiny, silver-walled room, maybe half as big as Pryor's office. Reeve moved up to the far end and opened the door on a narrow, brightly-lit tunnel. He turned to Tank. "You mind watching our backs?"

Tank hung at the rear while Reeve went ahead. I shivered, remembering the way our last trip down here had ended: Reeve "dead" and the rest of us stabbed with tracking devices.

The tunnel was a direct line to a big underground bunker at the base of the Shackleton Building. It was the only way to access the lift to the top level, short of strolling in through the front doors.

"Those things are all off, right?" said Amy after a minute, glancing at the security cameras that peered down from the ceiling every few metres.

"Should be," I said. "I assume they were hooked up to the same network as the ones outside."

"You *assume?*" said Amy.

"Shh!" said Luke. "Almost there."

Reeve slowed as we approached the foot-thick metal door at the end of the tunnel. The last time we'd come down here, it had opened automatically. But I guess the Co-operative were feeling a bit more cautious these days. The door stayed closed. No handle. No anything.

"Crap," said Luke.

Fire behind us. A locked door in front of us.

We were not off to a good start.

"Everyone quiet," said Reeve. He stepped up and pounded the door with his fist.

There was a moment's silence, then: "Yes? Who's there?"

I recognized the voice. It was Aaron Ketterley,

Phoenix's "residential liaison", the man who'd shown my family and me around town when we first arrived. He might have been a really nice guy if he wasn't trying to help exterminate humanity.

"Sir," said Reeve, deepening his voice slightly. "Officer Tracey here. We've had some hostile activity up above ground, and—"

"We're aware of that, Mr Tracey," said a second voice I couldn't place.

"Yes, sir," said Reeve. "The chief sent me to make sure everything's OK down here."

"We're fine," said Ketterley. "Thank you."

"Sir, the chief's orders are for me to get a visual on the two of you to confirm that you aren't being—"

A booming, clattering sound filled the tunnel as the door in front of us slowly shuddered open. "Mr Tracey," grumbled the second man, "you can thank Officer Barnett for his diligence, however—" He stopped short. It was Benjamin More, Shackleton's vice president.

"Down on the ground," Reeve ordered.

More edged backwards. "You."

"Yeah," said Reeve. "Down on the ground."

"Officer Reeve," said Ketterley bracingly, "I understand that these past few months have been traumatic for you, but you need to realize that hurting us is only going to—" His moustache twitched and he threw his hands in front of him. "Who's that? What is he—?"

Soren shoved his way forward, knocking me into the wall. He reached under his jumper, pulling something from the back of his jeans, and—

BLAM! BLAM! BLAM! BLAM!

Ketterley and More dropped to the ground, blood trickling from the holes in their heads.

I stumbled back, mouth open, air disappearing from my lungs. Luke caught me and hoisted me to my feet.

"Oh my goodness…" Amy shuddered behind me.

Soren stood frozen in the doorway, arm straight out in front of him, pistol clenched in his fist. He must have taken it from the armoury and hidden it in his room somewhere.

"Give it to me," I said, recovering myself, grabbing at Soren's arm.

He whirled around, pointing the gun back at the rest of us. "No."

"Soren—!"

BLAM!

I ducked to the ground as he fired again. Luke cried out behind me. I whirled around, but he was still standing. The shot had been fired at the ceiling above our heads.

"*What are you DOING?*" I roared, heart thundering.

Soren's hands shook. He brought the gun back down. "Step back! I will not be—"

Reeve launched himself forward, throwing a fist into Soren's jaw. He grabbed Soren's arm and slammed him into the wall, pinning his face against the gleaming metal.

"Get to the lift," he told the rest of us, wrenching the pistol from Soren's fingers. "We're not the only ones who heard all that."

Soren cursed furiously, but didn't try to take the weapon back.

We ran through the bunker, stepping around the bodies on the floor.

More death.

More stupid, senseless murder.

He might've just taken care of two our greatest

enemies, but still, I couldn't muster anything but disgust for what Soren had done.

The bunker was one big round room, stocked with everything Shackleton and his underlings needed to stay alive and unharmed in case of an emergency. And I guess the current situation qualified, because most of the beds off to our right were unmade and surrounded by bags of clothes and supplies.

"Oi! What are you doing?" said Tank.

I looked over my shoulder and saw Luke stooped over Ketterley, reaching a hand into his pocket, a nauseated look on his face. He pulled something out and tossed it to me. It was Ketterley's phone.

Luke took More's phone too and gave it to Reeve, who was already waiting at the lift. "Here. In case we need to talk to each other."

The words were barely out of his mouth when More's phone started vibrating in Reeve's hand. His eyes widened. He held up the phone, showing us the caller ID. *Bruce Calvin.* Wherever the chief had disappeared to these past few weeks, apparently he was back.

"What the crap?" said Tank, mesmerized by the

phone. "Those things actually work?"

"They can only call each other," I said. "The only way they can reach the outside is if…"

"What?" said Tank.

"External Communications," Luke said. "The room up on the top level."

The lift doors slid open.

"Right," said Reeve, stepping inside. "Bit late for a rescue party now, though." He stopped halfway through the doors, catching himself. "Besides Kara and your dad, I mean. I'm sure they're still—"

"Yeah," said Luke.

Reeve was right. Tobias was still our best hope at saving the world.

There were two lifts in the Shackleton Building: one that moved between the five floors that the public was allowed to know about, and this one, a direct line from the basement to the executive offices and the secret top floor above them.

We squeezed in after Reeve, and Luke hit a button on the wall, sending the lift trundling upwards.

"Here," said Reeve, handing Soren's pistol over to Luke.

Luke cringed. "I don't—"

"Just in case."

Soren scowled at him.

The lift came to a stop at the pretend-top floor of this place, and the doors opened on to an empty room, even smaller than the lift itself.

"This is us," said Reeve, stepping out and pulling open a steel door like the one at Pryor's office.

There was a guard standing on the other side.

He wheeled around at the sound of the door opening, hoisting his weapon up in front of him. "Whoa, whoa, whoa—" He broke off. It was Officer Hamilton, the guy from back at the graveyard. "Matt?"

"Ethan," said Reeve, raising his own rifle. "Listen, Miller and Ford are downstairs right now, taking control of the loyalty room. In about five minutes, you're going to have a fight on your hands. You need to choose a side. Now."

Hamilton hesitated.

"Come on, Ethan," said Reeve. "I know you want to do the right thing."

Hamilton held out for a moment longer, then lowered his weapon. Reeve patted him on the arm.

283

"Good on you, mate." He turned to the others. "This way, kids." He led them away down the hall, leaving Luke and me alone in the lift.

Luke hit another button and we started rising again. He looked at the pistol in his hands. His eyes flickered around the floor of the lift, like he was looking for somewhere to get rid of it, but in the end he stuck it into the back of his pants the same way Soren had done.

"Remember," he said, as the lift slowed again, "no dying."

"Neither of us is dying," I said. "Not tonight."

The doors slid open and we walked out into the darkness on the other side.

Chapter 28

As soon as we stepped clear of the lift, a series of loud *clunks* beat down from the ceiling as the automated lights came on.

Luke tensed for a second, then relaxed again. "Forgot about that."

"It's good," I said. "Means we're alone."

But it surely wouldn't be more than a few minutes before security realized we were up here.

On first glance, Shackleton's secret top floor could have been just another ordinary office building. A big open-plan central workspace – computers, desks, filing cabinets – with five doors leading away to other, smaller rooms. Nothing here that looked like it could stop the end of humanity.

Orange light flickered in the sky outside. I crossed to the edge of the room, where giant windows ran from floor to ceiling. One-way glass, like the rest of the building.

The mall was still blazing. Bits of the food court were scattered across the street, smouldering like campfires. A big slab of concrete had torn through the fence at the foot of the Shackleton Building, obliterating the fountain, but if any of the prisoners had escaped, they were long gone. I twisted around, pressing my face up against the glass. It was hard to get a good look at the school from this angle, but I was pretty sure the admin building was burning too.

A dozen or so security officers swarmed around the town centre, but it would be a while before they had the fire under control. In the meantime, that was a dozen fewer guards keeping an eye on things in the Shackleton Building.

"We should split up," I said, turning around again. "You take the main office, I'll—"

I froze. Luke was gone.

I jumped at the sound of a door opening, and he

emerged from one of the side rooms.

"It's empty," he said in a hollow voice.

He'd gone straight to the *External Communications* room. I went over to join him. The whole place had been gutted. Nothing left but a little hole in the wall with a cable hanging out where the computer used to be hooked up.

I guessed the Co-operative had moved the equipment somewhere else after we discovered it the first time. That or they were just past needing it. If all went to plan, by this time tomorrow there'd be no-one left to answer the phone.

"Reeve's right," I said, turning away. "If help's coming, it's already on its way. Come on, let's – hey. That's new."

A monitor had been mounted to the wall across from us, back over near the entrance to the lift. The monitor showed two digital clocks counting down in unison:

Final Lockdown Procedures
00:00:06:24
Tabitha Release
00:18:06:24

"Final lockdown procedures?" said Luke. "What's more locked down than a concentration camp?"

But it was the second countdown that had my attention. "Eighteen hours," I murmured. We'd been doing that countdown in our heads for months now, but there was something about seeing it up there on the screen in stark white numbers that made it seem so much more imminent.

This was all really happening.

"Five o'clock tomorrow afternoon," said Luke. "A hundred days after Mum and I landed."

"Better get to work, then," I said, tearing my eyes away, annoyed at being so easily distracted. "I'm gonna check some of these rooms we didn't get to last time."

Luke nodded and sat down at the nearest computer.

I moved to the next door over: *Research Centre.*

More lights clunked on as I went into a short corridor that had three gleaming silver doors spaced out along the opposite wall. Alongside each door was a bank of monitors, all switched off. The whole setup made me feel vaguely uneasy. *Get a grip,* I told myself, pushing the first door open. *It's probably just—*

I recoiled, almost falling over.

It was Dr Galton's testing room. The one from the DVD Bill had slipped us, way back in the beginning. The place where those two unsuspecting construction workers (and who knew how many others) had spent their last terrified moments before Tabitha tore them apart.

I forced myself to stay long enough to check the other two rooms – exact copies of the first – then backed out of the corridor and slammed the door, skin crawling like I'd been infected with something.

"What's up?" asked Luke, glancing up.

"Nothing," I said, cold shivers shooting up my spine. "Find anything?"

He sighed, typing something else into the computer. "Not yet."

I kept going, shaking off the rush of nerves. This was no time for a breakdown.

In the corner of the room was a door marked *Roof Access*. I tried the handle, but the door wouldn't budge. Funny that *that* was the one they bothered locking.

Not like they'll be keeping Tobias up on the roof, anyway.

But how did I know? What was I expecting? A shiny little box with *Tobias* stamped on the front?

You'll know it when you see it, I thought, pushing on. *You didn't come all this way just to end the night empty-handed.*

The next door was the conference room Shackleton and Calvin had dragged us into when they caught us up here last time. Nothing useful.

I pulled the door closed again. Luke had given up on the computer and was flipping through a filing cabinet next to one of the desks.

His head jerked up as a burst of gunfire rang out from somewhere downstairs. It sounded like things weren't going to plan for Reeve and the others either.

Luke slammed the filing cabinet shut. He started circling the desks, more and more frantic, not even looking properly, just scattering stuff across the floor.

"Luke," I said, "slow down. You're going to—"

"What if it's not even up here?" he snapped. "I mean, what are we basing this on anyway? *Rumours* from security. How do we even know they're—?"

"Stop. It's here, OK? It's got to be. Just keep looking."

Luke grabbed the back of a chair, fighting to calm himself. "Yeah. Sorry."

But *where* was it? As much as I didn't want to admit it, we were running out of places and time to look.

I left Luke rattling through a row of cupboards and went into the last unexplored side room. *Medical Analysis.*

More sensor lights flashed on, but not just from the ceiling this time. The walls flickered to life as well, revealing a sprawling grid of grey and white transparencies.

X-rays.

My feet echoed on the tiled floor as I took in the glowing images of arms and legs and heads, all labelled and grouped together by name.

Watson, Thomas, Reeve, Park, Lewis, Kennedy, Burke, Burke, Anderson, and a set labelled *Unidentified,* which I assumed belonged to Bill. Everyone who'd been dragged down under the medical centre by the Co-operative.

Mum and Amy had told us as much as they could about their time down there, but the reality was that they'd spent most of it locked up in their communal sleeping area or knocked out in the labs. Who knew what Montag and Galton were doing with them while they were unconscious?

After all the X-rays came some brain scans. There were only two sets, and my breath caught in my throat when I read the names.

Georgia Burke and *Bruce Calvin.* Side by side, like they'd been trying to compare their brains.

I turned away, revolted, and a monitor in the centre of the room caught my eye. It seemed to be running some kind of scan.

J_Thomas_Tissue_Modification_Treatment_4-3-1
Analysis: 51% Complete

"J. Thomas" was Jeremy, a Year 7 kid from school. Out of all the weird abilities that had resulted from the fallout, Jeremy's habit of imprinting his skin tone onto anyone he touched was probably the most useless. But it was enough to have him hauled off to the medical centre along with all the others. As far as we knew, he was still down there.

I stared at my right hand, at the place where he'd marked me with his fingertips back at school. The discolouration had faded by now, but—

Enough, I ordered myself, starting back towards the door. *This isn't what you're here for.* The best thing I could do for Jeremy and the others now was to hurry up and find—

I stopped moving, taking in a set of pictures across the room that I hadn't noticed before.

Ultrasound images. Pictures of Mum's baby lined up in neat rows, dated from the time Dr Montag first discovered the pregnancy right up until the day before we'd freed Mum.

I stepped closer to the wall, tracing a hand over the timeline of this tiny life. "We're going to get you out," I whispered, tears stinging my eyes. "You are *not* getting dragged into this—"

"Jordan!" Luke shouted from outside. "Get out here."

"What? What is it?" I asked, snapping out of it and sprinting back into the main office. "Did you find—?"

I grabbed the doorframe to bring myself to a stop. The lift doors had just slid open again.

Mr Shackleton stood on the threshold.

"Ah," he smiled, like he couldn't be happier to see us. "I was wondering when the two of you might pay me another visit."

Chapter 29

**Wednesday 12 August
1 day**

"Stop!" said Luke, pulling Soren's pistol from the back of his jeans and levelling it at Shackleton. "Stay there. Stay where you are."

Shackleton raised his hands into the air, opening his mouth in a caricature of fear, then smiled again and lowered them to his sides. "Come now, Luke. Do you really think yourself capable of that?"

"Where is it?" I demanded, charging over. "Where's Tobias?"

Shackleton eyed me curiously. "Tobias who?"

I slammed him into the wall, smashing his head into the countdown monitor behind him. "Listen," I said, shaking. "It's over, OK? We've got the cafeteria.

And any minute now, every guard in the building is going to know it. So either you tell us where you're keeping Tobias, or—"

I stopped as another round of gunfire echoed up through the floor. Was that our guys protecting the cafeteria? Had they even got that far?

Shackleton raised an eyebrow.

How much did he know? Clearly he hadn't come looking for us, or he would have brought security.

Shackleton reached up and touched the back of his head. It came back glistening with blood. "I assure you, there is no Tobias here – as you seem well on your way to discovering," he added dryly, casting an eye over the mess Luke had made. "However, if you would like to discuss the matter further, the conference room might be a more suitable place to—"

"No," I said, a desperate plan forming in my head. "Luke, see if you can find some rope or something."

"How is your mother?" Shackleton asked as Luke took off, like we were just catching up over lunch. "The poor dear. It can't be easy, out there on the run in her condition. It really would have been much kinder to—"

I punched him in the stomach. "Shut up."

Shackleton coughed, a tear trickling from one eye. He smelled like old man's cologne.

"And your sister?" he said, recovering. A smile crossed his face. "Precocious little monster. She gave Dr Galton quite a time until I suggested—"

More noise from outside cut him short. Not gunfire this time. These were deep whirring and clunking sounds, like heavy machinery warming up. The sound was coming from above us.

On the screen behind Shackleton, *Final Lockdown Procedures* had ticked down to zero.

"What's going on out there?" asked Luke, rushing back to us. He tossed me an extension cord.

"Well?" I said, giving Shackleton another shove.

His smile spread wider, exposing perfect teeth.

"Fine," I said, spinning him around and mashing that stupid smile into the wall. "You can tell us when we get outside."

"Wait – what?" said Luke.

Luke held Shackleton's arms in place while I tied them together with the extension cord. "Jordan, what are we doing?" Luke asked warily, as if he knew he wouldn't like the answer.

"We're taking him with us," I said.

Luke shook his head wearily. "Of course we are."

"We can't stay here. And I'm not leaving him. Either he tells us where Tobias is or we use him as bait so that someone else will." I shoved Shackleton's watch up his arm and pulled hard on the ends of the cord. "Done. Let's go."

Luke brought Soren's pistol out again, although I think it was pretty clear that we weren't going to use it. Shackleton didn't struggle at all as I dragged him back from the wall and shoved him inside the lift. His confidence unsettled me a bit, but I guess that was the point.

I hit the button to take us down to the bunker. The doors slid closed.

"You're remembering the fire, right?" said Luke.

"Plenty of other tunnels," I said, mind ticking over the options. "We can get out through Ketterley's office. Nice and close to the bush."

"Your attention, please," said a voice over the P.A. My heart leapt as I realized who it was. *"Repeat: Your attention please, all security staff. This is Matthew Reeve*

speaking. If you turn your attention to the video screen in the town hall, you will see footage, captured only a few minutes ago, recording the liberation of the Shackleton Building's cafeteria."

Shackleton's face registered only the slightest flicker of concern before returning to its normal wide-eyed amusement.

"The threat to your loved ones has been neutralised," Reeve continued. *"I invite you to join us in taking up arms against the leadership of this town."*

Reeve kept going, giving more instructions to anyone who wanted to join him and pleading with the rest of the town to stay calm and keep out of the fighting, but something else shoved its way to the front of my mind, distracting me from his speech.

Our lift wasn't moving.

I punched the button again. Nothing happened.

Shackleton frowned. "Perhaps your escape won't be as easy as you'd hoped."

I shoved him again and hit the other button, the one leading down to what everyone else thought was the top floor of this place.

The lift slid downwards. In a few seconds, we came

to a stop again, doors opening on the tiny room Reeve and the others had left through before. The entryway to the main office complex. The fire-fight downstairs now seemed a whole lot louder.

"Now what?" said Luke. "We can't exactly—"

"I know," I said. "Looks like we'll just have to take him out the front door."

Chapter 30

I pushed Shackleton through the little room and out into a corridor lined with offices, heading for the other lift, the one that would take us down to the ground floor. Abstract artworks hung along the walls on either side. Shackleton sighed wistfully at them as we passed. "I hardly ever seem to have time for my painting any more."

We reached the far end of the corridor. Luke hit the button on the wall and we waited for the lift to arrive.Shackleton started humming to himself.

Luke glared at him. "Stop that."

The lift finally arrived, and we got inside. Reeve's speech over the intercom had ended, but the machinery or whatever it was on the roof was still clunking away above our heads.

As we started moving again I realized the button for the floor below ours was lit up too. I glanced at Luke. "Was that you?"

Luke shook his head. He raised Soren's pistol again. I dragged Shackleton around. They wouldn't shoot if he was—

The lift stopped and the doors slid open on another office level. Gunfire blazed just out of sight. There was a rush of movement, and the first thing my eyes landed on was another weapon.

"Whoa, hey, stop!" said Luke. "Stop! It's us!"

I got a second look and realized who they were. Amy blurred into the lift, followed by Soren, who'd somehow managed to get his hands on another rifle.

"Close it! Close it!" shouted Amy, spinning in a circle.

A guard appeared at the far end of the room, spotting us just as the doors began to slide shut. He opened fire, and I dived sideways, dragging Shackleton with me. Bullets pelted the other side of the lift.

And then we were moving again. On our way to the ground floor.

Soren raised his rifle at Shackleton's chest. Shackleton flinched, backing into me, seeing straight away that Soren wasn't playing by the same rules as the rest of us.

"Wait – no!" I said. "We need him!"

"Where's Tobias?" Amy asked us.

"Not up there," said Luke. "At least—"

"That's why we've got Shackleton!" I said, eyes still on Soren. "We need to get him out so we can question him."

Soren relaxed his grip on the trigger but kept the weapon right where it was.

Shackleton straightened, the veneer of calm back up. He nodded at Soren, tugging slightly against my grip. "I don't believe we've been introduced."

Soren sneered.

The lift stopped again and we peered out across the enormous Shackleton Building foyer. As far as I could see, it was completely empty. Abandoned in a hurry when the explosions started going off outside. Food sitting uneaten on tables. Toilet doors hanging open. Water still running in one of the portable showers.

I balled up the end of Shackleton's tie and shoved it into his mouth. "Keep quiet."

"Where are the others?" Luke whispered.

"Busy," said Soren.

"Doing what?"

"Tank went back to help defend the cafeteria," said Amy, still jittering. "Reeve is – somewhere. We got separated, getting out of the A/V place."

The sound of weapons fire was almost constant now, but it looked like the fighting was contained to the floors above us for the time being. The entrances to the town hall were all closed, and I could hear shouting coming from inside, but no guns. At least, not yet. We moved out past the doors and I slowed to the back of the group. Dad was in there somewhere. He'd be able to help us if—

"No," said Luke, pulling on my arm. "We can't. We have to get out of here."

I gave it up.

I pointed through the front doors at the exercise area. A hunk of wreckage from the mall had punched a hole through the razor-wire fence. "There's our way out. Straight through there, and then follow me."

Surprisingly, Soren didn't argue about the following part. I peered out and then sprinted at the automatic doors, dragging Shackleton with me. I half expected the doors to be locked, but they sprang open and a gust of scorching air blew in from the street. Luke grabbed Shackleton's other side, and we dragged him down the front steps of the Shackleton Building. Out into the heat and the haze and the rubble.

We veered towards the gap in the fence, dodging the debris underfoot. Security were still way across the street and I was hoping they'd all be too caught up in fighting the fire to notice us slipping out.

I squeezed through the hole and then turned to pull Shackleton through. He winced as a bit of the fence dug into his back.

"This way," I hissed when we were all out, and we darted up the bike path between the Shackleton Building and what was left of the security centre.

I glanced back. It didn't look like anyone had followed us. And between the fire and the mutiny, I doubted there'd be any guards left on patrol out here.

Shackleton spat the tie out of his mouth. "I believe

you were wondering about the source of that noise earlier?"

I followed his gaze to the top of the Shackleton Building. A thick black pillar was slowly stretching up from the centre of the roof, ten metres tall and still growing. An antenna or something. It made the whole building look like a giant walkie-talkie.

"What is it?" I asked.

Shackleton smiled. "Just a bit of extra protection. It would be a terrible shame if all our efforts came to nothing at this late stage."

"Yeah, wouldn't that be a hassle?" I said, shoving him forward again. Whatever that antenna thing was for, I knew we'd find out about it soon enough.

We continued up the street, between the rows of abandoned houses, keeping to the shadows. My mind was racing, trying to work out what to do next. Taking Shackleton back to the Complex would be a mistake.

"In here," I said, opening the front gate of one of the houses.

We ran up the verandah steps. Soren smashed his rifle through the frosted glass of the front door. He reached through to the other side, unlocked the door and let us in.

I'd never set foot in this house before. I had no idea who it had even belonged to. But it could just as easily have been mine, or Luke's, or Peter's, or any other house in Phoenix, and all of those memories rushed at me as I stepped through the door. My parents sitting me down and telling me Mum was pregnant, Peter tackling a guard down the stairs, Luke sleeping up on the landing, Mum and Georgia getting dragged away at gunpoint… It was like the whole of the last hundred days was converging into this single moment.

I brought Shackleton through to the lounge room and threw him down on a couch. Soren stood over him, rifle trained on his chest, while Amy zoomed across to the window to keep watch. Luke closed the front door behind us, then came in and sat on the other couch. "What now?"

I folded my arms, staring down at Shackleton, the ultimate cause of all the suffering we'd been through, tied up at gunpoint on the couch in front of me. "Now we get some answers."

Chapter 31

"You're the one behind the attack on my security centre," said Shackleton, fixing Soren with a penetrating stare. "Aren't you?"

Soren's eyes shifted from me to Luke, like one of us must have told him.

"I must say, that whole business was quite a mystery to me. I knew none of your fellow insurgents had such violence in them." The smile returned to Shackleton's lips. "But *you*..."

I pushed between them, grabbing Shackleton by the front of his jacket. "Enough!" I snapped. "What's Tobias and how do we get it to the release station?"

"Now, that's interesting," said Shackleton, still

infuriatingly calm. "What has led you to believe that you need to take something out to the release station?"

I threw him back down against the couch. "Answer the question! What's Tobias?"

Shackleton furrowed his brow, a look of genuine curiosity on his face. Then his eyes lit up and he burst out laughing.

"Answer her!" Soren demanded, pushing past and poking the end of his rifle into Shackleton's chest. "Answer her or I will kill you!"

"He will," said Luke, looking uneasy.

"I am sorry." Shackleton shook his head, regaining his composure but clearly still amused by something. "I don't know how you came by the name Tobias, but this is all terribly ironic."

"What is?" I demanded. "What are you talking about?"

"Shh!" said Luke, glancing to Amy at the window. "Jordan, someone's going to hear you."

"If this 'Tobias' of yours really did hold the key to unravelling the work we are doing in this town," said Shackleton, serious again, "do you honestly think I would share that information with you, even in exchange for my own life?"

"Why don't we find out?" said Soren, jabbing his rifle into Shackleton again.

"No, *wait*," I said, pushing the weapon aside. "Just—" I crouched, eye to eye with Shackleton, a last, desperate hope springing up in my chest. "What if it was *her* out there? Your daughter. What if *she* was one of the people on the outside, about to get massacred?"

Another tiny glimmer of surprise registered on Shackleton's face. He wiped it away again. "I have no daughter."

"Dr Galton," I pressed. "*Victoria.* What if—?"

"Do not think you can sway me with sentimentalism, Jordan." Shackleton looked more engaged than he had all night. "I am well beyond the point of entertaining such trivialities. The new humanity being created in this town is of far greater importance than any *feelings* one might have about those who are to be jettisoned in the transition."

He smiled coldly over at Luke. According to the Co-operative, Luke and his mum were here by accident. A glitch in the system. Which meant they weren't immune to Tabitha like the rest of us apparently were.

"*Jettisoned*," repeated Luke.

Shackleton shrugged. "Or *killed*, if you prefer. The semantics are quite beside the point."

Soren barged forward again, smacking Shackleton across the face with his rifle. "If you *have* a point, *get* to it!"

Shackleton writhed on the couch, twisting his bound arms around to push himself back into a sitting position. His tongue ran over his teeth, smearing them with blood. When he spoke again, there was an edge of impatience to his voice. "The point, children, is that humanity is rapidly plummeting towards a depth of depravity and self-destruction so severe that we will soon be powerless to extract ourselves again."

"I think we might already be there," said Amy softly, speaking up for the first time since we stopped here.

"The human race is critically ill," Shackleton continued. "A cancerous wreck, sacrificing at the altar of its own vapid self-interest. For all our talk of progress and enlightenment, we are no less barbaric than when we were tossing spears and dressing in animal skins."

"Look around you, Shackleton!" I shouted. "You're not exactly helping the situation!"

"But that's exactly what we *are* doing," Shackleton said. "There comes a point at which the only viable means of saving something is by wiping the slate clean and starting afresh. You may question the cost involved, but Phoenix represents humanity's best hope of—"

"You don't get to decide that!" I shouted, shaking him. "What right do you have to choose who lives and who dies?"

A little trickle of blood spilled from the corner of Shackleton's mouth. "Everyone dies, Jordan."

"You're disgusting," I said.

"Come now, Jordan." Shackleton leant forward. "We have spoken about this before. Your great weakness is your insistence on viewing 'good' and 'evil' in such inflexible terms. Such ideas are merely human constructs. We invented those definitions, and we are free to adjust them as we see fit."

"That's *crap!*" I spat. "You can't just *change* right and wrong to suit yourself."

"Give it a year," said Shackleton. "Two, maybe. Give the people of Phoenix time to experience the new world that I will lead them into. Then ask them if they still think my actions were unjustified."

"It doesn't matter! None of that—" I balled up my fists, resisting the urge to throttle him. "It's still evil! Even if every person on Earth turned around and said you were right all along, you'd still be the same filthy monster you are now!"

Shackleton smiled again, teeth pink with blood. "Who says?"

"Enough!" barked Soren, pushing forward again. "I did not come here to argue philosophy!" He kicked Shackleton in the ribs, knocking him over on to his side, and jammed the gun under his chin. "You will tell us what we want to know, or—" Soren faltered, staring down at him. "What is that?"

Something was blinking behind Shackleton. A tiny blue light, flashing against the back of the couch. I pulled Shackleton over on to his stomach. "It's his watch."

"Yes," said Shackleton, dragging his mouth away from the couch cushion. "I'm afraid you're out of time."

There was a gasp from the window, and a half-second later, Amy was across the room, squeezing my arm with both hands. "They're coming!"

Chapter 32

**Wednesday 12 August
1 day**

Luke leapt out of his seat. "How many of them?"

"I think three," said Amy, the words spewing out at triple speed. "Officer Barnett and two more behind him. I couldn't really see. I don't know. I don't know. We have to get out!"

"It's a tracking device," I said, tearing off Shackleton's watch and throwing it on the ground. "Like the suppressors you put in us."

"Something like that," said Shackleton.

I dragged him up from the couch and started hauling him from the room.

"What are you doing?" said Soren.

"Back door," I said. "We'll jump the fence and—"

"He is not coming." Soren pointed at the carpet with his rifle. "Put him on the ground."

"Come on!" said Amy, already in the hall. "Hurry!"

I pulled Shackleton towards the door, but Soren grabbed the front of his suit.

"Just leave him!" said Luke. "Jordan, we don't have…"

He trailed off as a tinny burst of music suddenly filled the room, something classical I vaguely recognized. My pocket started buzzing.

Ketterley's phone. I'd completely forgotten about it. I pulled it out and checked the caller ID.

Andrew Barnett.

"Don't answer it," said Soren, but I was already sliding the phone open. Something told me it wasn't Ketterley he was calling for.

"What?" I snapped, holding it to my ear.

"Jordan," said the cold voice on the other end. "Why don't you have a look out the front window?"

"We have Noah Shackleton!" said Soren, listening in. "Leave, or I will blast his face apart!"

"Charming," said Shackleton.

"That would be a mistake," said Barnett. "Come

to the window, Jordan."

I got down low and edged my way to the front of the room, trying to keep out of sight. There was every chance he was just calling me out so he could get a clear shot.

"Jordan, come on," said Luke, "let's just go."

I peered up over the windowsill and almost dropped the phone. Officer Barnett was standing out in the middle of the street, lit up by one of the streetlamps. Officer Cook was next to him, holding a gun to the head of a sobbing 12-year-old girl.

It was Lauren. Hamilton's daughter. The Year 7 kid who'd helped us out with food and clothes while we were on the run from the Co-operative in town.

"You sick bastard," I breathed.

Barnett chuckled on the other end. "Let me speak to Shackleton."

I backed off from the window and lowered the mobile from my ear, hand shaking. I hit the speakerphone button. "He can hear you."

"Andrew," Shackleton leant towards the phone, "how nice of you to come for me."

"You OK, sir?"

"Oh yes, we're having a fine time," said Shackleton. "Although I do think I should head back to attend to our little disturbance in town."

"Yes, sir," said Barnett. "You still there, Jordan?"

"Let her go," I demanded.

"That's not how this works, Jordan. Either you release Shackleton to us or the girl takes a bullet. And let me tell you, we have plenty more where she came from."

"Do it then," said Soren.

"No!" said Luke and I together.

"Listen to me." Soren ripped the phone out of my hand. "I have already killed two of your superiors tonight. I will not hesitate to kill a third. If the girl dies, Shackleton dies with her."

"Stop!" said Luke, face white. "Everyone, just – just *stop* for a second."

The room fell silent. I could hear Lauren whimpering on the other end of the phone.

"Yes?" said Barnett.

"We'll swap you," said Luke. "Lauren for Shackleton."

Shackleton stretched towards the phone again.

"Do it, Andrew. We've lost enough candidates already tonight."

I took the phone back from Soren. "You hear that, Barnett?"

"All right," said Barnett, clearly not happy with the situation. "Get out here."

"No," I said. "You guys need to back off first. Into the yard across the street."

"Fine."

"There are four of them in here," said Shackleton quickly. "Burke, Hunter, Amy Park, and our trigger-happy friend to whom I've not yet been—"

Soren punched him in the face and he stopped talking.

I shut the phone. "All right. Let's do this." I turned to Amy. "Do you think you can carry her?"

"What? Oh." She zipped to the window and back again. "Yeah. Yeah, I think so."

"Good," I said, heading into the hall. "As soon as they give us Lauren, you pick her up and run her out of here, OK? Soren, I want your rifle trained on Shackleton the whole—"

"I am not a fool, Jordan," Soren snarled.

There were so many ways I could have responded to that statement, but this really wasn't the time.

Luke crawled up to the hole Soren had smashed through the glass on our way in. "OK, they're back against the other house."

He opened the door and I jostled Shackleton out on to the verandah. Soren rushed out after me, sweeping his gun around while I got Shackleton down the steps.

"Looks like it's just the three of them," said Luke, surveying the street. He pulled the pistol out of his jeans again.

The air outside was hazy with smoke. I could still hear the distant crackle of the fire and the shouts of the guards. Lauren let out a terrified moan as we approached, and I felt another surge of rage at Barnett for dragging her into this.

We marched Shackleton through the gate, stopping when we reached the footpath. We were maybe twenty metres apart from them.

"All right," said Barnett. "Let him go."

"On three," I called back. "One – two—"

I released Shackleton, raising my hands above my

head to prove that he was really free. Officer Cook shoved Lauren away and she ran towards us, tears streaming down her face. She screamed as Amy raced out to grab her, hoisting her awkwardly off the ground and running her up the street towards the bush.

The air splintered as Soren fired his rifle.

Barnett cried out, shuddering violently as the bullets tore through him. He dropped to the ground.

BLAM! BLAM! BLAM!

I dived behind the garden fence as Officer Cook returned fire.

"C'mon!" said Luke, heading towards the house.

I scrambled after him, sticking low to the ground. Amy and Lauren were already disappearing into the darkness at the top of the hill. I couldn't see Shackleton anywhere. He'd just—

BLAM! BLAM!

Soren shrieked and collapsed to the ground. Cook crossed the street, holstering his pistol and reaching for his rifle instead.

"Jordan, *run!*" Luke yanked me backwards.

Soren let out another horrible, agonized screech, clutching his arm. Impossible to tell in the darkness how bad it was, but he wasn't getting up. I hesitated. But what were we supposed to do?

Cook raised his rifle, aiming at us this time. Luke jerked at my hand again, and we sprinted away down the side of the house.

Chapter 33

Wednesday 12 August
1 day

We stumbled through the bush, returning to the Vattel Complex on autopilot, not even stopping to think whether going back there was a good idea.

I dropped to my knees at the entrance, overwhelmed by the sudden urge to vomit. Luke knelt beside me, breathing hard, probably thinking I was about to start slipping away again. But this wasn't a vision. It was just my guts finally registering the insane horror of everything we'd been through tonight.

Soren's cries had followed us for only a few seconds before abruptly cutting out. He was gone. I had no idea how I was supposed to feel about that.

I braced myself against the low, crumbling ruin

that ran past the entrance, and heaved my dinner into the dirt. Luke stayed with me, rubbing my back and trying to keep my hair out of my face.

"We should get inside," he said, when I was finished.

"Yeah," I coughed, wiping my mouth.

Luke pulled a paperclip from his pocket and started feeling along the ruin for the broken power socket that would pop open the trapdoor. I stared around at the bush, still dizzy from the vomiting. Amy and Lauren were nowhere in sight. Soren was dead or getting there. Reeve and Tank might not be any better off. And for all of that, we were still no closer to finding Tobias.

This isn't how it was meant to happen! I raged inside my head. *Where is it? Where's Tobias? If it's not even up there, then what's the point? What's the point of any of it? Why drag me into this and fill my head with visions and put me through all this misery if we were just going to fail at the finish line anyway?*

There was a whoosh of compressed air as Luke got the trapdoor open. Screams echoed up from the bottom of the stairs.

Mum. The baby was still coming.

I hurried down the steps, Luke right behind me. Mum's violent panting and groaning rang out into the empty corridor. I could hear Ms Hunter too, yelling at her to keep pushing. It sounded like she was crying.

I ducked into the girls' bedroom on the way past. Georgia was crashed out in her bed, somehow sleeping through it all. Paper and crayons littered the floor around her. No sign of Cathryn.

Then I spotted the picture Georgia had drawn before she fell asleep. I breathed in sharply, suddenly cold, bending to pick it up.

Almost the whole page was taken up by a huge man, dressed in black. A security officer. Somehow, I was sure it was Officer Calvin. The man stood in the middle of some scribbly trees with an enormous red smile on his face. He was holding the baby.

"That's not – it's just a drawing, right?" said Luke over my shoulder. "I mean, she can hear thoughts or whatever, but she can't see the future."

I tore my eyes away from the picture, almost ready to wake Georgia up and ask her about it. But then Mum cried out again from the lab and I decided it could wait. Georgia didn't need to hear that.

I spun around, looking to the doorway as footsteps came pounding up the corridor towards us.

Cathryn, I thought bitterly, striding out to meet her. *If you've—*

But it wasn't Cathryn.

It was Bill.

He reached out to Luke and me with filthy hands, his eyes wide and glistening with tears. Bill's mouth worked soundlessly for a moment, slowly opening and closing, before the words finally escaped his throat in a wild, breathless whisper. "It's time."

Chapter 34

**Wednesday 12 August
1 day**

Bill leapt forward. He latched on to Luke and me, fingers closing around my arm with shocking strength. "Quickly! You must come with me. You have a role. You must fulfil your function."

"What—?" I jerked back my shoulder. "Bill, what do you need us to do?"

"I need you to hurry!" said Bill, face contorted in a kind of wild, desperate glee. He dragged us into the corridor.

Ms Hunter's barely-contained panic was still streaming out from the lab. "OK – it's – oh. Oh my—" She swore loudly. "Here it comes. Just – just—"

Mum screamed again, long and gut-wrenching,

like she was being torn apart. I started for the lab door, but Bill yanked me roughly away. Finally, the screaming stopped. Mum shuddered for breath, and a tiny, strangled cry rose up in her place. Bill kept hauling us away out of earshot, forcing us down into the bowels of the complex.

"Let me go!" I said, almost skewering my head on a bit of pipe as I fought to get free of him. "I need to make sure my mum's OK."

"She's fine," Bill grumbled.

"You don't know that! Look, please, just give me five minutes to—"

"WE DON'T HAVE FIVE MINUTES!"

He pressed on, faster now, shoving me in front and dragging Luke along behind him.

We reached the open area outside Peter's room, and it wasn't until Bill crashed into me that I realized I'd stopped walking.

"Oh, crap," said Luke behind me, sounding sick.

The concrete slab we'd used to block the door was now lying in two pieces across the old couch on the other side. Peter's door was open a crack, the barricades scattered on the floor. I could hear him murmuring inside.

"*You*," I said, stumbling forward as Bill forced us on again. "You did this! Bill, stop, we have to close it again. If Peter gets out—"

"Inevitable," said Bill. "It has already happened."

"No, it's *not* inevitable! Not if you—"

Bill twisted my arm behind my back, heaving me deeper into the research module. "There is no time! No time! The ends are connecting. The timing – this is critical. Critical." He kept going, muttering to himself, more agitated with every step.

I kept struggling, but it was pointless. He was too strong.

I tensed up as we approached the tunnel Soren had dug into the side of the wall. The place where Luke was supposed to die.

"*Go!*" said Bill, pushing me straight past it.

"Can you at least explain what you're planning here?" said Luke. "I mean, how are we supposed to help you if we don't even—?"

"Redundant!" said Bill, stumbling into me as he tripped on something. "You will know. When it begins, you will know what is required of you. Now turn on my light."

327

"Huh?"

"You mean this?" I said, turning on his helmet lamp. It blinked on, blindingly bright against my face.

"Good," said Bill, bumping into me again. "Good."

We reached the room where Bill had first started his excavation. He brought Luke and me through the mess of smashed furniture and computer parts, and shoved us through the gap he'd made in the wall.

We stumbled into the blocked-up corridor I'd visited when I came to tie him up. The section of the opposite wall he'd been attacking back then was now a second gaping hole, big enough to crawl through. I clambered inside before Bill pushed me again.

Bill's helmet flashed around the room as he climbed in after us. Mouldy concrete spilled down two of the walls, but apart from that, it was completely empty. I glanced around, searching for another hole in the wall or whatever that was going to lead us on to the place Bill was so desperate to show us. But apparently this was all there was.

Bill reached back through the gap in the wall and picked up a faded yellow camping lantern. He switched it on, gave it a whack, and it flickered to life.

The battery seemed to be almost dead, but it lit up the room more brightly than his little helmet torch – enough to prove that there really *was* nothing in here.

Bill straightened up, rubbing his hands together, staring expectantly at Luke and me. Like either of us had any idea what was going on.

"Well?" I said.

Bill kept staring, eyes tearing up again, chest heaving under the filthy hospital gown he'd been wearing since we brought him down here. "Here I come. Here I come, Jordan. Get ready."

"For what? What are you expecting me to…?"

I swayed sideways, crashing into Luke, head swimming with an all-too-familiar nausea. But worse. Even worse than before. The ground warped under my feet, concrete reverting back to sludge, the whole room running together into a dull grey nothingness.

"No…" I murmured, eyes rolling back into my head, chest and throat heaving. Not now. Not with Bill right there, threatening to lose it if we didn't do what he wanted.

I tried to will myself out of it, to swallow it down and get back to reality, but since when had that ever worked? Luke held me for as long as he could, but I slipped away from him and crumbled to the ground.

And then Bill began to laugh. Wild, breathless, out-of-his-mind laughter, like he might explode from the excitement of it all.

"YES!" he cried. "Oh— Oh, yes! At last! Here I – here I come! Oh, Jordan – Jordan, I'm—!"

His voice cut out and the room fell silent. I shuddered on the floor, cradling my head to keep it from smashing against the concrete, until the world finally straightened itself back out and my body settled down again.

Someone was crying. *Sobbing*.

I opened my eyes. Luke and Bill were gone. Cracks had appeared in the walls around me, and there were bits of concrete strewn across the floor, but everything else looked pretty much the same. I got up, spinning around to locate the source of the tears.

It was *me*. Some future version of myself, collapsed on the floor, half-hidden in the shadows in the corner. Mouth open. Nose running. Face twisted up in desperate, uncontrolled misery.

"Luke…" she moaned, sucking in a spluttering breath. *"Luke…"*

My insides went cold. I felt my hands rise to my face, knowing what this meant.

It had happened. Not just in a grainy image on some old surveillance tape. It had actually happened. Here, in the real world – or future, or whatever. He was gone.

I staggered back from the other Jordan, distancing myself, wanting to run screaming from the room.

The light from Bill's lamp caught me in the face. It was still there, still glowing. How long did the batteries last in those things? Surely I couldn't have jumped ahead more than a few hours.

I gasped as Luke burst into view in front of me, arms already outstretched to bring me back, but we passed straight through each other. He reached for me again, glancing sideways at the hole in the wall. Whatever Bill was doing back there, Luke didn't like it. I reached out my hands, getting ready to head back.

Surprisingly quickly, Luke and I made contact again, and I felt myself being drawn back to the present. The gagging started up again and Luke wrapped his arms around me, holding me steady as my body was wracked with shakes.

Everything spun out of focus for a second, and then the two timeframes collided. I could still see the other Jordan, but I could see Bill again too. He was even more worked up than before. Laughing, bouncing from foot to foot, eyes streaming.

Why? Did he even understand what was going on? Had someone told him about my visions?

It almost seemed like he'd *known* this was going to happen. But how was that possible? There was no way to predict my visions until they happened.

The other Jordan sat up. She stared straight at me, like she knew I was there. Which I guess she did, given that she *was* me only a few hours ago. She wiped her eyes, breathing deeply, like she was trying to get herself together enough to speak.

But she was already evaporating, growing fainter as I was sucked back into the present. I clamped down on Luke's arms, swallowing hard, trying to hold on, to calm the shakes, to stay connected to the vision long enough to hear what the other Jordan had to say.

Luke jolted back from me, staring into my eyes

like something horrible was happening. I remembered what he'd said before about me *glowing* or whatever.

Fine. Let me glow. Just as long as I got to hear whatever Future Jordan was trying to tell me.

I looked back. Her face was in her hands again. *Come on!* I thought. *If you've got something to say, then—*

Luke whirled around, letting go of me with one hand. A dark silhouette had appeared through the hole in the wall.

Peter.

He skulked through the shadows, and for a moment I couldn't work out what timeframe he was in. But, no, of course, if Luke could see him, then he must be in the present. He must have—

Peter leapt through the hole, sights locked on Luke. His hands were flecked with blood.

Luke panicked, letting go of me completely and drawing the pistol that was still stuffed down the back of his jeans. He thrust the weapon out at Peter.

I grabbed my stomach with one hand as the nausea soared to new heights. I opened my mouth to yell at Peter, but I couldn't get the words out. Everything

333

was blurring. But not like before. Not like the room was collapsing. This time, *I* was collapsing.

Luke took a shaky step forward, waving the pistol, and Peter backed off, shouting something I couldn't hear. I glanced back at the other Jordan. She was down on the ground again.

The room was getting even hazier now, like I was staring at it through a thick fog. A wall of sound rose up against my ears, like rushing wind, blocking out everything else. I squeezed my eyes shut against it all, trying to pull myself together.

When I opened them again, Bill was striding towards me. He'd stopped laughing, but the crazed, ecstatic look was still etched across his face. He kept coming until we were face to face. Hesitated for a moment, taking a breath.

And then he dived. Straight into me. Straight *through* me.

I whirled around to where he should have landed, but he wasn't there. He'd just *disappeared.* I stared down at my chest, as if I was expecting to find him hiding inside me or something. But, no, he was definitely gone. I turned around again. Past Luke, trying to focus on me and fend Peter off at the same time. There had to be something I'd missed. Something—

And then Bill was back, soaring through the air like there'd been no interruption to his dive. He crashed to the ground next to Future Jordan.

She looked up. Her expression turned dark. She scrambled to her feet, backing up against the wall. She could *see* him.

Bill advanced on her, weeping openly, reaching out to Future Jordan like she was his long-lost child or something. She opened her mouth, but whatever she said to him was drowned out by the roar of noise in my ears.

The fog around me was so thick that I could barely see anything now. Just glimpses. Jordan slamming a fist into the side of Bill's face. Bill waving his arms, trying to say something. Jordan lashing out, screaming.

I blinked hard, swaying on legs that were barely there any more. The fog swirled around my head. The wind howled. I was falling to pieces.

Somewhere through it all, I saw Bill looking back at me, a horrified expression on his face. He glanced at the Future Jordan, mouth open, hands clutching his head. Then he ran at me again – whatever was left of me – diving through my body and disappearing again and finally coming out the other side. Luke gasped, reeling back.

And then all of it collapsed and I blacked out.

When I came around, the fog and the noise were gone and I was on the ground, convulsing as if my whole body was trying to turn itself inside out. Everything was shaking. There was a loud cracking sound as chunks of concrete rained down around the room, and then I must have blacked out again because suddenly Luke was kneeling under me, stroking my face, begging me to wake up.

I opened my eyes. Luke shuddered with relief and bent down to kiss me on the forehead. I took hold of his arm and he helped me sit up.

"Where's Peter?" I asked, looking around, still struggling to focus on anything.

"Gone," said Luke. "He ran when he saw the gun. But, Jordan, what just happened? Bill was right there, and then he was gone, and then—"

"I don't know," I said. "In my vision, I was – it must have been tomorrow. I saw myself. A future version of myself. I think she was trying to tell me something. You started to bring me back to the present, but I held on again. Tried to hold on to both timeframes at once. You know, like I did out in the bush."

"Yeah, you were – you were doing the glowing thing again. But so much – so much worse this time. When Peter ran, I looked back and – you were getting all, like, sucked up into this mist stuff. Like you were fading out, but also kind of – I don't know. I don't even know how to describe it. But it looked like..." He trailed off, pale and shell-shocked. "Well, it *looked* like..."

"Like the thing you appeared through in the video," I finished, feeling suddenly hollow. "Right before you got stabbed."

That was how it was going to happen.

That was how Luke and Peter would wind up rocketing back through time.

It was me.

"I'm so sorry..." said Bill. "I'm so, so sorry..."

My head snapped up. I'd forgotten he was even here.

Bill was over in the corner where I'd seen the other Jordan. Slumped on the ground, crying, just like she had been. There was something different about him. Something about the way he moved, the sound of his voice, the way he put the words together. Somehow, he didn't seem quite so out of his mind any more.

Bill's teeth clenched. He held his head in both hands, fingers clawing into his scalp. "I'm so sorry…"

I stood up, completely thrown by his sudden mood shift. "It's – it's OK. Just—"

"No it's not!" he choked. "It's not. Not after what I did." He stared up at the ceiling, mouth open in a silent wail.

"Bill," I tried again. "Tell me what—"

"I'm not Bill."

I shook my head. "What do you mean?"

"My name's not Bill," he said. "It's Peter."

Chapter 35

**Wednesday 12 August
1 day**

"Peter," said Luke. "You have the same name as—?"

"No," said Bill. He got up, wiping his face on the sleeve of his gown. "No, mate, I *am* Peter." He leant against the wall with one arm, head down, gathering himself. And again, I noticed the change in him. He was still a total emotional wreck, but he was *here* in a way he hadn't been before.

My brain was about ready to explode. "Bill, you're not – what are you saying?"

"Look," he said, "Kara and Soren showed you the video, right? They showed you what I did."

"The surveillance tape?" said Luke. "Peter appearing through that portal thing and killing me?"

339

"That was me. Twenty years ago. I was…" Bill reached out for Luke, and he flinched away. "I'm sorry."

"That doesn't even make sense!" I said, struggling to understand, let alone figure out if I believed him. "Peter came back. We saw him go back through the portal again, right after he stabbed Luke."

Bill shook his head. "No. I *tried* to go back, but I never made it. The whole thing – the portal or whatever you want to call it – collapsed around me before I could get through. You must have broken the connection. It exploded – this massive bright light all around me – and I got spat back out again, into the past. And then this whole place started caving in, and—" He shrugged, pulling an uncannily Peter-like face. "I must've got knocked out, I guess, because the next thing I knew, I was waking up in hospital."

I sat down again, the hollow feeling intensifying, as if someone was scooping out my insides like a jack-o'-lantern.

"It was me," I said eventually. "All of it. If I was the one who sent you back there – if that portal thing we saw in the video was me – that means the explosion was me too. I was the one who destroyed the Vattel Complex."

It was insane. Unbelievable. All those people dead…

"Jordan, listen," said Bill, "you're not the one who—"

"Wait," I said, realizing something. "That portal – that was one of the 'events' Kara was studying. That was why they built the Complex in the first place! To figure out what those things were! If that last one was me… Then all the others were me too, right?"

I glanced between Luke and Bill, desperate for one of them to contradict me. "Right? Something to do with my visions. When I went back to their time, it must have left some kind of a trace or something. Something Kara's people could measure with all their lab equipment. That's what they were studying. Me."

Luke came over and joined me on the floor. "Jordan … even if that's true – none of this is your fault. This isn't something you did. It's something that happened *to* you."

"He's right," said Bill. "Nothing you could've done. This was already set in motion way before you guys

341

got here. This is my fault. No-one else's." He heaved a heavy sigh and went on with his story. "When the Vattel Complex collapsed, they flew emergency crews in to rescue the survivors, and I guess they picked me up along with them. No-one knew who I was, though. I mean, I hadn't even been born yet. They questioned me in the hospital, but what could I tell them? Besides, you know what I was like. What your Peter is like now. They couldn't have got a straight answer out of me even if they tried."

"So then what?" I asked. "What have you been *doing* for the last twenty years? You didn't try to find your family?"

"I didn't *have* a family. My parents hadn't even met yet. And, anyway," Bill sniffed loudly, tears coming back again, "the only thing I cared about – the *only* thing – was getting back to Jordan. That's why I killed Luke. To get rid of him. All I had to do was find a way back to Jordan and there'd be nothing to stop us from being together." He screwed up his face, disgusted with himself. "I know. I know. It was insane. Monstrous. But that was where my head was at."

I hugged myself, suddenly overcome with shivers.

Luke leant in and put his arms around me.

Bill looked down at us, expecting some kind of response. But what was there to say?

"So, yeah," he went on, "when I woke up in the hospital a few weeks later, the doctors said it was a miracle I was alive. I'd lost so much blood, and I had burns pretty much everywhere, and – I mean, look at me." He held out his scarred, mangled hands. "Not surprising you guys never realized who I was. Anyway, as soon as I could, I broke out of the hospital."

"Where were you?" asked Luke. "What hospital?"

"I don't know," said Bill, looking up again. "Somewhere in Sydney, but I didn't care where I was. All I cared about was getting back to Phoenix. Which was stupid. Phoenix hadn't even been built yet. But I wasn't thinking like that. I mean, my brain was totally screwed. It was all…" He closed his eyes again, clenching his fists in front of his face. "Mate, you have to understand, this is the first time I've actually thought about any of this. When I went through Jordan just then – I don't know what happened, but it was like waking up. Like I've just got my brain back for the first time in twenty years."

He broke down again, shaking with tears. Part of me wanted to get up and leave. I needed to check on Mum. Make sure *our* Peter wasn't doing anything stupid. But I couldn't just walk out. Not yet.

Bill took a couple of spluttering breaths. "I had nothing," he said. "No money. I didn't even *exist*. Plus, I had no idea where Phoenix even was. All I knew was that I had to get back here." He waved a hand at the room around us. "Back *here*, to this moment. I remembered coming in here and seeing Bill disappear. I needed to make that happen again. I needed to get the two of you back together in the same place and open another portal and get back to my own time.

"So I waited. For nearly twenty years, that was *all* I did. I was totally obsessed. All I had to do was wait it out, and then I could be with her again. When the time got closer, I tracked down Shackleton's old office in Sydney. I stole a computer and hacked into the Co-operative's candidates register. I had to make sure you were both on the list, that you were both coming." Bill turned to Luke. "You weren't there. You or your mum. I deleted two of the other names and added you guys in their place."

"That's why we're here," Luke breathed. "Even though we're not candidates. It was you."

"But *why?*" I said, finally finding my voice again. "Why did you have to make all of this happen again? Why go out of your way to *bring* Luke to Phoenix if he was your whole problem in the first place? And why put *me* through all of this? All the clues and messages and dragging us out to the airport – if you were that obsessed with me, why not just break into my house?"

"Because I wasn't looking for *you,*" said Bill. "I was looking for *her.* My Jordan. The one I'd left behind when I went through to the past."

"We're the same person!"

"I know!" Bill choked. "I know that! I mean, now I do. But that wasn't – I told you, my mind was – I had a *plan.* Get Luke out of the way, and get back through the portal to my own time. Get back to the Jordan I'd left behind. Right from the beginning, I knew that was what I had to do. And even after I got stuck, I couldn't look past my perfect freaking plan. Nothing else mattered. When I got back here and saw you— You might as well have been a completely different person. I mean, I knew who you were, but by that point you weren't even people to me. You were just tools I could use to get what I wanted."

Bill's eyes dropped to the concrete. He laced his hands around behind his neck. "I sneaked into Phoenix in a cargo plane, and started gathering information, waiting for you to get here. As soon as Luke landed, I put those memory sticks into your rooms and used the threat of Tabitha to bring you together."

"But, hang on," said Luke, "when you got us to come and meet you that first time, why did you choose the airport? Why not just bring us straight here if that's where you wanted us to be?"

"I didn't know where here *was*," said Bill. "I was unconscious when Mike and the others brought me down here. And the only other time I'd been up to the surface since then, you guys had stuck me with a sedative. But I knew we'd all get down here eventually because I'd seen it happen the first time." He shrugged his shoulders. "The airport was a mistake. I'd already seen Calvin and his guys show up and drag Bill away last time. I thought maybe I could change it. Speed things up. But I couldn't. I can't. All of it was fixed, because it had already happened before. That whole night turned out exactly the same way as it had the first time around. But I'd left myself a backup plan. I'd left clues for Peter – the other Peter – to find."

"The map out to the wall," said Luke. "And those pictures. And the Tabitha DVD."

"Why didn't you just tell us who you were?" I asked. "Or why didn't you warn *Peter* what was going to happen?"

"*I don't know!*" Bill shouted, getting to his feet. "I couldn't – I wasn't thinking like that. He was just like you. Just a tool. A piece of the puzzle. I didn't even think of … of…"

He cried out, tearing at his gown, and I backed off. He might be thinking straighter, but for all I knew he could still throw me across the room if he wanted to.

"It's happening again! Just like before. Just like—" Bill's hands shot to his head. "I have to stop it. I – I have to stop it."

He turned in a circle and bolted from the room.

Chapter 36

Wednesday 12 August
1 day

We ran, grazing against the walls, sprinting to keep up with the light that danced from Bill's helmet as he raced through the passageway ahead of us. He didn't look back, didn't seem to care whether we were following him or not.

I felt like I was going to burst into tears any second. It was all too big, too weird, too overwhelming. I couldn't even begin to wrap my mind around it all. But I could run. I surged forward, pushing through the darkness, blocking out everything else and concentrating on putting one foot in front of the other.

We tore past the scene of Luke's death and kept running, through the minefield of wreckage and back into the entryway to Peter's room. A figure staggered through the door and I dug my heels in, ready to fight him off with my bare hands if I had to.

But it wasn't Peter. It was Cathryn. Bleeding from deep scratch marks in her arms and face. Terrified beyond anything I'd ever seen in her before.

"He almost k-killed me," she shuddered, hands shaking over her blood-smeared cheeks. "Pete— he almost… He almost…"

"Where did he go?" I demanded. "Which way?"

Cathryn's eyes flickered towards the living area. "Out there. But I don't know what he was—"

I took off again, Luke right behind me.

"Wait!" Cathryn begged, stumbling after us.

Bill hadn't stopped. He was way ahead now, already out of sight.

In a minute, we were bursting into the undestroyed corridor that led up to the entrance. The laboratory door was open. I veered inside and found Mum sitting up in her bed, holding a tiny, wrinkled baby wrapped up in a towel. Georgia was curled up next to her, still half-asleep, gently stroking the baby's cheek.

Luke's mum was resting against a bench, looking

completely shattered. She jumped up as we arrived, brushing Luke's arm on the way past and then rushing over to help Cathryn.

"You're back already?" asked Mum sleepily. "What happened? Where are the others?"

"Where's Bill?" said Luke. "Did he come through here?"

Ms Hunter looked up. "No. We heard footsteps, but—"

"What about Peter? Have you seen—?"

"No, we haven't seen anyone since you left. Luke, what's—?"

Luke ignored her, racing through to the surveillance room.

I crossed to Mum's bed and gazed down at the baby and for one tiny moment, everything else faded into the background. Despite everything – the weirdness of the pregnancy, the less-than-ideal birth – the baby looked completely healthy. Completely normal.

I clutched on to the head of the bed, forcing myself not to cry, knowing I probably wouldn't be able to stop.

"She's amazing," I murmured.

"He," said Mum. "It's a boy. Abraham. We always said that if we ever had a son, we'd name it after—"

Georgia looked up, brow furrowed. "That's not his name."

Mum smiled. "That's what we've picked, sweetheart. He's going to have the same name as Daddy."

"No," said Georgia firmly, shaking her head. "That's wrong. He already told me his name. He's called Tobias."

Chapter 37

I let go of the bed frame. "Georgia, no— You might have heard us talking about that name, but—"

"No, that's not why," said Georgia. "He knew his name already, even when he was in Mummy's tummy. He *told* me."

Mum stared at me, the colour draining out of her face. "Is that – is that possible?"

"I don't know," I said, reeling away from the bed. "Georgia, are you *sure?* Are you sure it was the baby who told you that?"

"*Yes,*" said Georgia emphatically. "I'm not lying. He said it in my head just before he got born."

"What about that drawing you did?" I asked, trying

352

to keep my voice even. "That picture of the security man holding the baby."

"That's Mr Calvin," said Georgia. "Luke said, "Draw a picture for the baby." That's what the baby wanted a picture of." Her eyes narrowed. "Why are you angry?"

"We're not angry, sweetheart," said Mum faintly. "We're just trying to understand."

"Jordan!" said Luke, rushing into the lab again. "He's upstairs. He just ran out into the… What? What happened?"

"It's the baby," I said. "*Tobias*. Georgia just— She can communicate with him, or read his mind or something."

"He told me," said Georgia. "That was always his name, ever since he got into Mum's tummy."

Luke walked across to the bed. "Did he tell you anything else?"

"No," Georgia shrugged. "That's all. He only started talking today."

I glanced at Luke, then out into the corridor. If we were going to catch up with Bill, we had to do it now. I turned back to Mum. "Wait here. But get ready to— Do you think you can walk?"

"I think so," she said. "But, Jordan, I don't think—"

"OK. Stay here. But get ready to run if you have to."

"Run *where?*" asked Luke's mum.

"I don't know," I said. "Just get ready."

We shot back into the hall. Up the stairs. I hammered the trapdoor button and we leapt out on to the surface, pacing in a circle, searching the darkness.

No Bill. No Peter.

"Where would he go?" Luke panted. "Where would either of them—? Surely they haven't gone back into town?"

But who knew *what* was going through Peter's head right now? He could be anywhere.

Luke rested an arm around my waist. My head pounded. I could smell the vomit from before, and I thought I might throw up all over again. I closed my eyes for a minute, focusing on my breathing, leaning my head against Luke's shoulder.

"I believe her," I said. "Georgia. She's telling the truth about the baby. About Tobias."

Luke blew out a lungful of air. "Yeah."

All our searching, and he'd been right here with us

all along. But what now? What hope did that tiny little baby have against a Co-operative super-weapon?

"Hang on," said Luke. "What about all the rumours in town? If *he's* Tobias, then—?" He stepped away from me as something flashed in the sky behind us. "Whoa. Was that lightning?"

There was a loud crackle, and a sound like one of the rocket things that had launched at Kara and Mr Hunter's helicopter. A line of sparks lanced through the air, far above our heads, shooting towards town from somewhere out in the bush.

"Not lightning," I said.

There were more of them. Dozens. Tearing through the night in every direction, all converging on the town centre.

"Missiles?" said Luke, voice brightening. "Maybe Dad got the army or something. Maybe—"

"I don't think so." I started jogging through the bush, gazing upwards. A dark line cut across the sky overhead, marking out a path behind one of the projectiles. Some kind of big, thick cord.

There was a rapid series of *thunks* as the cords converged above the town centre.

"That antenna thing on top of the Shackleton Building," I said. "I bet that's where they've—"

An explosive crackle of electricity filled up the sky, impossibly loud, like lighting smashing into the ground right next to me. Sparks rained down on us, and for a moment the bush was bright orange as all the cords above our heads lit up at once.

Luke gaped up between the trees. I could see his lips moving, but couldn't hear a thing over the noise. The cords had laced themselves together into a massive, electrified grid. A dome, stretching out as far as I could see in every direction.

All the way out to the wall, I thought, mind dredging up an ancient memory from the night we scaled the giant barrier surrounding the town. Peter had spotted this deep metal groove in the top of the wall, running the length of it. None of us had ever been able to work out what it was for. It looked like we might have our answer.

"Final lockdown procedures," Luke murmured, as the light and the sound faded away again. The grid still crackled and spat, but not so ferociously now. I guessed maybe that had just been while it was powering up.

Whatever the case, it looked like our trip out to the release station had just ratcheted up from "dangerous" to "impossible".

Luke hit the backlight on his watch and I glanced down. The time had just ticked over to midnight.

"Doomsday," he said.

Seventeen hours until the end.

I could still hear the distant echoes of gunfire from the centre of town. How much of Phoenix was even going to be left by the time this was all over?

And then another sound. Heavy breathing and pounding feet, and then the dark shape of a person exploded from the bushes in front of me. The figure pitched forward, face illuminated for a fraction of a second as the grid sparked above us.

Soren, bruised and bleeding. He collapsed at our feet.

"Soren? You're alive!" I said. "How did you—?"

Soren shook his head wildly, scrambling to get up. His legs gave out and he stumbled to the ground again.

"Help!" he shrieked. "Help me! We have to get away from here!"

"Why? Soren, what's—?"

"Calvin!" Soren gasped. "He's back! They know where we are! They're coming!"

Catch up on the rest
of the series...

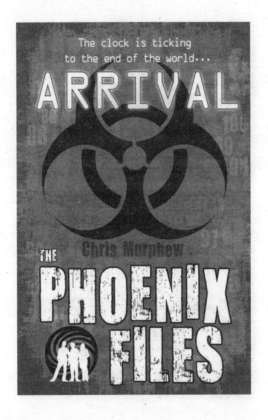

"The end of the world is
one of those things that you
never really expect to wind
up being your problem..."

There are 100 days until the
end of the world...

88 days until the end
of the world...

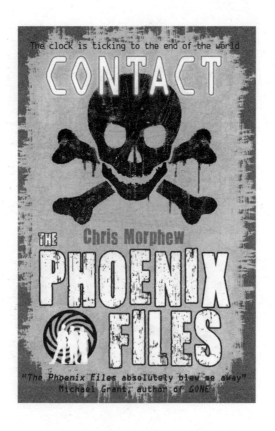

The clock is ticking to the end of the world

CONTACT

Chris Morphew

THE PHOENIX FILES

"The Phoenix Files absolutely blew me away"
Michael Grant, author of GONE

"One day off between suicide
missions. Was that really so
much to ask?"

63 days until the end
of the world...

"Phoenix was the one
place where people weren't
supposed to die..."

49 days until the end
of the world...

"Luke Hunter," said the woman,
horribly calm, arms folded
across a dirty lab coat. "You
have no idea how long we've
waited for you to arrive."